URBAN CHANGE AND RENEWAL: THE PARADOX OF PLACE

In dedication to those countless men and women in the north of England who continue to have their lives blighted and disrupted by successive phases of "modernisation".

Urban Change and Renewal: The Paradox of Place

Edited by

PHILIP GARRAHAN
University of Teesside

PAUL STEWART
*University of Wales
College of Cardiff*

Avebury

Aldershot · Brookfield USA · Hong Kong · Singapore · Sydney

© Philip Garrahan and Paul Stewart, 1994

All rights reserved. No part of this publication may be reproduced, stored in a retrieval system, or transmitted in any form or by any means, electronic, mechanical, photocopying, recording or otherwise without the prior permission of the publisher.

Published by
Avebury
Ashgate Publishing Limited
Gower House
Croft Road
Aldershot
Hants GU11 3HR
England

Ashgate Publishing Company
Old Post Road
Brookfield
Vermont 05036
USA

British Library Cataloguing in Publication Data

Urban Change and Renewal: Paradox of Place
    I. Garrahan, Philip   II. Stewart, Paul
    307.76

ISBN 1 85628 648 7

Printed and Bound in Great Britain by
Athenaeum Press Ltd, Newcastle upon Tyne.

Contents

Acknowledgements   vii

Contributors   viii

1   Progress to decline?
   Philip Garrahan and Paul Stewart   1

2   Something old, Something new? The Great North in the 1990s
   Fred Robinson   9

3   Wearside in the 'new' North East: Longer term perspectives on industrial restructuring
   Ian Stone   21

4   Continuity and change in urban governance: urban regeneration initiatives in the North East of England
   Keith Shaw   49

5   What's in a name? The invention of Wearside
   Pete Rushton   67

6	Is Andy Capp dead? The enterprise culture and household responses to economic change *Jane Wheelock*	81
7	Back to the future? Preparing young adults for the post-industrial Wearside economy *Bob Hollands*	99
8	Transnational corporations, human resource management and regional regeneration *John Knell*	127
9	Foreign direct investment and local economic recovery *Philip Garrahan and Paul Stewart*	143
10	Condemnation and closure: The Wear shipyards *Ian Roberts*	163
Bibliography		185

Acknowledgements

We wish to thank Louise Jones at the Cardiff Business School for her professionalism in creating a finished manuscript from a very diverse range of software.

Contributors

Philip Garrahan is Principal Lecturer in Politics at the University of Teesside.

Robert G. Hollands is a Lecturer in Sociology in the Department of Sociology and Social Policy at the University of Newcastle-Upon-Tyne.

John Knell is a Lecturer in Industrial Relations in the School of Business and Economic Studies at Leeds University.

Ian Roberts is a Lecturer in Sociology in the Department of Sociology and Social Policy at Durham University.

Fred Robinson is a Lecturer in Sociology in the Department of Sociology and Social Policy at Durham University.

Peter Rushton is Principal Lecturer in Sociology at the University of Sunderland.

Keith Shaw is a Senior Lecturer in the School of Government at the University of Northumbria, Newcastle-Upon-Tyne.

Paul Stewart is an Industrial Sociologist and Lecturer at the Cardiff Business School, University of Wales.

Ian Stone is Principal Lecturer in Economics at the School of Government at the University of Northumbria, Newcastle-Upon-Tyne.

Jane Wheelock is Reader in Social Policy in the Department of Sociology and Social Policy at the University of Newcastle-Upon-Tyne.

1 Progress to decline?

Philip Garrahan and Paul Stewart

Introduction

The interrogative 'progress to decline?' in the title above sets the context for this book. It has by now become commonplace to identify countries like Britain as undergoing a problematical transition to which there appears to be no single remedy. Explanations for the causes of this transition alternatively stress factors internal to the nation-state, or forces external to it, or a combination of both. They lead to positions being staked out in theoretical debates about post-industrialism, post-Fordism and the primacy of flexibility, long wave theories of change, or the like. (Allen and Massey, 1988; Stewart et al. 1990). In this book, the contributors prosecute their different themes with these debates in mind, and draw their material from the contemporary study of the north of England. The contributions start from a shared concern with the current transformations which, whatever their origins or effects (cultural, economic, political, or social) also clearly share a spatial dimension. (Hudson, 1989; Massey and Allen, 1988; Sadler, 1992).

The decline of the northern region of England which has been precipitated by a process of deindustrialisation has also recently been accompanied by the championing of signs of improvement. However, as our title indicates, this apparent progress has in reality hastened the relative decline of the region, positing questions of a fundamental nature for academics and policy makers alike. These questions arise in areas to do with managing the local economy, investment and training, youth policy, small businesses and the enterprise culture, and so on. The issues range widely across the complex architecture of modern industrial society. They are especially relevant for the appreciation of the processes of change whereby old industrial regions are compelled by force of circumstance to embark on the path of modernisation. This brings with it the potential for the imposition of severe economic dislocations and for the aggravation of existing social divisions. While not pre-judging the outcome of these processes of change in the longer term, at the time of writing there is a perceptible worsening of the health, life chances and standard of living of those at the bottom of the social ladder, while the benefits of the consumer society are exclusively enjoyed by others.

The themes of this book

At the heart of this book then are evidence and theoretical argument about the reconstruction of modern industrial society. In the chapters which follow, a multi-disciplinary approach is employed to address the nature of contemporary cultural, economic, political, and social change. The most successful studies in this field focus on the relationship between the broader political economy and specific exemplars of current transformations. Our theme is clear: that there is a fundamental paradox evident whenever we study these exemplars of change in particular places. This paradox of place is a consequence of the enduring aspects of urban and regional life which clash with the claims made about the speed and nature of change. Our emphasis is on the inter relationship between continuity and change, rather than on what would become an invalid understanding of the current transitions as amounting to change and renewal. Change and renewal assume a disembodiment of the social and political organisation of space and time. It has to be acknowledged, as many of the contributions to this book do, that a significant degree of restructuring is emerging in the UK. However, even where substantial movement occurs, continuities with the past are sustained. This means that we reject any notion of simple linearity in the development of new forms of life in urban and regional spaces.

Given this focus, the chapters draw upon the combined interests of a number of leading academics and researchers in the north of England and upon the proceedings of a seminar convened at the University of Sunderland. The preoccupation of the seminar was the interconnectedness of two public perceptions of reconstruction. On the one hand a rhetoric of renewal and public and private affluence, and on the other a public perception of dissonance and decline. Of course, this assymetry is born out of at least two public (and private) agendas - one conveying a utopia of privately sponsored leadership, the other a less optimistic view of the new world as a recommodified public sphere. The difference between the two perceptions lies in their respective origins. The first is concerned largely with a myopic acount of the limited experence of the few who have succeeded in the new "Great North", whilst the other derives its perspective from an understanding of the relationship between the limited success of the few and the disappointment of the many. Since the seminar, the contributors have refined and updated their chapters in the light of more recent developments.

Some of these recent developments confirm the north of England's depressing economic trajectory, whatever the relative position given the greater susceptibility of other regions of the UK to the effects of the recession in the early 1990s. The 'rollercoaster economy' , as Robinson describes it in his chapter, is very much still with us. Despite the public image building in the north of England, the reality continues to be of higher than national average levels of unemployment in the region. The history of the north as the state-managed region par excellence is now being re-written as major industries formerly in the public sector such as coal, iron, steel and shipbuilding close,or contract prior to privatisation. The region's reputation as ailing from the branch-plant economy syndrome has not been much reduced following limited successes in the process of re-industrialisation. Fewer people are in work and increasingly the gender recomposition of the labour force indicates a trend for well paid jobs for skilled male workers to be replaced by low paid and insecure work for women. Where new initiatives to create employment occur, they have often proved to be heavily publicly funded, as in the cases of Nissan or the region's two Urban Development Corporations.

Despite this the claims for a market-led pathway to recovery remain the mainstay of public policy rhetoric. That there has been some economic growth in some places is the focus of Stone's chapter, but there are questions about the extent of employment generation and its unevenness. Given the general movement in the region to deindustrialise the economy, the fundamental and often deliberately avoided question is whether such economic change will threaten the stability of the social order. That there is the inclination to deny this question is indisputable, and it is consistent with talking-up the region's prospects in order to promote investor confidence. There is strong evidence of the achievements in attracting foreign direct investment in this way, and the north of England has been targetted by companies from the Far East as a result. Presumably these companies would have been less enthusiastic about their investments if the gains of a slack labour market, public subsidy, low start-up costs, and a weakened trade union movement had been contrasted with the potential for urban unrest in places of high unemployment where the whole social fabric of urban life is in jeopardy. The well known Tyneside riots of 1992 were in inner city places and have been followed by regular incidences of public disturbances in towns like Stockton and Darlington and outlying areas of County Durham.

One argument could be that this respresents an unpleasant but necessary step in the process of readjustment via the enterprise culture to leave behind the culture of dependency on state intervention. On the contrary, there is evidence to suggest that this is less to do with economic retrenchment and more to do with the particular dynamics of economic restructuring. Urban social decay has been a feature of the transition from corporatist politics in this state-managed region, to state-sponsored commitment to private ownership and control. The necessary consequence of this was bound to be the exclusion from new patterns of consumption and from the restructured labour market of large segments of urban youth. This is hardly a contradiction within the rhetoric of the 'New North', since it is an indispensable precondition for what Shaw describes in his chapter as the local growth coalitions and boosterists. The increasing social divisions between those excluded from the new consumerism and those who enjoy its benefits are reflected in Shaw's characterisation of the development of a non-elected urban political elite. The latter ensures the reproduction of an economic regime sustaining the recommodification of public utilities and services.

This process could be defined as a suitable case of renewal under the auspices of responsible private citizens. The unchallenged dominance of the latter allows for these private citizens to broker a new version of reality to sit alongside their creation of the new urban and regional space. To change a battered old world is considerably easier when the name of that world is recast. In the case of Sunderland, consigned to the dark industrial ruins of an old urban dystopia, a new past has been "invented". As Rushton shows in his chapter, this has been done in order to accomodate the agenda of the new policy makers. They are intent upon refocussing interest in a positive way around the possibilities provided by economic restructuring. This demands an optimistic appraisal of the past and a new vision of the present. Foreign direct investors are unlikely to be attracted to the image of `Sunderland, the shipbuilding capital and coal mining centre of the world`. A new name needs to be given if a new space and locality is to be discovered. Thus, whilst the present is displaced and the past is, in Rushton`s term "sanitised", the future can become a place of true endeavour.

This new future is taken to task in Wheelock's chapter. There are serious doubts about whether economic imperatives genuinely figure at all levels in the process of modernisation, so it is worth addressing the micro-level analysis in some detail. Rising levels of male unemployment, as we noted above, have been paralleled by more job opportunities for women. In a declining industrial region like the north of England this translates into male job losses being replaced by low wages in women's work. Two other aspects of the same development are involved in this analysis. One is a benefit system with its own poverty trap, sometimes making it financially irrational for women with unemployed husbands to contemplate working for low wages. The second is the enterprise culture with its pressure towards small and family businesses to create work. The conjunction of these two forces determines a highly exploitative environment, where more rather than fewer households are likely to be driven into dependency on the welfare state.

Indeed, it is the question of what happens to the majority of individuals who either fail in small enterprises or who never make it into employment, whether due to age, gender or skill attributes, that the purveyors of a new culture of place and a better economy and society fail to address. How are those entering the labour market for the first time made ready for it and can their training and acculturation for the future be assimilated to the notion of a `post-industrial` society? For Hollands' chapter, the provision of youth training on "Wearside" highlights the discrepancy between the prognostications of the `post-industrial society theorists and the reality of youth training. Whatever the profound changes in industrial policy, and the attendant labour market restructuring, vocational training is still fundamentally tied to the agenda of industrial culture. The destination of many is still the tough and onerous job in the old fashioned industrial labour market. Rather than finding progress in a highly skilled post industrial labour market, the majority are increasingly locating in short term, part-time and insecure employment - or unemployment. The certainties of `post-industrialism` are unsustainable in this context.

This persistence of industrial societies and cultures in the context of industrial renewal is addressed in Knell`s chapter. He argues that the human resource policies of direct inward investors sustains (and often reinforces) the low skill gradient in the local labour market. The training needs of foreign direct investors and of local labour markets often become congruent. In this interface in places marked by industrial decline, new inward investment can often be seen to be reinforcing the drift towards a low wage economy. Whatever the dominant role of the enterprise in the local labour market, there is necessarily a reciprocity in the training itinerary provided and the capacity of the local labour market to accomodate or to provide for the company's unique pattern of skill. This suggests that whilst the new investor may seek to impose its culture upon the locality, a process of adaptation at the level of human resource management is inevitable.

Garrahan and Stewart's chapter sustains the essential tenets of Knell's thesis with respect to the interaction of company requirements and the local labour market. A significant dimension of foreign direct investment from Japan into the north of England has been the assumption of a more skilled and flexible workforce which, at the plant level, operates more efficiently when organised in teams. This is often used by power brokers and policy makers to uphold claims about the benificent effects of foreign direct investment, and in this context detailed attention to training policies is justified. Long-term economic decline in the north of England has highlighted the failure of policy remedies designed to boost training and use new investment as a catalyst for local economic recovery.

The final chapter of this book is a reminder of the workplace struggles generated by contraction and closure. By focusing on shipbuilding in Sunderland, an account is provided of the period leading up to the virtual demise of this industry in the region. Given what has been said about government funding for foreign direct investment and training programmes, the considerable extent to which the shipbuilding yards supposedly had been modernised to make them highly competitive seemed to matter little. Management attempted to secure greater efficiencies through changes in working practices and against this backcloth trade unions consistently fought the pressures to de-skill work in the yards. Roberts vividly documents the collective and individual resistance to this process and highlights the timeless significance in production of workers' knowledge of the labour process.

Conclusion

As the chapters in this book demonstrate, reconciling the declared aims of market-led solutions with their actual consequences is more and more problematical even for the most dedicated ideologue of 'Thatcherite' or New Right politics. Regulated regional economies have prospered elsewhere in the advanced industrialised world, but this is a lesson wasted on contemporary government policy makers in the UK. Instead, de-regulation continues apace, and this is happening despite the accumulated evidence of a drift towards a low investment, low skill, low wage economy as a result. Since this book was conceived, general recessionary forces have continued to have their impact on the UK's national and regional economy. Many of the gains, however questionable, made by some regions of the UK during the late 1980s, are now being diminished. This short term narrowing of regional differentials has led some commentators in declining areas like the north of England to look optimistically at the prospects for the longer term. This has the immediate effect of heightening ever more the assymetry between perceptions of change which are the heart of this book.

2 Something old, something new? The Great North in the 1990s

Fred Robinson

Abstract

For many years, the Northern Region of England has been experiencing deindustrialisation and consequent high unemployment. In an attempt to 'sell' the region to inward investors, the 'boosters' have sought to downplay the North's problems and promote a new image of regional revival. In reality, however, any revival that has occurred is patchy and fails to address the needs of those most affected by the negative impacts of economic change. The region - like the country as a whole - has become increasingly internally divided. A new 'Great North' now co-exists with an impoverished and redundant North.

Introduction

The Northern Region of England is a textbook example of nineteenth century industrialisation based on 'carboniferous capitalism'. Coal mining stimulated the development of railways, shipbuilding and heavy engineering, together with iron and steel-making (McCord, 1979). In the region's economic heyday - from the mid-nineteenth century until the end of the post-war boom in the early 1920s - its economic power was virtually unparalleled. Like Japan today, the North then was an internationally-renowned economic powerhouse: it was a world leader in shipbuilding and heavy engineering, and the 'Great Northern Coalfield' was one of the most productive in the world.

Like other older industrial regions in the 'rustbelts' of Europe and the U.S., the North has since witnessed the erosion and destruction of its industrial base and supremacy. Here, the decline - that process encapsulated by the term 'deindustrialisation' - has been long and drawn out, sometimes rapid, at other times gradual and punctuated by cyclical revival. In some other parts of Western Europe and the U.S. it has been a more recent and rapid decline, while in post-Communist eastern Europe, it looks set to be a short, sharp and consequently painful process. There are inevitably similarities and differences in the pattern and process of deindustrialisation between each case and each 'rustbelt' region. But there are some particularly intriguing lessons to be learnt from the Northern Region of England as one of the first places into, and one of the first places to move out of, 'traditional' industrialism. It offers some lessons about the limited nature and impact of ameliorative public policy and - perhaps most intriguingly of all - how subsequent 'uneven re-development' has produced stark contrasts and contradictions. Today a new 'Great North' coexists with an impoverished and redundant North - is that the inevitable fate of such regions, and is it sustainable?

Historical background - The roller-coaster economy

It is easy to accuse the North of living in the past and it is not surprising that, in many respects, it seems a justifiable accusation (Hetherington and Robinson, 1988). Like Britain as a whole, it is a place mourning the loss of empire and still looking for a role. Its people feel comforted by the re-packaged history celebrated at Beamish, the huge open-air museum in County Durham where Edwardian certainties last forever. Likewise, Catherine Cookson's portrayal of life on Tyneside in the 1920s is enormously popular (and that popularity extends far beyond so-called 'Catherine Cookson Country'). There is a sense in which everything that was great in the region happened decades ago, in the age of Victorian industrialism - or even centuries ago, in 'Hadrian's Wall Country', 'Bede's World' or in the 'Land of the Prince Bishops'. Many people hold on to memories of a harsh, but honest and homely, past and speak proudly of grandfathers who worked in the pits or built the world's finest ships (see Colls and Lancaster, 1992). Thus, in the 1990s, the closure of the few remaining collieries and the threatened closure of the last shipyard on the Tyne is widely regarded not just as economic stupidity but also as a profound psychological blow, robbing the region of its economic and cultural heritage and distinctiveness.

The process of decline in the traditional industrial base has continued for seventy years and is now approaching the end: there is little left to go. Seventy years ago, following the abrupt ending of the post-Great War boom in the early 1920s, the region was plunged into deep depression (Mess, 1928). The sheer deprivation and desperation of those times is well remembered, and the Jarrow March remains a potent image (Wilkinson, 1939; Armstrong and Beynon, 1987). Britain's economic centre of gravity shifted as consumer industries developed in the south, while the North, a victim of industrial specialisation, had to wait for work until re-armament, when its products once again had a market.

The beginnings of what Hudson (1989) aptly calls a 'state-managed region' are to be found in this period. Very modest state intervention - in the form of government-funded public works schemes and the provision of industrial estates - was initiated in the mid-1930s. The best-known of these projects is undoubtedly the Team Valley Trading Estate in Gateshead which now, incidentally, provides 15,000 jobs and represents the region's most important centre of manufacturing industry. (By way of an aside: will the much more expensive London Docklands development - much more heavily state-subsidised - stand the test of time so well?)

The experience of the Depression, of wartime planning, the need and enthusiasm for reconstruction, and the ascendency of Labourism, combined to create the post-war 'state-managed region'. Nationalisation of industries of key importance to the North (coal, iron and steel, railways) provided a measure of job security and much needed investment. Regional policy and planning helped to bring branch plants of newer, lighter industries to the area (Allen et al., 1957; Loebl, 1988). In the long boom of the 1950s, the region enjoyed (now unbelievable) unemployment rates of around 2%; and successive Conservative governments (from 1951 - 64) adhered to 'one nation' Toryism, Keynesian management, the welfare state, regional development and 'modernisation'. The region had 'never had it so good'.

And even in the 1960s and up until the mid-1970s, as the economy weakened and was restructured, the region coped with change; it was painful and difficult, but nevertheless bearable and managed. What we now might call the 'dash for oil' at the end of the 1950s led to a radical pit closure programme which decimated the coalfield. But relatively strong regional policy, including the large-scale programme of infrastructure investment flowing from the 1963 Hailsham Plan, helped attract new branch plants. Then, it was possible for ex-miners to find new jobs in factories or else transfer to other coalfields. Through this period there was also a continuing growth in employment opportunities for women, both in factories and in the service sector. As elsewhere, there was substantial growth in public sector services providing an important source of new jobs. Nevertheless, new employment growth proved insufficient to prevent rising unemployment in the 1970s (Robinson et al., 1987) and even before the onset of the severe recession that was to come, the region was already experiencing economic difficulties. It is worth noting, however, that an unemployment rate of 6.5% in the North in the late 1970s then seemed severe and certainly unacceptable; it is sobering to think that today it would be widely regarded as modest, even an indication of successful economic management and development.

This very brief outline of the region's economic history has now taken us as far as the end of the 1970s and heading for a steep descent on the roller-coaster. The severe economic recession of the first Thatcher term undoubtedly had a catastrophic economic and social impact on the region, with massive job losses in all manufacturing industries. In 1981 alone there were more than 40,000 redundancies in the Northern Region, mainly in the manufacturing sector. The traditional industries witnessed a sharp decline, with the closure of steelworks (Consett, Hartlepool, Workington), shipyards (on the Tyne, Tees and Wear) and engineering plants as well as job-displacing capital investment in the Teesside chemicals industry. What remained of the coal-mining industry also witnessed further contraction. At the same time, the 'branch plant economy' - factories established with regional policy support - proved vulnerable to corporate restructuring prompted by the recession; there was an exodus of British (and American) multinationals out of the region. The long term growth of the service sector also came to a halt, affected especially by cuts in public expenditure (Robinson and Goddard, 1982; TUSIU, 1985).

Between 1978 and 1983 the number of employees in employment in the region fell by 185,000, a staggering decline of 14.9%. Most of this loss comprised full-time jobs, about three-quarters of them held by men, predominantly in manufacturing industry. Over this same period, the region's official unemployment count increased by more than 100,000 to over 200,000, rising from a rate of 6.4% in 1978 to 14.6% in 1983 (Table 1), despite repeated fiddling of the figures and the growth of short-term government schemes for the unemployed.

The North was thus left devastated by a recession rooted in a variety of causes (strong competition impacting upon an 'open' economy, underinvestment, low productivity), made much worse by an over-valued pound and government indifference to domestic industrial production, coupled with ideological opposition to Nationalised - and unionised - heavy industries (Byrne, 1992). The south, by contrast, fairly soon moved out of a much shallower recession - and did not understand what Northerners were complaining about. The North-South Divide sounded like a cliché but was real enough: the North's 'moaning minnies', as Thatcher haughtily dubbed them, had much to moan about. Small wonder, then, that in the recession of the early 1990s, Northerners find it hard to feel much real sympathy for those (equally stereotyped) filofax-carrying yuppies, committed Thatcherites once boasting telephone number salaries, now experiencing the economic roller-coaster for themselves.

Partial recovery - then recession again

In the late 1980s, the North at last experienced a degree of economic recovery, stimulated by national economic growth and the consumer boom. This recovery was belated but, of course, welcome, and was seized upon by the region's 'boosters' as evidence that the North's troubles were largely over. In the event it was a false dawn, an upturn which proved fragile and short-lived.

Figures for unemployment fell steadily and substantially in the second half of the 1980s, from the peak of 15.4% in 1985 to the trough reached in 1990 of 8.7% (Table 1). Since then, unemployment in the Northern Region has again risen, though later and more slowly than in the south, reaching 12.0% by April 1993. For the last twenty years, the Northern Region has continued to have the highest regional rates of unemployment in mainland Britain, as well as some of the highest local (travel-to-work area) unemployment rates in the country. The only (somewhat perverse) consolation is that the strong impact of recession in the south has meant that the difference between the level of unemployment in the North and in Great Britain as a whole has significantly narrowed in recent years.

Employment figures (Table 2) provide a similar picture: recovery in the late 1980s and a particularly sharp recent fall when the green shoots of economic growth failed to appear. The number of employees in employment has never returned to the levels reached a decade ago and before (and the scale of decline since the late 1970s is even greater in terms of full-time equivalents). Male employment has fallen very significantly and continues to do so while female employment has fared much better, especially for part-time employees. After a slight increase in the late 1980s, manufacturing employment has resumed the long term trend of decline and service sector employment has fallen back after some expansion in the 'Lawson boom' years. Self employment rose in the 1980s but from a low base and much less substantially than in the south, and has shown itself not only to be very vulnerable to recession but also unable to significantly offset job losses elsewhere in the economy.

Table 1: Unemployment: North and Great Britain, 1978-93

	Northern Region No. (000s)	% rate	Great Britain % rate
1979	93.9	6.5	3.9
1980	115.6	8.0	5.0
1981	165.6	11.8	8.0
1982	187.2	13.3	9.4
1983	202.6	14.6	10.4
1984	214.5	15.3	10.6
1985	221.1	15.4	10.8
1986	221.5	15.2	10.9
1987	203.9	14.0	9.8
1988	174.0	11.9	7.9
1989	140.0	9.9	6.1
1990	122.7	8.7	5.6
1991	143.4	10.3	7.9
1992	157.1	11.3	9.7
1993 (Apr.)	167.8	12.0	10.4

Source: Dept. of Employment: Employment Gazette

Notes: Rates are calculated by expressing the number of unemployed people claiming benefit as a percentage of the estimated total workforce (the sum of unemployed, employees in employment, self-employed and participants in work-related government training programmes). These unemployment rates are annual averages, based on seasonally adjusted figures.

The Northern Region comprises the five Counties of Northumberland, Tyne & Wear, Durham, Cleveland and Cumbria.

Since the mid-1980s, continuing decline and deindustrialisation has been accompanied by some re-industrialisation and physical regeneration. The development of Nissan's new car plant on Wearside is by far the best-known and the largest example of re-industrialisation and has been followed by the arrival of other overseas companies (including several others from the Far East), most of them anxious to establish a low-cost base within the post-1992 European Market. At the same time the region

Table 2: Employees in employment: Northern Region, 1978-93
(Thousands)

	Total	Male	Female All	Female Full time	Female Part time	Manufacturing
1978	1,242	749	493	297	196	415
1979	1,248	741	506	298	208	410
1980	1,209	716	493	286	207	387
1981	1,122	654	468	269	199	339
1982	1,093	633	461	264	197	321
1983	1,057	605	451	252	199	291
1984	1,059	593	466	256	210	277
1985	1,057	593	464	255	209	278
1986	1,061	585	476	254	222	272
1987	1,068	582	486	258	228	272
1988	1,094	595	499	269	230	278
1989	1,088	588	500	272	228	281
1990	1,115	591	524	274	250	273
1991	1,081	567	514	272	242	261
1992	1,088	562	525	267	258	256
1993 (Mar.)	1,052	539	513	257	256	241

Source: Dept of Employment: Employment Gazette
Estimates for June each year.

has seen the development of high profile projects like Gateshead's MetroCentre (said to be the largest retail scheme in Europe) and various waterfront developments promoted by the two Urban Development Corporations (UDCs). As elsewhere, there are business parks with post-modern buildings in the region, much lauded by the local boosters but in reality representing a quite limited level of investment compared with many other parts of the country (and leaving behind a legacy of vacated and unwanted space at other locations in the region). Perhaps most significantly and ironically - in view of the free market rhetoric of the 1980s - almost all of these new developments have been heavily subsidised by the public sector. Nissan and other inward investors received regional policy assistance; the MetroCentre had Enterprise Zone benefits and the UDCs have, in a variety of ways, subsidised property development. (All of which raises pertinent questions about the truth behind the ideology of the 'enterprise culture' and the image of businesses operating in an environment of minimal state intervention - as well as indicating who are the real major beneficiaries of a 'dependency culture'.)

Over this last decade or so the North has undoubtedly changed, but by how much? The North still has the highest level of unemployment of any region in mainland Britain and a per-capita GDP which remains more than 10% below the UK level. The North's cultural underpinnings still seem quite firm, with a strong loyalty to the Labour Party (50.5% voted Labour in the 1992 General Election) and to trade unionism. (41% of those in work in the region in 1992 were in a union, compared with 24% in the south east outside London and 35% nationally.) In spite of everything, it is still easy enough to find men wearing cloth caps, keeping pigeons and whippets and drinking Brown Ale. In contrast, however, one can also point to the demise of male manual industry, the rise of the non-unionised 'flexible' worker, the pervasive consumer culture, the central importance of women as wage earners, and the erosion of working class communities.

The North may not have embraced Thatcherism but the region has certainly been shaken up and changed, especially since 1979. What those changes have been, which of them are really important, what they mean and, moreover, whether they are to be welcomed - these are strongly contested issues which we now move on to explore.

The Great North?

Since the mid-1980s there has been an interesting, though often unedifying, competition between two very different interpretations of the region, its recent development, its problems and prospects. On the one hand there is the long-standing portrayal of the North as a region of chronic unemployment, deep-rooted structural economic problems and as a place significantly worse off than the south. This view, easily sustained by almost all the Tables published in *Regional Trends*, has become distinctly unfashionable. It has proved useless in attempts to secure help from the government although is still of some use in submissions to the European Commission. On the whole, this 'moaning minnie' approach is now the preserve of academics, dissenters and - most revealing of all - is the view which seems to be held by many 'ordinary people' in the region.

The competing interpretation is that the region has undergone a remarkable transformation. The region's 'boosters', the economic development agencies, the local authorities, the urban development corporations, much of the local media - the region's key institutions and personalities - have been vigorously promoting an image of a new 'Great North' involving not just advertising campaigns but also efforts to counter 'negative' comments about the region (see Wilkinson, 1992). According to this 'Great North' view of the world, the past decade has witnessed the renaissance of the region, exemplified by selected symbols: inevitably, the Nissan car plant; the MetroCentre development; and the UDCs' waterfront schemes on Tyneside, Wearside and Teesside. The region's traditional industries and culture are seen as 'heritage'; the region has acquired a new 'enterprise culture', and 'good news' stories are the order of the day. Problems are recognised - but secondary.

This image building, frequently degenerating into 'hype', is regarded as necessary to build self-esteem and investor confidence. Above all, it is supposed to help attract inward investment - though whether it does or not is unknown, probably unknowable. It is sometimes justified on the grounds that all regions (or, at least, all those with serious economic problems) engage in image-building.

The trouble is that, not only is it a very partial view of the region and not only is it disbelieved, even by many of its promoters; it also gets in the way of realistic interpretation, analysis and - therefore - action. The reality is unfortunately much closer to the dismal theses of the 'moaning minnies' camp, and is inevitably much more complex than the advertising copy of the Great North Campaign.

Crisis? What crisis?

Amid the gloom of the recession of the early 1990s, it has not been easy for the region's 'boosters' to sell the idea of a regional renaissance. Eighties' slogans like the 'Great North' (from the Northern Development Company), 'The New North East' (Tyne & Wear Development Corporation) and 'Talent, Initiative, Ability' (Teesside Development Corporation) now seem even more hollow, generating cynicism rather than enthusiasm. Thus the NDC's most recent campaign, recruiting 'Great North Ambassadors' to spread positive publicity about the region armed with their Ambassador Files, fell rather flat even in the region's loyal press. It certainly did not help that the campaign was launched in the same week as the announcement of the first wave of redundancies at Swan Hunters shipyard and at a time when the last of the region's pits were being shut.

Nevertheless, those whose business it is to talk up the region have been able to point to the fact that the North has, so far, weathered recession this time better than the south. Again, there are differing interpretations of this but two points are clear enough. First, the current recession undoubtedly hit the service sector hardest, undermining an insupportable sector bloated by the mid-1980s Lawson boom. Quite simply, since these activities - things like financial and business services - did not really take off in the North this region largely escaped the impact of their collapse. And, secondly, the North started the recession from a position of high unemployment - other regions have been catching up. It is of little comfort to the North, however, that others are now suffering, or that the region missing out on the Thatcher economic miracle has turned out to be a blessing in disguise (though at least very few of the region's house owners are now saddled with negative equity). It is quite apparent, though, that the North-South Divide does not now adequately describe the economic and social geography of the UK as many formerly - and recently - prosperous areas in southern Britain have witnessed massive increases in unemployment.

Other divisions have become more evident, divisions which are found everywhere across the country and which today appear more significant than regional divisions - although the old regional differences are certainly still there. More than a decade of divisive government, which broke with the welfare state consensus and has redistributed income, wealth and power to the already privileged, has created a deeply divided society. Comfortable Britain - some of the working class, most of the middle class, as well as the rich - has seen a real increase in prosperity (if not in security, public services, or contentment). Meanwhile, the poor minority - at least a quarter, perhaps a third, of the population - has been further impoverished, carrying the burdens of deindustrialisation, privatisation, tax giveaways and cuts in welfare benefits and public services. Recently released figures which, incidentally, caused no surprise, no storm of protest and were hardly reported, showed the poorest 10% of the population had seen their living standards (after housing costs) drop in real terms by 14% over the period from 1979 to 1990/91 while each group above them saw a real increase, the higher the starting point the larger the increase (DSS, 1993).

Returning to the issue of whether and how the region has changed, these divisions provide a key to the conflicting interpretations. To the 'boosters' and to many of those still in well-paid jobs the last few years can easily be seen in a positive light. They have personally become more affluent and have been able to partake of much greater opportunities to spend their money, consuming at the MetroCentre or buying out of public services. The boosters' glossy brochures (now not actually glossy and presented in tasteful pastel shades) celebrate these lifestyle opportunities, showing - quite truthfully, in fact - that an executive moving to the region can have a good life here. To those at the other end of the socio-economic spectrum, things look very different. To them, the region has changed, but their experience has been negative and destructive: high unemployment, low household incomes, poor prospects, reliance on declining public services, crime and disorder, shortened and wasted lives. These are the realities which confront a substantial minority of people in the region, which make for the North's poor position in the league tables of *Regional Trends* (CSO, 1993), and which the boosters (not much aware of these realities themselves) must ignore except insofar as they 'sell' a readily available and keen supply of labour.

So, as we noted at the outset, a new Great North co-exists with an impoverished and redundant North, and the separation of these two worlds within the one region helps to maintain the separation and strength of the two competing interpretations. The 'comfortable' Northerner can literally by-pass the West End of Newcastle and not see the hopelessness, fear and destruction; he or she may never enter the redundant pit villages of east Durham and can easily be oblivious to the massive Council estates where much of the region's poor are now concentrated and 'residualised'.

It remains unclear whether this divide is sustainable. At present, much, but by no means all, of the now unmanageable crime and disorder of the disaffected youths in economic ghettos does not spill over into the owner-occupied suburbs but it could well do so. And the assumption that poor communities will hold together in spite of, or even because of, long term adversity and marginalisation was decisively shattered by the Tyneside 'riots' of 1991. The government appears to believe, however, that it is possible to continue to tighten the screws on the poor (through cuts in benefit, new taxes on fuel, and so on) and simply offer occasional crumbs of comfort; such an assumption seems dangerous in view of the levels of dislocation now seen in places where unemployment has become by far the most likely prospect for young people whose own parents have never had the chance of a job themselves.

Finally, moving on from these real fears about social stability in a blatantly unjust society, we should raise the even larger and more complex question of whether the region's economy is sustainable. In the longer term it is evidently not environmentally sustainable, but in the medium term can a service-based economy work? This takes us back neatly to our starting point: deindustrialisation. Failing to maintain, restore and develop manufacturing is the biggest economic failure of the Thatcher years, just as the creation of deep social divisions was its greatest moral failure. Without reconstruction of the manufacturing base the outlook is almost certainly a real decline in living standards, especially when all the 'family silver' has been sold through privatisation and North Sea oil revenues tail off. Moreover, to add insult to injury, the poor and the peripheral regions are likely to suffer most. It is hardly a recipe for either a United Kingdom or a 'classless society'.

3 Wearside in the 'new' North East: Longer term perspectives on industrial restructuring

Ian Stone

Abstract

This chapter contributes to current debates on the 'new' North East through a study of de-industrialisation and attempted re-industrialisation on Wearside over the period 1973-90. Based on a comprehensive database of Wearside manufacturing establishments, it includes an analysis of aggregate change in the number of units and related employment over the period, and uses components of change analysis to identify the contribution of key elements to the restructuring process. The importance of closures and employment contraction is assessed against that of new creations and expansions to provide a perspective on the comparative strengths of the forces of de-industrialisation and those of re-industrialisation. Changes in Wearside's industrial structure are identified, principally as they relate to establishment size, ownership characteristics, sectoral specialisation and location. Dramatic changes have occurred in relation to each of these structural elements, indicating extensive restructuring of the sector and the way it is organised. The final section discusses the implications of changes identified, and assesses the current strengths and weaknesses of the Wearside manufacturing economy with reference to its broader (spatial and temporal) context.

Introduction

The 'new' North East. The concept of a 'new' North East, which has been enthusiastically promoted in recent years by development agencies, the media and other regional interests, is founded upon the supposed renewed strength of the region's productive capability. The apparent robustness of Northern manufacturers in the face of the early 1990s recession is taken as evidence of this change. Newer firms have continued to grow, while the survivors of the last recession - much slimmed down and fitter than in 1980 - have proved themselves able to withstand conditions of prolonged market downturn. A stronger improvement during 1992 than most other UK regions even led to suggestions that the North would lead the national economy out of recession (Cambridge Econometrics, 1993; The Times, 13 May 1991). This re-birth of an old industrial region is attributed to a radical change in attitudes occurring since the early 1980s, including an increased willingness on the part of labour to embrace new employment practices (eg. numerical and functional flexibility), a reduced commitment to unionisation and less adversarial forms of industrial relations. Such changes are considered to have made the region an attractive location for inward investment, particularly from the Far East, and to have assisted management in the process of modernising operations and work practices at longer-established plants.

This view is not an uncontested one. There is certainly a considerable body of opinion in the region which questions the extent and significance of change in the recent past. Some writers have expressed doubts about the achievements claimed for the 1980s on the basis of the limited extent of employment generation and unevenness with which the benefits of growth have been distributed (eg. Hudson, 1991; Robinson and Shaw, 1991) . Others have disputed the dynamism of the 1980s developments and questioned the extent to which there has been a shift in the local production system away from a Fordist regime (eg. Garrahan and Stewart, 1992; Sadler, 1992; Amin and Tomaney 1993).

This chapter contributes to the debate on the nature of change in the Northern economy through an analysis of the impact of industrial restructuring processes on Wearside's manufacturing base. It is founded on the author's comprehensive database of establishments operating in the local economy over the period 1973-90, and thus offers an insight into the anatomy of change associated with de-industrialisation and attempts at job creation in manufacturing which could not be obtained using published statistics. At an aggregate scale it identifies the relative and absolute performance of Wearside manufacturing, and the comparative strength of de-industrialisation processes *vis-à-vis* those of job generation. It also unpacks the restructuring process in terms of the main components of change to reveal the radical shifts which have occurred in sectoral specialisation, ownership characteristics, size profile of establishments and spatial location. On the basis of detailed knowledge concerning the structural trends in Wearside's manufacturing, it is possible to identify the longer-term trajectory of the sector, its strengths and weaknesses, and capacity for future growth.

Wearside is an appropriate case study through which to inform debates on the emergence of a 'new' North East. In the early 1970s, its manufacturing economy was very much representative of the wider region. It was sectorally relatively specialised, organised predominantly in terms of large production units belonging to companies with headquarters elsewhere in the UK, and spatially concentrated upon the town (now city) of Sunderland which was overwhelmingly dominant in terms of its share of the Borough's manufacturing employment. External control had increased steadily over the post-war period as a result of both takeovers and the establishment of branch plants by non-local companies to stand at over 80% of employment. New branch factories undoubtedly diversified the economy away from the traditional staples of coal, glass, shipbuilding and marine engineering towards new light engineering industries. Apart from the mining and processing of coal, Wearside's industry in the early 1970s was in private rather than state ownership, although this was shortly to change, notably in relation to shipbuilding facilities which were nationalised later in the decade.

Today's Wearside is promoted as very much an integral part of the 'new' North East. Indeed, for many, the region's economic transformation is symbolised by the closure of Sunderland's last remaining shipyard - a remnant of an industry identified with public subsidy, workforce inflexibility and a culture of unionisation - and its replacement by an emerging cluster of new internationally-competitive activites centred upon Nissan's Washington car factory, with its much vaunted 'Japanese' manufacturing and employment practices. Having watched helplessly the avalanche of closures and redundancies in local industry in the late 1970s and early 1980s, local policy-makers seized on inward investment successes to promote Wearside as 'the advanced manufacturing centre of the North' and exhort investors to 'Make it in Wearside'. The Wearside Opportunity (TWO), a local private sector initiative in partnership with the local authority, the DTI and development agencies, was specifically created to foster regeneration by building on Wearside's manufacturing traditions, including the attraction of further inward investment (capitalising on Nissan's decision) and support for local manufacturing enterprises.

The database of Wearside manufacturing establishments covers the period 1973-1990. The terminal dates are comparable in terms of the stage of the business cycle they represent (ie. relatively buoyant conditions); 1973 is also a benchmark year in that it immediately precedes the first oil shock to the UK's industrial base. The database, compiled from numerous sources, including direct interviews and telephone surveys, achieves near 100% coverage of establishments, with only the occasional very small (<5 employees) short-life plant escaping inclusion. The definition of 'Wearside' used here relates to the area of Sunderland Borough, made up of two significant urban settlements, Sunderland itself (population 191,000) and Washington New Town (60,000), together with the mainly rural former coalfield zone to the south consisting of Hetton-le-Hole and Houghton-le-Spring (population 45,000).

Context and relevant concepts De-industrialisation is central to any analysis of the longer-term process of industrial change affecting urban areas. The industrial experience of any urban centre reflects this phenomenon as a specific outcome of interactions between external forces and local conditions. Government policies, at different spatial scales, have combined with more general processes in the business and technological environment to create the context in which industrial change has occurred; both the overall dimensions of change and the emerging pattern of manufacturing activity have been influenced crucially by these outside factors interacting with local structures and processes.

De-industrialisation refers to a process whereby an economy experiences an absolute and proportional decline in industrial employment (declining output is not necessary to most definitions, although in the case of the UK there has been a marginal decline in production since 1973). While there is debate over the phenomenon's cause, it is commonly thought to have been exacerbated in this country by the ability of foreign manufacturers to out-compete their British counterparts through achieving higher levels of productivity and a greater willingness to adopt new technology (see review by Caslin, 1987; also Dintenfass, 1992). If mining is included, then de-industrialisation in this coalfield area pre-dates the emergence of the phenomenon at the national scale by around a decade. As far as manufacturing is concerned, the de-industrialisation phenomenon has only been of significance since the early 1970s in this region. Although the national economy began losing manufacturing employment after 1966, the redistribution - through regional policy inducements and controls - of the new jobs generated within the country favoured the North. This meant that the region more or less held its employment level in the sector up to the early 1970s, in spite of the contraction in traditional manufacturing activities (NRST, 1977). It is thus only since that time that job generation via the attraction and development of industry has become one of attempted *re*-industrialisation - in the sense of reversing the proportional and absolute decline in manufacturing employment. This phase reflects an adverse structural shift in the balance of employment turnover resulting from a combination of enhanced levels of contraction and closure and a dramatic fall in the number of mobile investment projects. The extent of this shift - and its implications - are examined below with reference to Wearside's experience.

The main characteristics of the industrial re-structuring process at the sub-regional level - the extent and timing of contraction, the establishments affected by rationalisation, the number of new creations and associated jobs - are conditioned by the broader context of business environment and government policy. Significant changes have occurred in this context since the early 1970s, and the structural developments in the Wearside economy reflect this. Prominent among these changes are the internationalisation of business, the greater emphasis within production upon flexibility, and the enhanced competition to which UK manufacturers have been exposed resulting from the increasing openness of the economy. Competition for mobile investment projects has intensified due to internationalisation, and the location requirements (environmental and social) of such investors have become more precise.

At the national scale, government policy since the late 1970s shifted radically away from interventionism and demand management primarily aimed at achieving full employment, towards monetary measures designed principally to control inflation. Within this framework, measures to improve the supply-side of the economy and market determination of economic outcomes have been dominant (for details of policy changes, see Stone, 1994). Thus, the 1980s were marked by anti-union legislation and other measures to make the labour market more responsive to price signals, increased support for innovation and small businesses, privatisation of state enterprises, and an unwillingness to support loss-making activities. Government has resisted the notion that it should take a generally more interventionist stance in relation to industry; indeed, for virtually an entire decade it showed scant concern for the requirements of manufacturing where these came into conflict with other priorities, particularly controlling inflation. While regional policy subsidies and coverage have been reduced sharply, much emphasis - nationally and regionally - has been placed upon attracting inward investment. Central government's resistance of EC attempts to establish common policies on employment has meshed with its labour market reforms to make the UK the prime European location for foreign capital in the 1980s.

Within the framework of this external environment, changes on Wearside have also been conditioned by more local processes. The extent and pattern of rationalisation affecting the stock of establishments existing at the beginning of the period is influenced by the nature of those investments - for example, age of plant and equipment, on-site functions, labour relations, products, markets and skills - and the specific outcomes reflect an interaction between external and local factors. The process of industrial renewal, whether through investment in existing plants, incoming greenfield investments or new start-ups, is similarly influenced by Wearside's industrial past and its experience of restructuring, particularly as these impact significantly upon the character of the labour market. De-industrialisation and re-industrialisation are thus not discrete processes, but ones which are linked in a complex manner. Earlier waves of investment in Wearside combined to give rise to particular forms of social structure, which in turn have conditioned the character of subsequent waves. In the manner described by Massey (1984) the emerging character of Wearside's manufacturing sector, and particularly the investments of the 1980s, cannot be understood without reference to the specific history of the locality in terms of its industrial structure and related labour market characterstics (see also Sadler, 1992). These are important in determining the role the area plays in the broader spatial division of labour.

Trends in Wearside's manufacturing employment 1973-90

In overall terms, manufacturing employment in Wearside has declined dramatically over the period 1973 to 1990, falling by 43% from 43,150 to 24,580. The largest losses occurred during the recession of the early 1980s, when 11,000 manufacturing jobs disappeared between 1979 and 1983 alone, representing a massive 30% drop in only four years. Manufacturing employment's slow recovery from its 1986 low of just below 24,000 jobs was interrupted in the late 1980s by the closure of North East Shipbuilders Ltd (NESL). Largely because of this labour market shock, there was virtually no improvement in the level of employment in manufacturing during the boom of the late 1980s, and Wearside's factories actually employed *fewer* people in 1990 than they had in 1983. The new jobs being created by inward investment and small firms were outweighed by those being lost in the traditional sectors, even at a time when, notwithstanding NESL's closure, the overall pace of de-industrialisation had slackened markedly. In net terms, therefore, forces for industrial contraction were such that, even in the boom period of the 1980s, re-industrialisation was not taking place.

In spite of its 43% fall, Wearside's manufacturing employment actually held up better than that in the rest of Tyne and Wear, where the contraction was even greater (down 54% between 1973 and 1989). Wearside's contraction is substantially worse, however, than the national performance (a loss of one third), although research into industrial employment change within the UK suggests that this pattern is consistent with expectations, given Wearside's position as an industrial district within a conurbation in the northern half of Britain (Champion and Townsend, 1990). Wearside began the period with 38% of its employment in the manufacturing sector, which was substantially above the figure for the UK as a whole (32%) and represented an unambiguous specialisation in manufacturing. By the end of the period it had fallen to 25%, which is not significantly above the national average for 1989 (23%) and the same as figure as for the Northern Region.

Even the 25% proportional figure is achieved only because of the overall shrinkage of the total employment level on Wearside. While the employed population at national level actually increased over the period, Wearside's declined (according to Census of Employment figures for 1973-89) by around 18%. This is due primarily to the scale of shrinkage in manufacturing, though job losses in coalmining (from 8,600 down to 2,000), and construction (8,000 to 4,800) - combined with service sector growth which was sluggish compared to national trends - have been important elements. Even allowing for some rise in self-employment, job opportunities have fallen sharply. Official unemployment doubled over the two decades since 1973 (from 8,750 to around 17,500 in 1993), and would have been higher but for a fall of nearly 6,000 in Wearside's population in the decade to 1991.

Components of change analysis gives a more detailed breakdown of the contribution respectively of job loss and re-industrialisation efforts to the net reduction of manufacturing employment. Closures have played a particularly prominent part in the restructuring. Of the 1973 stock of 329 establishments, over half (178) had closed by 1987, resulting in the loss of 19,245 jobs (Table 1). Further employment loss was incurred through *in situ* employment change. The 65 surviving establishments which contracted accounted for a loss to the local economy of 9,663 jobs, which far outweighed the job gains (amounting to 3,048) among the 73 establishments which expanded their employment. There was thus a net contraction due to *in situ* change of some 6,615. New creations, consisting of those establishments formed on Wearside or moving in from outside the area, were the chief source of jobs to replace those lost through closures and contractions. However, due to their small average employment size, such units were more impressive in terms of numbers (293) than in their contribution to jobs (7,400). The 1973 stock of manufacturing establishments thus experienced a net decline of almost 26,000 in its workforce over the period to 1987, while the inflow from new creations amounted to little more than a quarter of that total.

Table 1: Wearside manufacturing: components of change, 1973-87

	Number of Establishments	Employment change
Initial stock 1973	329	43,150
New Creations	293	+7,400
Closures	178	-19,245
Expansions in situ	73	+3,048
Contractions in situ	65	-9,663
Unchanged	13	-
Stock 1987	443	24,580
Net change 1973-87	+115	-18,460

Source: Author's Wearside industrial database, 1973-90

Predictably, the net job losses were more marked in the post-1979 period, when the largely recession-induced fall in employment was 11,480, compared to 6,980 for 1973-79. While during the second period the closure rate increased from 8,560 to 12,960 and *in situ* employment change worsened, there was also a rise in both the number of new creations and associated employment (which doubled, from 2,590 to 5,050). Altogether, the rate at which new jobs were being generated in the Wearside manufacturing sector - either from new firm formation, in-movers or growth among existing firms - though improving, did not rise significantly over the two periods (up from 7,380 to 8,130). At the same time, the rate at which factory jobs were being lost through closure and contraction increased markedly, resulting in a sharper overall rate of decline in employment during 1979-87.

Performance and structural change

This section breaks down this overall performance into its component parts to identify the structural change in more detail. The changes are summarised in the Appendix (sections 2-5 in Table).

(a) Establishment size

The poor performance of the large employers on Wearside was central to the dramatic fall in manufacturing employment. In 1973 the local economy was dominated by large units; there were no fewer than 24 plants with 500 or more workers, accounting between them for 28,500 jobs (two-thirds of the total). While establishments with 50 or fewer employees made up nearly 70% of the total number of operators, these accounted for just 3,400 jobs, or less than 8% of the total. By 1990 there were just *eight* manufacturing plants on Wearside with over 500 workers, employing altogether just under 8,000 people. In 1973 Wearside had three establishments with over 3,000 employees, and a further two with over 2,000. By 1990, there were only *three* plants (Corning's glassworks, Grove Coles cranes and Nissan) with 1,000 or more workers.

Wearside's bigger plants, those with 500+ workers, have been less prone to outright closure than smaller ones - though by virtue of their size such shutdowns have had a profound effect on the local economy. The nine plants of this size which had closed by 1987 resulted in the loss of 11,000 jobs, more than a quarter of the 1973 total. These plants have also tended to be more vulnerable to contraction: labour shedding by thirteen of the big plants led to the loss of 8,400 jobs. Only two of the plants in this size category expanded over the period. However, this contraction occurred at a time when there were few large replacement investments available to peripheral economies, compared to the period before the mid-1970s when there was much more industrial mobility and many branch plants moved to the North East. Only one such greenfield project - Nissan - came to Wearside; it is not surprising, therefore, that it has been accorded such significance.

The net employment losses among the large plants (-17,040) dwarfed the changes in other size brackets. Those in the 50-199 and 200-499 size groups each incurred net losses in terms both of unit numbers and employment, though these were moderate by comparison (net losses of 19 establishments and 3,100 jobs). It is the smaller size bands where the growth occurred, although, again, the net gains were small alongside the scale of losses among the large plants, as indicated by the fact that the growth in the number of establishments (from 329 to 443) was accompanied by a fall in the average size of manufacturing establishment (from 131 employees to 55). Over the period 1973-87, establishments with less than 50 employees showed net gains in terms of numbers (+142) and employment (+1,670). These establishments performed better in terms of *all* the components of change than those in larger size bands, and are the only ones which as a group finished the period larger in employment terms than they were in 1973.

In 1990, establishments with 50 or fewer employees accounted for 82% of the 443 units and 21% of manufacturing employment. The employers with 500 or more workers now account for less than a third (32%) of total employment. In Wearside, therefore, as elsewhere, small and medium-sized enterprises have increased their share of employment due to the combined effect of contraction among large units (causing them to be re-allocated to lower size bands) and a relatively good employment performance by small firms.

Urban economies like Wearside's thus face an awkward coincidence of changes: first, any growth of smaller and medium enterprises (SMEs) derives from a small base given the historical dominance of large employers; secondly, the contribution that this growth in SMEs can make to local employment is heavily offset by the contraction in employment among the larger establishments. Similar urban economies undergoing a long-term process of de-industrialisation are thus paying a double price for their previous dependence on a small number of key industrial firms.

(b) Ownership

Employment performance within Wearside manufacturing is mainly differentiated in terms of ownership category, although the influence of this is also bound up with less distinct factors relating to establishment size, product specialism and location. There are clear differences in growth between the indigenous or Wearside-owned firms and the externally-owned sector, and within the external sector itself. The latter can be divided into non-Wearside owned plants belonging to UK companies and those in foreign ownership. The Wearside and overseas-owned establishments have both been, proportionately and absolutely, less affected by de-industrialisation and made a greater contribution to re-industrialisation than the non-Wearside UK plants, which performed abysmally over the period.

The fact that the majority of Wearside's larger plants were part of UK companies, while indigenous firms controlled the bulk of the small establishments, undoubtedly helps account for the sharp divergence in performance by size identified in the last section. It is important, however, to note that the observed contrast in growth between the indigenous and externally-owned UK sector applies regardless of size: on Wearside, the performance of smaller externally-owned UK plants was not only worse than that of the indigenous small firms, but also worse than the larger plants in the same ownership group. It is also worth recording that separate analysis of the group of plants with headquarters elsewhere in the Northern Region revealed that the latter's performance was not significantly different from that of plants with headquarters elsewhere in the UK. *Regionally*-owned companies, it seems, proved no more useful in retaining employment in their non-headquarter plants than nationally-owned ones, reflecting the crisis for UK firms in general and the vulnerability of branch plants during company rationalisations.

Reflecting their poor performance at a national level, employment in externally-owned UK establishments has collapsed in the period since 1973 and is the chief cause of the huge aggregate fall in Wearside's manufacturing jobs. Over the period to 1987, the indigenous and foreign-owned sectors both managed to avoid substantial contraction overall, with net losses of 5% and 9% respectively. These ownership groupings actually made gains in terms of number of plants (62% and 57%). In contrast, the external UK sector experienced a fall of 27% in terms of number of plants (down from 102 to 74) and a reduction of 62% in employment. This sector's net decline in jobs (17,440) was not far short of the 18,460 reduction in manufacturing employment overall. Moreover, these trends have continued since 1987. While the indigenous sector remained unchanged over 1987-1990, and the foreign sector, in spite of a large divestment, had expanded to almost 7,000 jobs (making an overall gain of 2.4% since 1973), the external UK sector continued to shrink, falling to 9,800 (a 65% fall compared with its 1973 level of 28,150). Such a percentage fall was immensely significant for Wearside, given that 66% out of the 83% of jobs in external control in 1973 were in the factories of UK companies.

Available evidence relating to another urban centre in the UK periphery suggests that the scale of the collapse in the external UK sector on

Wearside was not untypical. In the only comparable UK study covering this period, Hart (1989) shows for Belfast that employment in the original stock of externally-owned estabishments fell by 67% over the period 1973-86. This compares with an equivalent figure of 61% for Sunderland during 1973-87.

The poor performance by the external UK group was particularly pronounced in the branch plant sector. This consisted of mobile investments attracted to Wearside since the 1950s through infrastructural investment in industrial estates, the availability of labour, and capital subsidies. These incoming plants, a number of which were large employers, were the prime source of new jobs replacing those being lost in the 'sunset' industries. They consisted of mainly light industries, many of which broke with the past in offering job opportunities for women. The relative absence of local linkages, their limited range of functions and the simple semi-skilled assembly operations which characterised many of these plants made them cheap to close and thus vulnerable in company rationalisations (Watts, 1981). In the event, branch plants of UK companies have proved particularly susceptible to recession and the sector declined precipitously over the period, as closures halved the number of establishments (from 41 to 21) and employment fell by almost three-quarters (from 11,900 to 2,750). Closures affecting just six plants, combined with a dramatic contraction in a seventh (which has subsequently closed altogether), resulted in the loss of over 10,000 jobs.

Only two closures of plants of significant size occurred among the foreign-owned branch plants (Timex and RCA Records, which together accounted for just over 1,000 of the initial stock of jobs). The overwhelming losses occurred among the *UK-owned* branch plants, due in some cases to a market contraction giving rise to consolidation of production at sites elsewhere (eg. TI Tubes and Cape Insulation), and in others to product obsolesence. Examples of the latter include Plessey (electro-mechanical telephone exchange equipment), Hepworth and Jackson the Tailor (made-to-measure suits), and Thorn-EMI (TV and radio components) (for more detail, see Stone and Stevens, 1986). These branch plants were typical of many established in the 1960s and 70s in lacking the capacity to develop their own new products (and markets), and being dependent on corporate decisions made outside the region for new product lines.

At the heart of the 'traditional' sector of Wearside industry - and, as subsidiaries, a substantial element of the UK-owned sector of the local economy - was the integrated shipbuilding and marine engineering complex, which in 1973 accounted for a quarter of manufacturing jobs. At that time Wearside could boast a fully-comprehensive shipbuilding capacity consisting of five shipbuilding yards (two of which were about to undergo wholesale modernisation and the installation of covered building facilities), a repair and refit yard (Greenwell's), two marine engine building facilities (George Clark and Doxford Engines), a marine electrical installation, propshaft and propeller service unit (Sunderland Forge), and a specialist marine coatings factory (Camrex). Numerous small establishments specialised in supplying castings and componentry for the vessel construction and outfitting activities. Although the key firms in this sector had, by the early 1970s, been acquired by companies headquartered elsewhere in the UK (and in some cases - notably Austin and Pickersgill and Sunderland Shipbuilders - were subsequently nationalised), these were mostly operations with considerable local autonomy and a wide range of on-site operational functions, including design capability.

This core industry has now virtually disappeared. The drawn-out recession in merchant shipbuilding, which lasted from the mid-1970s through to the late 1980s, saw extensive corporate re-organisation and rationalisation undertaken (following nationalisation of the industry in 1977) by British Shipbuilders. This rationalisation, which began with a reduction in the number of berths on the Wear, resulted in the creation of North East Shipbuilders Ltd in 1986. Shipbuilding activity on the Tees and the Wear was concentrated in Sunderland, with the closure of Smith's Dock in Middlesbrough and the amalgamation of the two modernised Wearside yards, Sunderland Shipbuilders and Austin and Pickersgill (Stone, 1989). When an orders crisis arose shortly afterwards, attempts at privatisation became enmeshed in the financial arrangements associated with the sale of the Govan shipyard to a foreign buyer and EC rules on subsidies, culminating in the yard's closure in 1989 (Hinde, 1993). The contraction of the core business locally and throughout the UK led to re-organisation and rationalisation among other subsidiaries in the complex. Unlike the branch plant sector, the establishments of which have tended to be relatively isolated within the local economy, the contraction of the shipbuilding core gave rise to decline throughout the whole complex of associated activities (Raby, 1977; Stone and Stevens, 1986). Only the smaller, less specialised or less dependent suppliers have been able to survive this through diversification into other markets.

Surviving plants, both subsidiaries in the 'traditional' industries and post-war greenfield branch factory investments, have undertaken bouts of labour-shedding as production has been intensified. Plant-level re-organisation, the introduction of more flexible work practices, investment in new process technology and increased use of sub-contractors contributed to the total of 6,000 jobs lost through *in situ* contraction in external UK plants during the period 1973-87. The contracting-out of work formerly undertaken in-house by large plants is just one of the developments encouraging the growth of the indigenous sector. Others include the introduction since the late 1970s of a panoply of measures (including financial support, information and advice, and tax concessions) designed to encourage the formation and growth of small businesses, the growth of opportunities in *niche* markets and higher level of unemployment which has 'pushed' individuals made redundant by larger firms to seek to make use of their skills (and redundancy money) by setting-up their own business.

The contrast in performance between the indigenous and externally-owned UK sector is striking (see Table 2). The 238 new indigenous creations is equivalent to over seven times the number (33) created by firms from elsewhere in the UK over 1973-87. Moreover, these local firms gave rise to two-and a half times as many jobs (3,820 compared with 1,570 in the externally-owned UK establishments). Even the closure rate among indigenous firms, in spite of its domination by small firms, was lower (47% compared with 66%). More Wearside firms expanded (55) than contracted (31) over the period, resulting in a net gain of 580 jobs; the reverse was true of the external UK plants, where surviving units experienced a net *fall* in workforce of 4,500. Moreover, the performance of the indigenous firms actually improved in the 1980s compared with the 1970s (net growth of 1.5% and -6% respectively), while, conversely, the externally-owned UK firms declined in employment terms by 19% in the 1970s and 41% during 1979-87. Finally, it should be noted that, in addition, there was a net transfer (via acquisition) of some 1,500 jobs *from* the indigenous *to* the externally-owned sector.

Evidence suggests that the performance by the Wearside indigenous sector was relatively good in comparison with its counterpart in other local economies. During the period 1986-90, employment growth in the surviving small (<50 employees) indigenous firms grew at an annual rate of 11.4%, compared with 7.7% for Northern Ireland, 4.8% for Leicestershire and 3.0% for the Republic of Ireland (NIERC, 1992). In addition, figures indicate that the contribution of new indigenous firms to the stock of manufacturing jobs may also have improved. Storey *et al* (1982) calculated that new jobs established in the county of Tyne and Wear over the period 1965-78 amounted to 3.7% of the total stock in manufacturing. Wearside data (relating to part of that county) suggests a figure of 15.5% for 1987, which is a considerable improvement, even allowing for the greater fall in the size of the stock of jobs.

Table 2: Wearside manufacturing: components of change 1973-87 by ownership categories

	New creations	Closures	Expansions	Contractions	Net change
External UK	+1,568	-13,940	+1,660	-6,422	-17,438
External overseas	+2,009	-2,071	+223	-2,653	-638
Indigenous	+3,823	-3,234	+1,165	-588	-384

Source: Author's Wearside industrial database, 1973-90

The foreign-owned sector also performed better than the external UK plants, reflecting a trend identified regionally (Smith and Stone, 1989). As a result of recent (ie. post-1985) expansion, the overseas-owned establishments in aggregate recorded a slight gain (2.4%) over the period 1973-1990 in terms of employment, which stood in 1990 at just under 7,000. Since 1973 there has been a near doubling in the number of plants, with 20 of the 38 establishments in 1990 being set up in the 1980s. The influx of new plants has thus more than compensated for rationalisation since 1973 affecting foreign branch plants (eg. closures of Timex and RCA Records) and acquired establishments in 'traditional' sectors (notably contractions at Corning's glassworks and the electronics components factories Electrosil and Philips, plus the closure of Domtar's Hendon papermill).

The recent expansion also means than the overseas sector's performance on Wearside for the period since 1978 is more or less in line with that for the Northern Region as a whole. While this might seem unimpressive, given Nissan's arrival, it should be remembered that, unlike the situation in the region as a whole - where net acquisition of UK establishments by foreign companies has been important in counterbalancing the effect of losses through closure and contraction - on Wearside growth has been virtually entirely through *new greenfield* investments. By 1990, with quite a few of the recent investments still in their development stage, the foreign plants together accounted for just over 28% of the manufacturing total (up from less than 16% in 1973); the estimated figure for 1991 is 33%. Set against an equivalent figure for the Northern Region of just under 20% (Smith and Stone, 1989), this indicates a high degree of concentration of Wearside's manufacturing employment in foreign plants.

(c) Sectoral composition

Significant change in the pattern of industrial specialisation has taken place in the Wearside economy as a result of the processes of de-industrialisation and re-industrialisation. In 1973, the most important sectors (SIC two-digit classes) were all engaged in branches of engineering - mechanical; electrical and electronic; and shipbuilding and marine. These three sectors were virtually identical in terms of their employment, with 18% of the total in each. Together with the next largest sectors, clothing (12%) and glass (10%), they made up over three-quarters (76%) of the total employment in manufacturing. While the number of jobs in mechanical engineering and clothing fell over the period to 1990 at a rate slightly below that of manufacturing as a whole, the employment reductions in electrical engineering (down by 64%), shipbuilding (-86%) and glass/non-metallic minerals (-73%) has meant a dramatic deterioration in their absolute and relative importance, with the latter two sectors falling respectively to just 4% and 5% of the total by 1990.

Actual increases in employment have been achieved in just four sectors, most prominently motor vehicles (up from 135 jobs to 3,300 in 1990), but also in rubber and plastics (+59%), paper and printing (+31%) and timber and furniture (+4%). By 1990, as a result of the differential growth, mechanical engineering (with 19% of manufacturing jobs) - still the largest sector - was followed in relative importance by the rapidly-growing motor vehicles sector (13%), clothing (12%) and electrical engineering and paper and printing (both 11%). These five leading sectors now account for two-thirds (66%) of manufacturing employment. Although this might be taken as indicating a shift towards a more diversified economy, the rapid projected growth in vehicles is likely to result in a significant increase in specialisation over the 1990s.

Large plants have exerted a dominating influence over the changing sectoral characteristics of the Wearside industrial economy. The disengagement of large employers noted above has been the main factor in the decline in those sectors which lost most jobs (mechanical engineering, electrical engineering, shipbuilding and glass). Employment in these sectors declined from 27,500 to 9,580 over the period to 1990. Similarly, the emergence of the motor vehicles sector as an important employer is crucially related to one key large firm. The employment loss attending the demise of the large establishments in each of the main sectors experiencing decline has not in any way been compensated for by the substantial number of new firms established *in these very sectors* during the period. Increases in terms of number of establishments have taken place virtually across the whole spectrum of sectors, and the increases since 1973 are by no means proportionally in favour of the sectors which have shown employment growth. Growth in the better performing sectors for the most part reflects the absence of large declining employers whose contraction more than nullifies the job generation impact of new enterprises.

The pattern of sectoral specialisation is differentiated by ownership. Indigenous firms have a significant presence across a wider range of sectors compared with the externally-owned enterprises. Mechanical engineering, the industry with by far the largest number of plants (62), together with paper and printing, accounts for 38% of total manufacturing employment among Wearside-owned firms. These and four other SIC classes with a further 45% of employment (other metal goods; food and drink; clothing; and timber and furniture) are the sectors where new creations have been most numerous over the period. UK-owned external plants are more concentrated sectorally. Mechanical engineering and clothing together account for 54% of employment in the establishments of this group, followed by electrical engineering, shipbuilding, timber and furniture and paper and printing with a further 31%. The limited number of new plants formed over the period by this group have been mainly in mechanical engineering and the labour-intensive clothing sector. The foreign sector has shown little interest in the traditional specialist Wearside sectors, particularly mechanical engineering. Moreover, this group is even more highly concentrated, with 68% of employment in motor vehicles and electrical engineering, and a further 20% in rubber and plastics (mainly related to the car industry) and glass products.

(d) Location

The clear differences in manufacturing performance by zone within Wearside suggest that spatial re-organisation is a strategic element within the restructuring process. The older industrial centre of Sunderland itself has shed more jobs since 1973 than Wearside as a whole. In aggregate, more than 20,000 manufacturing jobs have gone in this part of Wearside, and the fall continued, albeit at a slower rate than during the early 1980s recession, right through to 1990. Although the overall number of manufacturing jobs in Wearside remained fairly stable during 1983-90, 3,500 jobs disappeared in Sunderland itself during these years. From an initial 1973 total of nearly 34,000 jobs (79% of the total), employment in manufacturing had by 1990 fallen to 13,734 (56%) (see Appendix). This compares with a figure of 8,531 for Washington, which has seen its share of total Wearside manufacturing employment rise from 14% in 1973 to 35%. Indeed, Washington has gained almost as many jobs since 1983 as Sunderland has lost.

These figures, moreover, *understate* the shift in the manufacturing locus away from Sunderland and towards Washington. This is because Sunderland's total, based on post-code designation, includes employment at Nissan's factory (and that of one of its satellites), which is located to the west of the A19 and perceived by many to be properly part of Washington. To credit the Nissan complex jobs to the New Town would significantly alter the balance, and would mean that Washington in 1992 is, in employment terms, the prime manufacturing centre of Wearside.

In terms of components of change, Washington's strong performance in comparison with Sunderland has been achieved in spite of the fact that losses through closures have been higher in the New Town than in the old urban core. Washington attracted a considerable proportion of branch plant investments, which, as has been seen, were especially prone to closure in this period. It is largely because of this that Washington's losses through closure over the period 1973-87 amounted to 47% of initial employment, compared to 32% in Sunderland. Washington's main strength has been its ability to generate jobs through new creations. In spite of its smaller employment base, the New Town has, throughout the period, created more employment than Sunderland (even including Nissan within the latter's figures) through new creations; more than twice as many jobs during 1973-79 and 31% more during 1979-87. Furthermore, proportionately, in both periods, Washington's surviving establishments performed better than their Sunderland counterparts: relatively more of them expanded than contracted; those expanding gained more jobs and those contracting lost fewer.

The job gains due to new creations achieved by Washington are in part a reflection of the New Town's appeal to inward investors. If Nissan and Nissan-Yamato are left aside, ten out of twelve foreign investments during the 1985-90 period went to Washington, and only one (small) project to Sunderland. This is at least partly related to investors' perceptions regarding the nature of local labour markets and their attempts to develop in greenfield sites particular forms of industrial relations (Lever, 1991; Peck and Stone, 1992). But Washington's performance is in relation to new firm formation and is also significantly better than that of Sunderland. Precisely why the New Town should offer a better environment for start-ups and growth is an interesting question. Its performance is consistent with the argument of Fothergill and Gudgin (1982) that factors such as access and the availability of premises are important. Equally, it may reflect linkages between small firms and the role of the Development Corporation, which for most of the period promoted the locational attractions of its restricted area and offered support, including rent and rate discounts, to new firms and to businesses seeking to re-locate from outside. Whatever the explanation, the growth achieved by indigenous firms located in Washington - the 'New Town effect' - is an important factor behind the relatively good performance of Wearside's small firms in relation to other areas for which data is available.

Wearside's manufacturing sector in the 1990s

It is clear from the preceding analysis that the Wearside manufacturing economy has undergone radical restructuring over the past decade or so. In terms of the indicators included in the appended table, the manufacturing economy of today is markedly different from that of 1973. The sector is markedly smaller, the change in the balance of sectoral activity has made it more diverse (although this is probably a transitional phenomenon), and there are many fewer really large employers and a much larger number of small ones. There has been a strong tendency for Washington New Town rather than Sunderland to be favoured as a location for business, and Wearside's ownership profile has shifted sharply away from plants headquartered in other parts of the UK and towards indigenous and overseas sources of control. Outwardly these are substantial changes. Indeed, to anyone returning to Wearside after an absence of 20 years, the impression of change in the industrial fabric would be striking. Indeed, the cessation of shipbuilding and of coalmining, and the replacement of these industries with a brand new car manufacturing facility, would appear a momentous change, both industrially and psychologically. This section assesses some of the major developments and their implications for the sector's growth prospects.

The failure of the externally-owned UK establishments, both in the private and public sectors, is central to the structural transformation of recent years. It reflects the relative failure of British manufacturing industry during the 1970s and 80s, in the face of increased international competition, an uncompetitive pound and lack of domestic support for industry. Indeed, on the basis of longer-term trends, by the mid-1990s both the indigenous and overseas-owned sectors on Wearside will be larger in employment terms than the externally-owned UK sector. Reflecting the low-technology specialisation within British manufacturing in general, the group of UK establishments are generally in labour-intensive sectors of limited technological sophistication: mechanical engineering and clothing alone account for over half the employment. The basis for endogenous expansion within this group is limited, and unless prospects for growth in UK manufacturing improve markedly, further contraction of this sector is indicated.

A continuation of the "re-indigenisation" of manufacturing can be anticipated, although external takeovers of successful local companies will, as in the past, restrict the growth of indigenous firms as a group. In spite of such takeovers, the indigenous sector has increased its share of employment from 19% to 32%, which suggests a shift back towards the situation existing up to the 1950s, when capital was mainly under local control. It is predictable, given trends in technology, the organisation of production and policy relating to smaller firms, that the indigenous sector - which is composed mainly of small firms - should show a relatively improved performance. This development, for a number of reasons, is less significant than it appears, however. In fact, the data shows that the growth in Wearside firms' share of employment has been almost entirely due to the overall fall in the number of manufacturing jobs, although this is not to discount the fact that the sector has held its employment in the face of severe industrial contraction, and that the number of units has increased markedly.

More significantly, a question mark must be placed over the *dynamism* of the indigenous sector and its capacity for further growth. The Wearside economy, like that of the Northern Region as a whole, lacks a significant core of small to medium-sized locally-controlled companies with significant growth potential. Altogether, in 1990 there were 33 Wearside-owned firms (out of a total of 443 establishments) with 50 or more employees, accounting for 17% of the total employment. Of these firms, just *four* (Berghaus, Rite-Vent, E.P.Thompson and Vaux Brewery) had in excess of 250 employees. Apart from Berghaus - which was actually the subject of a takeover by a UK company in 1993 - these firms are engaged in sectors which are hardly those most affected by intensified international competition. The local economy has, in fact, recently lost (through re-location to Team Valley, Gateshead) Bonas Machines, an indigenous company manufacturing computer-controlled weaving equipment based on on-site design and development, which had a successful record in world markets.

There is a core of small indigenous businesses which have established themselves making products for *niche* markets serving customers beyond the region, both in the UK and abroad. Examples include firms producing specialist chemicals, medical diagnostic kits and electronic random number generators for lotteries. The rationalisation at Corning's glassworks factory has given rise to numerous small businesses established by skilled glass-blowers made redundant over the years. Many of these are turning out quality glassware products conceived and designed in-house for markets overseas. These are, nonetheless, all small employers. Indeed, empirical research suggests that very few new firms are likely to become significant employers (eg. Storey, 1982). Wearside's experience is consistent with this finding: of the 39 firms which were established since 1973 and are of at least ten years' standing, *none* were found to have more than fifty employees.

The majority of indigenous firms typically compete in a regional market, usually on a sub-contract basis. This particularly applies to mechanical engineering, metal goods and clothing firms. Where they have their 'own' products, they are largely to be found in markets sheltered from overseas competition and mainly in those where entry costs are comparatively low. It is no coincidence that the sectors with the best record in terms of spawning new enterprises (mechanical engineering, clothing, printing and timber products) are the ones where employment performance at the national level has been better than the average due, at least in part, to natural protection. Many of the firms, particularly those in mechanical engineering and metal goods, have introduced new process equipment over the last decade, as a means of widening the range of sub-contract services they can offer, but they remain reliant upon major firms for their orders, carry out no design function, and do little in the way of marketing. In the light of the structural weaknesses of the indigenous sector as a whole, it is unrealistic to expect that it will expand substantially into the vacuum left by the collapse of externally-owned UK plants.

The foreign sector has to be regarded as the engine of growth within the Wearside economy, though it should be remembered that it is currently narrowly-based sectorally, with two-thirds of the employment in just two sectors, vehicles and electrical engineering. The recent prediction (Foley, 1990), that around 40% of UK manufacturing capacity will be in foreign-ownership by the mid-1990s, is undoubtedly in need of revision due to the impact of the latest recession. It would nonetheless be reasonable, given government efforts to ensure that labour market conditions in the UK relative to those elsewhere in the EC preserve this country's advantage in attracting inward investment, and the continued growth of activity related to Nissan, to anticipate that in the second-half of the 1990s around 50% of Wearside jobs will be in foreign-owned plants. Figures for 1993 would probably show employment in the foreign sector to be larger than either the indigenous or UK ones, although - as noted with regard to the indigenous sector - the performance of the foreign component is exaggerated by the extent of contraction among UK plants.

Unlike the earlier influx of investment from overseas in the 1960s and 70s, when many of the foreign plants were specifically designed to mainly service the UK market, this latest phase is more explicitly linked to exports, given the UK's position within an increasingly integrated EC economy. These plants, by virtue not only of the market orientation but also of the scale and character of investment involved, may prove to be more enduring than many of the past branch plant investments. Although the European car industry is suffering from over-capacity, the ownership advantages enjoyed by the major Japanese producers should see them continue to grow through gaining an increased market share. This, of course, means that the 'new' Wearside exhibits continuity with the past in that it is marked by a lack of local control and relies for its future growth impulses upon outside forces. With the relative demise of the UK manufacturing sector, Wearside has been increasingly incorporated into the broader division of labour via foreign rather than domestic investment, and is having to conform, both socially and politically, to the requirements of foreign capital to maintain its development impetus.

One of the ways in which the incoming companies are altering the social aspects of production is by bringing with them new managerial techniques and personnel practices, many of them involving changes in the status and role of trade unions. They are helped in this by the fact that de-industrialisation has increased the pool of unemployed to an extent which has made labour (and unions) on Wearside, and elsewhere in the region, much more acquiescent than formerly; indeed, this is plainly one of the 'attractions' of this location for such companies, and constitutes one of the ways in which de-industrialisation is related to the form of re-industrialisation. The smaller plants especially are likely to be operating as non-union workplaces, while some of the large plants have opted for single union agreements in which the union's role is very much circumscribed (Peck and Stone, 1992). The decision to locate almost all of these plants outside 'old' Sunderland is, in part, related to the attempt to socially distance these operations from the old institutions and practices which prevailed in the traditional core of the Sunderland manufacturing economy.

The emergence of a new integrated system of production built around vehicles assembly similar in some (though by no means all) respects to the agglomerative production system centred on shipbuilding and marine engineering existing prior to the early 1980s constitutes another element of continuity in the evolution of Wearside's industrial sector. The establishment of a network of suppliers around Nissan has been encouraged by government insistence upon 'local content' agreements, and by the fact that production in the specialist vehicle component supplier plants (eg. Ikeda Hoover, Calsonic, Nissan-Yamato) is synchronised with that of Nissan on the basis of frequent deliveries through the day (Peck, 1990). While a proportion of the parts are being supplied from producers elsewhere in the UK and Europe via a (part Japanese-owned) local transport/warehousing intermediary - which has itself involved the creation of local jobs - the requirements of synchronised production, combined with expanding quantities of individual components as Nissan's production expands, will continue to act to draw suppliers to the area. The integrated nature of this development contrasts with earlier branch plant investments typified by limited local linkages.

Examination of this development cluster indicates, however, that the plants involved by no means defy the 'rules' of functional differentiation by space normally associated with the organisation of production in multi-plant enterprises. Thus, it is the production of the less sophisticated components - though manufactured using sophisticated *processes* - which are located in Wearside, with more complex inputs and components supplied from elsewhere (eg. Nissan's European design and research is mainly located in the South East, at Cranfield). The concentration on items at the low end of the production chain places limits on the potential for localised growth based on a complex of spin-off effects. Such considerations have led researchers to take a cautious view of the direct and indirect impact of the car production complex upon employment generation in the regional economy (eg. Amin and Tomaney, 1991). From Wearside's perspective, many of the jobs which have been generated by the new complex have been filled from outside its boundaries, while the vast majority of shipyard-related employment was for Wearsiders.

Some local firms are being drawn into the network as Nissan personnel especially work with the management of these sub-contract firms to help them achieve the necessary quality and reliability to qualify as approved suppliers. There is undoubtedly a transfer of technology occurring via this process, and some small firms have achieved considerable growth in consequence. One Wearside firm has altered its product specialism entirely in response to Nissan's requirements and doubled its workforce over the last five years on the basis of becoming dependent on supplying the car factory. There are, of course dangers in such dependence. Indeed, some firms have found difficulty in incorporating the car company's exacting requirements into their production activities as a whole. While many local firms have had to cope with the problems caused by the loss of their skilled workers to the incoming plants (Peck and Stone, 1992), management in other companies operating in the area have found that the presence in the locality of a high profile company, the new manufacturing and personnel techniques of which are well-publicised, has made it easier to introduce new methods within their own plants (Peck and Stone, 1993).

Conclusion

Close examination of the Wearside manufacturing economy reveals the presence of underlying structural weaknesses which make it unrealistic to regard the developments of the 1980s as foreshadowing a return to a golden age of economic growth and technological progress. It could be argued for Wearside - as it has in relation to national manufacturing - that changes have taken place which will improve its prospects of achieving a significant degree of re-industrialisation over the longer-term. The problem with this argument is that any competitive gains arising out of new industries, changing attitudes and the spread of modern management techniques and personnel practices have to be set against two vital considerations. First, in proportional terms, Wearside's manufacturing is now dramatically smaller as a source of employment than in 1973 (or indeed *any* time in the postwar period). The *extent* of re-industrialisation needed, given the limited sources of alternative employment in the local economy and the high levels of unemployment, is very substantial indeed. Secondly, the local economy - narrowly or broadly defined - is still confined by its inherited resource base and the framework of policy existing at the national level. The full exploitation of development opportunities arising out of the new industries is held back by well documented deficiencies in the region's capacity relating to educational attainment, the generation of new firms producing sophisticated products and services, and the development and exploitation of innovations (see eg.CURDS, 1992). The absence of a meaningful industrial strategy at national level - such as that found in Japan or Germany - has contributed to this weakness.

Wearside, in manufacturing terms, is a microcosm not just of the region but of the British economy; 'leaner and fitter' than in the 1970s, but in a number of important respects structurally deficient and far too small to allow the generation of anything like full employment. While the prospects of further significant de-industrialisation are reduced by the diminished weight of 'older' relative to recently-established plants in the manufacturing sector as a whole, genuine re-industrialisation will still be, at best, a slow process. The policy pendulum has shifted recently in favour of giving priority to industry. It needs to go further. A concerted strategy for industry at a national level, backed up by appropriate training and infrastructural policies, regionally-based institutions and support, and appropriate incentives for employment-intensive growth, would begin to address long-standing national problems (eg. balance of payments constraints and the long-term rate of growth) and at the same time offer improved prospects of employment for Wearsiders left stranded in the gap between the unequal forces of de-industrialisation and re-industrialisation.

* I am grateful to Alice Sharp for her assistance in updating the Wearside industrial database and to the Northern Ireland Economic Research Centre for helping to fund the 1990 survey of firms. Thanks are also due to Kevin Hinde and the editors of this volume for helpful comments on the draft of this chapter, although the usual caveat applies. The full range of tables on which this chapter is based can be found in *Restructuring of Manufacturing on Wearside*, NERU Research Paper no. 2, December 1992 (available from the author).

Appendix

Wearside Manufacturing: summary of main structural changes, 1973-90

	1973	*1990*
1. Employment		
Manufacturing employment	43,150	24,580
Total employment #	112,000	*91,000
Manufacturing share #	38.7%	25.2%

2. Establishment size
Employment (and number of units) by size band:

	1973	*1990*
1-20 employees	1,377 (164)	2,457 (283)
21-50 employees	2,027 (62)	2,678 (79)
51-100 employees	3,158 (42)	2,522 (32)
101-500 employees	8,051 (37)	8,000 (41)
501 or more	28,536 (24)	7,922 (8)
Total number of establishments	329	443
Average size (employees)	131	55

3. Ownership
Employment (number of units) by ownership category:

	1973	*1990*
Indigenous Wearside	8,192 (206)	7,802 (334)
External UK-owned	28,147 (102)	9,800 (71)
External overseas-owned	6,810 (21)	6,977 (38)
Share of manufacturing employment:		
Indigenous Wearside	19.0%	31.7%
External UK-owned	65.2%	38.9%
External overseas-owned	15.8%	28.5%

4. Industrial sectors

Main SIC classes (% of total mfg empl)	*1973*	*1990*
	mechanical engineering 18	mechanical eng. 19
	electrical engineering 18	motor vehicles 13
	shipbuilding/marine eng. 18	clothing 13
	clothing 12	paper/printing 11
	glass/non-metallic mins 10	electrical eng. 11
Employment share of largest five sectors	76%	66%

5. **Spatial distribution**
   Employment by zone (share of total):

Sunderland	33,925 (79%)	13,734 (56%)
Washington New Town	6,169 (14%)	8,531 (35%)
Hetton/Houghton	3,055 (7%)	2,314 (9%)

\# Figures from Department of Employment, Census of Employment
* Refers to 1989

4 Continuity and change in urban governance: Urban regeneration initiatives in the North East of England

Keith Shaw

Abstract

The increasingly competitive battle for post industrial economic activities has seen cities in America and Britain developing more and more sophisticated place-marketing strategies in order to 'sell' themselves as suitable locations for investment. This chapter argues that useful insights on the process of <u>change</u> can be generated by emphasising both the emergence of a more 'entrepreneurial' urban agenda, and the influential role of local spatial coalitions. However, it also argues that too strong an emphasis on change ignores important elements of <u>continuity</u> in urban governance - particularly in older industrial areas like the North East of England - where the longevity of economic decline has ensured that corporatist alliances of local politicians, capital and labour have long engaged in local boosterism.

Introduction

Recent accounts of urban regeneration initiatives in Britain have emphasised both a shift in the style of urban governance and the emergence of new institutional structures and coalitions. Thus, for Harvey, the post-Fordist regime has led to a shift in the economic development agenda of urban governments away from 'managerialism' towards 'entrepreneurialism' (Harvey, 1989a). In particular, urban decline has forced cities to develop more proactive and innovative strategies that increasingly involve inter-urban competition in order to attract mobile investment and employment, tourism and consumerism, high-status corporate activities and central government expenditures (Meegan, 1993: pp. 64-65).

Such entrepreneurial approaches have also been linked with the emergence of inter-organisational partnerships through which a range of business interests (in particular) are becoming more influential at the local level (Boyle, 1990). In this respect comparisons can be made with developments in American cities during the last two decades, where observers have come to emphasise how the urban development process has been hi-jacked by business-led growth coalitions that have engaged in vigorous campaigns to promote city redevelopment (Logan and Molotch, 1987).

For land and property owners, developers and the built environment professionals, growth means the increased utilisation of land and buildings within a specific locality to boost their profits. They are often joined in promoting their 'place-marketing' strategies by large retail interests, local utility companies and the local media who benefit in general from economic growth, because there is an increased demand for their goods and services. It is also the latter grouping that act as growth 'statesmen' spreading the ideology that growth is in everyone's interest (Wolman and Goldsmith, 1992, p. 133).

This emphasis on the transformation of both the agenda, and the institutional structures of urban governance has been increasingly utilised in the recent UK urban literature. Firstly, in terms of explaining the general shift of priorities at the local level away from social welfare objectives and towards economic development goals - what Cochrane has refered to as the shift from 'welfare state to enterprise state' (Cochrane, 1991, p. 290)

Secondly, in terms of depicting the increased involvement of business (particularly property) interests within non-elected regeneration agencies, and the subsequent downgrading of the local authority role (Harding, 1991; Lloyd and Newland, 1988). Whatever the comparative insights to be gained about the *transformation* ofurban governance in the UK (through emphasising the shift to urban entrepreneuralism and the emergence of growth coalitions) it is important to acknowledge that such frameworks have their roots in the particular experiences of American cities, and thus may not adequately capture the element of *continuity* in both the structures of urban governance and the nature of urban leadership in the UK.

It can be argued that this may be particularly true of the UK's older industrial urban centres, where the longevity of economic decline and the early involvement of the state in regional policy interventions has long generated corporatist alliances intent on regenerating the local economy. This corporatism 'at the local level' had often been conducted *outside* normal democratic channels, saw *business*, political and labour interests predominating and was primarily concerned with local *economic* development. It can be argued that in such areas the contemporary transformation in urban governance is therefore less marked, with recent changes of approach (such as the growth of place-marketing strategies) being articulated and implemented by the existing corporatist interests already predominant at the local level.

To consider these issues further we will now look at the politics of urban regeneration in one such older industrial area, the North East of England (in particular the Tyne and Wear metropolitan area). This is a relevant area of study because of it's long-term economic decline, the well-established local corporatist traditions in the region and because of the recent expansion in public-private coalitions that has served to increase the formal involvement of business in urban regeneration (Shaw, 1990).

We will argue that there are important changes in the contemporary approach to urban regeneration in the North East - such as the expansion in the formal role of business interests within inter-organisational coalitions, and the shift towards a more post-industrial economic development agenda. However, such changes also need to be considered within a context that stresses the longevity of alliances (traditionally based on tripartite representation) which have operated within non-elected agencies and which have long advocated embryonic versions of the strategies now associated with local growth coalitions and with what Harvey has refered to as urban entrepreneurialism (Harvey, 1989a).

Urban regeneration in the North East: the institutional context

Urban and regional development in the North East of England has long been associated with corporatist political structures. The area has, since the 1930s, provided an almost 'classical illustration' of corporatist political structures dominated by the labour movement, local/regional capital and representatives of regional governmental agencies (Byrne, 1989, p. 34). It was this constellation of interests for example that lay behind attempts to modernise the economic and social structure of the region during the 1960s. A 'strongly local corporatist' grouping (Cooke, 1988, p. 194) of unions, capital and professionals - with Newcastle's Council leader T.Dan Smith at it's core - lobbied strongly for improved regional infrastructure, financial support for industry and increased spending on housing, education and training, in such regional planning documents as 'Challenge of the Changing North' (Northern Economic Planning Council 1966).

Initially it is important to note then, that the specific pattern of inter-organisational coalitions that characterise the North East in the 1990s reflect not only the contemporary concerns of both Conservative ministers and the business sector to ' do something about those inner cities ', but also the more traditional localist response to the region's long-term economic decline. The region has certainly been a policy 'laboratory', being the target of policy interventions since the 1930s (from local as well as central government).

This has meant that recent developments (particularly during the 1980s) have been superimposed on an already complex patchwork of agencies. The significance of this is that in an area where local corporatist interests had always taken their civic duties seriously - and where the use of appointed agencies to implement urban and regional initiatives has a long pedigree - this has served to produce a ready-made pool of local 'notables' from which to choose the board members of the 1980s and 1990s.

Hence, traditional forms of representation in the area have managed to survive the Thatcherite downgrading of 'tripartite' forms of representation which has occurred within other areas of the public sector. Well established agencies such as the Northern Development Company (NDC), the Port Authorities, Tyne and Wear Enterprise Trust (now simply called ENTRUST) and the Tyne and Wear Economic Development Company (TWEDCO) have served as a fertile source for the boards of the newer bodies such as the Tyne and Wear Development Corporation (TWDC), The Newcastle Initiative (TNI), The Wearside Opportunity (TWO) and the Tyneside and Wearside Training and Enterprise Councils (TECs).

If we now examine the structures, interests and policies that go together to make up the dominant local response to urban regeneration in the North East, three issues can be highlighted which suggest the need for a framework which is able to assess *both* change and continuity in the contemporary politics of urban regeneration. Firstly, while the lead role of local authorities has been challenged, they clearly remain important co-ordinators and facilitators within the new institutional arrangements. Secondly, while there has been an increase in formal business involvement within the new partnership organisations, the traditional grouping of tripartite interests continue to dominate their board membership. Thirdly, while 'place-marketing' strategies have been developed as part of the increasingly competitive battle for post-industrial economic activities, such approaches can also be seen as extensions of pre-existing policies rather than merely as the product of the contemporary shift to entrepreneuralism.

The continuing importance of local authorities

Local authorities in the Tyne and Wear area have long been involved in economic development initiatives. From the creation of the North-East Development Board in 1935 to the passing of the Tyne and Wear Act in 1976, emphasis has been placed on industrial attraction, infrastructural provision and direct financial support for industrial development. And a strong measure of local economic intervention has been continued by the five metropolitan districts - building on the expertise developed by Tyne and Wear County Council between 1974-1986. Indeed, all the remaining districts: Newcastle, Sunderland, Gateshead, North and South Tyneside have maintained strong economic/industrial development capabilities. Thus, in Newcastle,

> Economic development is one of the City Council's top priorities for action, and the establishment of a new Development department demonstrates the Council's strong commitment to this area of activity (Newcastle City Council 1990).

As well as developing their own local strategies, the individual councils are also involved in supporting (either financially or through providing councillors to sit on the boards) such ventures as NDC, ENTRUST, and TWEDCO. This is evidence of the fact that they have long accepted the need to work with (and within) other agencies to further local economic development objectives such as inward investment, small firm development, provision of factory units and skills training.

Given both the existing strength of local authorities in the area of economic development and their pragmatic response to the setting up of organisations such as UDCs and TECs, local authorities have been able to exert continuing influence within the new partnership agencies. Thus, local authority influence 'continues to inter-penetrate other local and sub-regional agencies extensively' (Dunleavy and King, 1990, p. 7).

Examples from Tyne and Wear include: councillors from Sunderland, South and North Tyneside, and latterly Newcastle, accepting seats on the board of TWDC; both the council leader and chief executive of Sunderland being involved with the board of TWO, and Newcastle's chief executive sitting on the board of TNI; a senior Newcastle council officer being seconded to work for the chief executive of TNI; while the chief executives of Sunderland, Gateshead, and South Tyneside, are all board members of one of the areas two TECs. The provision of personnel to sit on the boards of the new agencies, coupled with the strength of the partnership ethos within a 'stable political culture that emphasises pragmatism over ideology' (Moore and Pierre, 1988, p. 177), has meant that local authorities have worked closely with the new agencies to promote several key economic development initiatives in the area.

This is not surprising given the comments of one local councillor on the initial development proposals of the TWDC,

> all they've done is to go around all the local authorities asking for any development schemes we've got on the shelf and can't afford to implement because the government has cut back our resources (quoted in Hetherington and Robinson, 1988, p. 207).

Moreover, the close involvement of Newcastle City Council in the subsequent development of some of The Newcastle Initiatives' key schemes, such as the Grey Street Renaissance, the Cruddas Park Initiative and the Theatre Village development (TNI 1988), points to the continuing importance of the public sector role within partnership agencies. Indeed, as Harding argues,

> ..the city council had to produce strong planning guidance for the Theatre Village area in the attempt to forestall speculation and the ruination of an arts based strategy which TNI adopted (Harding, 1991, p. 311).

The restoration of the local authorities' central role can also be seen in the formation of the Westgate Development Trust, a joint TNI / Newcastle Council initiative to combine the regeneration of the Theatre Village with that of the nearby Chinatown area in the west of the city. Indeed, this project now takes pride of place within the economic section of Newcastle Council's successful 1991 City Challenge bid, with over £19 million to be allocated to the area within a five year time period (Newcastle City Council, 1991).

The picture that emerges from the North East's experience of recent urban regeneration initiatives is one in which local authorities continue to play a key role: private sector involvement may prove useful - but public sector involvement is vital. Such a view is at odds with the negative vision contained within American accounts of the growth machine which sees local democratic and public agencies effectively by-passed by business interests. We need to highlight then, not the demise of local government's role in urban regeneration, but how this has altered to accommodate both the increased role of the business community and the need to ensure co-ordination between different agencies. As Cooke argues,

..gone are the days when local government could dictate terms.... new skills centred upon ideas of negotiating and partnering are having to be developed (Cooke, 1988, p. 199).

The continuation of the corporatist basis of board membership

In the North East it is important initially to stress the continued representation of the region's traditional corporatist elites within the structures of urban regeneration. Thus, on all the major regeneration agencies - such as Urban Development Corporations, Training and Enterprise Councils, Business Leadership Teams and Regional or Local promotional agencies - the predominant source of board membership continues to be drawn from traditional tripartite sources.

Firstly, the Labourist political machine - such as leading local politicians and trade union leaders. For example: councillors remain important actors on the boards of the TWDC and NDC, and maintain an influential role via membership of City Challenge boards in Newcastle North Tyneside and Sunderland ; the regional secretary of the TUC sits on the boards of both NDC and the Tyneside TEC; and the recently-retired regional secretary of the TGWU sits on the TWDC and the Port of Tyne Authority. Secondly, Local capital - particularly drawn from the brewing and engineering sectors - remains an important source of local influence. For example, representatives of Scottish and Newcastle Breweries are involved with TNI, Tyneside TEC and ENTRUST; while members of the Vaux Brewers Group sit on TWO, TWDC, NDC and the Wearside TEC. Indeed, one of the Vaux managing directors - who was appointed chairman of TWO - was described as being 'dynastically ideal for the job' as his brother and fellow Vaux director was already Chairman of TWDC (TWO 1990 p 1). Even in the North East, where there has always been a well-organised and homogeneous business community, recent developments can be seen as further integrating organised business into the conduct of public affairs. As Peck notes of the TECs for example,

TEC boards and their various sub-committees are drawing together members of the business community - many of whom are active in other areas of local politics such as UDCs,school boards and economic development agencies - thus enabling the business elite to cohere and consolidate in quite new ways (Peck 1992 p 344).

Thirdly, State 'professionals' - drawn from local government (see earlier), the urban and regional development agencies themselves or the regional offices of government departments. For example the former deputy regional director of the DTI was for a period the Chief Executive of TNI, the Chief Executive of the NDC is himself a board member of TNI and the Chief Executive of TWDC is involved with both TNI and TWO.

Not only do representatives of the traditional sectors continue to dominate the boards of individual agencies, they also constitute a pervasive grouping that operates across the different agencies. For example, a former Leader of one of the region's major Trade Unions is on the boards of TWDC, NDC, and the Port of Tyne Authority; the former Managing Director of the Cookson Group has been involved with TWDC, NDC, ENTRUST and the Tyneside TEC; while the Chief Executive of NDC sits on the boards of TNI and TWO.

While there is some evidence in Tyne and Wear of the emerging representation of the sectors associated (in the American literature) with the growth coalition, such representation is still limited: a local property developer sits on TWDC and TNI; the regional director of a high street bank sits on TWDC, TNI and ENTRUST; while a managing director of a local building society sits on TNI and the Tyneside TEC. Elsewhere we can point to single agency involvement only, from representatives drawn from local newspapers (TNI,TWO), regional television companies (TWO), building societies (TEC), Universities and Polytechnics, (TWDC,TNI,TWO), and the retail sector (TECs, TWO). Clearly, this does not amount to the widespread colonisation of the agencies operating in the region by a 'new' growth coalition of interests. Indeed, recent evidence suggests a diminution rather than an increase in the representation of the newer 'growth' sectors; for example, the property developer noted above has now withdrawn from the boards of TWDC and TNI.

Moreover, it can be argued that the involvement of a wider range of interests in the region pre-dates the 1980s. Thus, representatives from such sectors as finance, the building societies, insurance companies, retailing, non-local capital and higher education have all (at some time) been involved within corporatist agencies in the region. For example, the board members of the 1960s Northern Economic Planning Council included a building society managing director, an insurance company chairman, two senior university academics, a retail manager, and a representative of the region's largest international corporation (NEPC 1969).

Two factors can be seen to influence this early involvement of a wide range of sectors within the region's development agencies. Firstly, the region's long-term economic decline (and the accompanying state interventions) has persuaded a wide range of public and private interests to co-operate in promoting regional solutions to the North East's problems (Cousins et al, 1974). The subjugation of these different interests to the 'lets-sink-our-political-differences-in-the-interests-of-promoting-the-region philosophy' has long characterised the North East (Hetherington and Robinson, 1988, p. 208).

The willingness of Nissan and Komatsu to invest in the region has seen them quickly accepted as 'northern nationalists' keen to promote the regions interests. This assimilation into the region's corporatist elite (representatives from both companies now sit on the boards of the TECs, TWO and TWDC) is indicative both of this triumph of regionalism over politics and of the increasing similarities between recent local promotional campaigns (by NDC in particular) - that emphasise the virtues of teamwork, collective loyalty and the quality ethic - and the Japanese model of management (Wilkinson, 1992, p. 208). In such an atmosphere of teamwork and partnership,

> A multinational company with little time for organised labour and openly endorsed for its management style by Mrs Thatcher was brought to Sunderland's strong Labour setting with no open dissent (Garrahan and Stewart 1992 p 33).

Secondly, where representatives of the new agencies are drawn from commerce and the professions this may reflect the traditionally influencial role played in the region by representatives of the 'old ruling class', both as a status group and as a source of business and civic influence. As the Benwell Community Development Project's 'The Making of a Ruling Class' argued, the region's traditional capitalist families who made their 19th century fortunes from coal, iron foundries or engineering, (such as the Strakers, Ridleys, and Dickinsons) moved in the 20th century,

> into the finance capital sector, into banking, insurance, investment holding companies, property companies,building societies,and into professions, such as stockbroking and the law... (Benwell CDP, 1978, p. 58).

Indeed, later generations of the three families noted above continue to play an important role within the region as, respectively, Chairman of the region's largest building society, Chairman of the Northumbria Water Company and senior partner of the biggest firm of local solicitors.

Moreover, as these key families gradually lost control of elected local government they continued to exercise an influential role within a variety of non-elected state agencies and appointed boards such as New Town Corporations, Water and Health Authorities, regional development agencies, Tourist boards, Port Authorities, Transport authorities and the governing bodies and councils of local universities and polytechnics. This has continued in the 1980s and 1990s, persuading *The Economist* to comment in an article on the region, of the existence of a traditional elite, whose names 'appear on the boards that run everything' (3/6/1989).

From managerialism to entrepreneuraliasm?

On one level it can be argued that recent promotional campaigns to recreate the 'Great North' or to construct the 'New North East' signify the move towards a more entrepreneurial form of urban governance. Thus while the traditional managerialist approach called for public sector infrastructure, financial support for industry and interventions to maintain the region's manufacturing base this has now been replaced by a new 'vision' dominated by a concern for image-building, attracting Far Eastern investment, fostering entrepreneurship, creating 'flagship' property and retail developments and promoting the cultural, media and leisure industries.

For Amin and Tomaney, Thatcherite attempts to create an entrepreneurial culture in the North-East during the 1980s have been faced with the obstacle of the area's labour and collectivist political traditions. Accordingly, a new local growth coalition has emerged in recent years to challenge the dominant structures of the old order. Local elites covering such coalitions as TNI, the TECs and the TWDC now share a post-industrial vision that views the purpose of urban regeneration as turning cities into,

> a play-pen and centre of consumption for citizens re-cast as potential entrepreneurs, professionals, and new model workers with insatiable appetites for Marinas, garden festivals, 'Chinatowns', and 'Theatre Villages' (Amin and Tomaney, 1991, p. 487).

While in a study of how agencies such as NDC, TNI, TWDC and Newcastle City Council have attempted to market and promote the City of Newcastle as a locality for inward investment, Wilkinson notes how image improvement strategies have now become an important aspect of public sector economic development activities,

> The city is now to be repackaged as an attractive and progressive business location, boasting a high quality of life and a progressive, entrepreneurial attitude. In terms of urban governace it has resulted in ....an emphasis on consumption-led strategies in urban regeneration (Wilkinson 1992 p 209).

The adoption of post-industrial solutions to the economic problems of the North East is also noted by Byrne in his analysis of the approach of the TWDC,

> TWDC has explicitly rejected a strategy for the regeneration of industrial Tyneside (and in practice,though not explicitly, industrial Wearside) which is based on the revival and further development of a marine manufacturing and port-trade base. Instead it has adopted a property-orientated approach, which seems to be based on imitating development ' successes' elsewhere (Byrne, 1993, p. 102).

It is important to note however, that while such concerns have become more influential in the last decade, the shift from managerialist to more entrepreneurial strategies has arguably been a more gradual process in the North East - an area in which the longevity of economic decline has ensured early experimentation with a variety of local responses to revive the region's economic fortunes.

Reviewing some of the earliest reports and surveys on the region (going back to the 1930s) the Rowntree Research Unit noted that,

> The North Eastern Economy.....is predominantly seen as deviant (an undue preponderance of fairly heavy industry) and backward (the failure to develop light or new industry and services) and this failure is the failure to develop new native entrepreneurs and to promote itself to outsiders (Cousins et al, 1974, p. 141).

Moreover when compared to what have become known as the 'growth' strategies of the 1980s and 1990s, the remedies advocated to tackle the North East's problems over the years do have a familiar ring to them. Three areas of continuity can thus be noted.

Firstly, agencies in the North East have long been concerned with trying to promote the region as a suitable place for inward investment. The longevity of economic decline, coupled with the need to attract new companies to aid the diversification of the narrow industrial structure, ensured that the North East was an early player in what was to become the more extensive 'place marketing' game of the 1980s and 1990s (Storey, 1983).

From the 1930s up to the present day the region has always had some form of development agency promoting the 'special' features of the area to outside firms. The North of England Development Council (set up in 1962) played an important role in attracting some of the American companies that invested in the region in the 1960s; being able to lure companies with the promise of extensive government grants, local authority industrial estates, and a loyal and docile workforce. In this sense recent (successful) attempts to attract Japanese companies - such as Nissan, Komatsu and Fujitsu - to the region, are thus contemporary examples of what is an established priority. Both TNI (with its Japan Links Project Team) and TWO (with its Civic Pride and Publicity groups) reflect this continuity in policy.

Secondly, alongside this general concern to engage in the competitive battle for employment, agencies in the region have also long emphasised the particular need to create a suitable environment to attract 'high-status' corporate activities within which work the managers, administrators, and professionals. For Harvey, this involves creating 'an atmosphere of place and tradition that will act as a lure to capital and people "of the right sort"' (1989b, p. 295). And while some observers see the particular significance of agencies like TNI and TWDC as fostering consumption-based growth strategies aimed at creating a new urban middle-class (Amin, and Tomaney, 1991), such concerns were also echoed by more traditional structures of urban governance.

Describing the redevelopment of Newcastle in the 1960s one observer summed up the message of the 'new society' as,

> ...Andy Capp must go; and along with him must go the jobs, houses, and general urban environment which made such a creature possible and necessary. New industries must be attracted to the area; executive-type houses must be built for executive-type wives; slag-heaps must be landscaped, dingy back-lanes must disappear, St James' football ground must be transformed into a minor version of the Houston Astrodrome. Andy Capp must learn to prefer creme de menthe to brown ale, and to spend his weekends polishing the second car or ski-ing with his 2.5 children on the plastic ski slopes.....(Davies, 1972, p. 2).

Similarly a quarter of a century before TNI, TWDC and Newcastle City Council (via its regional capital and urban development sub-committee) engaged in a campaign to promote Newcastle as 'one of Europe's most stylish cities', and T.Dan Smith spoke of transforming the city into the 'Venice of the North' or the 'Brasilia of the old world'. Thus, the city planning department under Wilfred Burns (later to become chief planner at the DOE) embarked on a series of large comprehensive development projects which are now permanent landmarks to that period of modernisation. And given the contemporary focus of some of the growth strategies of the 1980s, it is illuminating to note that in judging his efforts to create the 'city of the future' as a success, T Dan Smith commented that, 'one of the most remarkable and tangible results was the tremendous increase in land values in the city' (Smith, 1970, p. 58).

Thirdly, the contemporary concern to 'foster an entrepreneurial, enterprise culture' (TWO, 1990, p. 21) and to counteract the 'relative shortage of business men and women with the skill, courage and ambition to take advantage of the new opportunities that are becoming available' (TWDC, 1989, p. 5) also has strong roots in the region's past. The bemoaning of the absence of 'budding entrepreneurs' (Hudson, 1991) has long characterised debates on the region's development. According to the Rowntree Research Unit, the analyses of the North-East's problems have long included a concern with the,

> organisational and psychological backwardness of the North-East with a particular stress on the need to develop native entrepreneurial skills (Cousins et al., 1974, p. 141).

The Strategic Plan for the Northern Region, drawn up in the 1970s, noted that a lack of entrepreneurship was one of the fundamental reasons for the region's long-standing economic difficulties and hence, public policy should show a 'deliberate bias' in favour of small-firm development (NRST, 1977). This emphasis on nurturing local entrepreneurs and aiding small firm development became a central feature of the expansion of local authority economic development in Tyne and Wear during the late 1970s/early 1980s and influenced the setting up of the Tyne and Wear Enterprise Trust (later renamed ENTRUST) in 1981. The trust while not providing financial aid was set up to provide advice on starting up a small firm; general management training; special entrepreneur training programmes; and a counselling service for developing businesses (Clough, 1982).

To summarise: recent urban regeneration strategies in the North East are very much an amalgam of the old and the new. While there has certainly been an increase in the influence of more post-industrial strategies certain strands of this approach have already been articulated within the areas existing corporatist structures. This particularly applies to: the concern to attract new investment and employment ; the emphasis within place marketing strategies on promoting the tourist, leisure and cultural facilities on offer to the entrepreneurial middle-class; and the desire to nurture an indigenous enterprise culture.

In this sense, the recent growth of locally-differentiated promotional campaigns, under the banner of either the 'Great North' (a NDC campaign) or the 'New North East' (a TWDC initiative), can be understood as much as a response to the increasingly 'intense inter-urban competition for inward investment' (Wilkinson, 1992, p. 210) than as being indicative of the emergence of new local growth coalitions. As Garrahan and Stewart have argued of the Nissan move to the site at the former Sunderland Airport, this involved,

> a concerted attempt by local power-brokers (regional government officials, elected local councillors,the Washington New Town Development Corporation,p rivate sector firms, regional trade unionists and the media) to conform with Nissan's preferred public image...There was a tangible fear that the potentially high employment opportunities Nissan might bring could be lost to competitor localities (Garrahan and Stewart, 1992, pp. 32-33)

Moreover, the increasingly competitive nature of such campaigns has required not only the creation of an idealised image of the region's economic advantages, but has also necessitated it's continual re-enforcement by local authorities, local trade unions,local business organisations and representatives of government agencies. It is this 'filtering out' both of criticisms of the strategies adopted and of any alternative approaches to economic regeneration that is particularly characteristic of the new organisations of regeneration. Hence the very critical local reaction from local 'opinion formers' to recent studies that have either questioned the extent of the region's economic recovery (Robinson 1990) or made substantial criticisms of Nissan's development on Wearside (Garrahan and Stewart, 1992). As Hudson has argued,

> As the political economy of Thatcherism switched the emphasis to regional self-reliance and to competition between places as the only route to economic growth, revived sorts of corporatist bodies...emerged to sell the region, or particular locations within it, to potential private investors.Consequently,any attempt even gently to question the correspondence between the realities of life in the North

and the projected image of the 'Great North' can provoke charges of treachery and betrayal (Hudson, 1991, p. 48).

New wine in old bottles: the growth of a new urban corporatism ?

Some useful insights into the contemporary nature of urban regeneration in the UK can be generated by utilising a framwework that stressess the shift towards more entrepreneurial strategies - not the least in emphasising the emergence of a more consumption orientated approach to economic development and the (related) rise of marketing strategies aimed at altering the 'image' of an urban area. However we would also argue that too strong an emphasis on change prevents an adequate explanation of recent developments in areas such as the North East where economic decline has ensured that corporatist alliances between local politicians, capital and labour have long engaged in civic boosterism.

It is also the continuity in structures, personalities and policies that need to be explained as well as the changes. We would argue then that the key feature of experiences in the North East is how the existing local corporatist structures (rather than a business-dominated growth coalition) have been able to articulate a more entrepreneurial agenda. We would agree with Wilkinson when she argues that the existing local corporatist structures have more actively engaged in the marketplace and assumed a more marketing-orientated approach compared with their more traditional roles as regulator and policy maker (Wilkinson, 1992, p. 210). And as Harvey has noted,

> Corporatist forms of government can ...take on entrepreneurial roles in the production of favourable business climates and other special qualities (Harvey, 1989b, p. 295).

As we argued earlier, it would be more appropriate when depicting the key interests involved in urban regeneration in the region to draw not on the growth coalition model but on the corporatist framework. Such a view has traditionally emphasised the formal representation of organised producer interests, state mediation and bargaining and a specific policy concern with the 'sphere of production'.

Moreover, it can be argued that the significance of recent developments in the North East lies not in the transformation of existing power structures, but in the reinforcment of the specifically localist qualities of existing corporatist structures. Hence when we talk of a 'new' urban corporatism it is in terms of challenging the earlier scepticism of writers such as Cawson that genuine corporatist structures could emerge at the local level (Cawson, 1985). From this latter viewpoint, existing examples of corporatism at the local level are derivative,

> since the local dimension is the *target* of intervention rather than the basis for the organisation of the participating bodies (Cawson, 1985, p. 144)

Thus, one effect of the developments discussed in the North East may be to create the three conditions under which Cawson thought that a genuine local corporatism might arise (Cawson, 1985, p. 146). In particular: the need to be seen to support local inter-organisational coalitions sees producer group representation now more clearly reflecting *local* rather than *national* interests and priorities; local authorities have survived and are now increasingly acting as *mediators* between the different interests involved in urban regeneration rather than as the pre-eminent agency in local economic development ; while the growing importance of the,

> competitive local or regional level as a loci for economic policy decisions...is likely to encourage the development of internationally orientated urban and regional strategies in which public and private sectors will both need to be involved (Harding, 1991, p. 315).

Finally, it is worth noting that focussing on the distinctive local corporatist structures that dominate the urban regeneration agenda may also produce a useful general model through which to understand the growing network of non-elected agencies and 'quangos' that now operate within British cities (Colenutt and Ellis, 1993). As Dunleavy and King suggest, one answer to the question of '" Who (or what) runs British cities in the 1990s"' is to explore the development of a ' new urban corporatism' (1990, p. 11) within which existing elites are able to expand their influence via membership of a wider range of appointed agencies.

Indeed, it can be further argued that a systematic attempt to understand the interests now coming to dominate the wider range of non-elected agencies operating in the North East (in such areas as higher education, health, housing, transport, tourism and the arts) would need to take account of the view that,

> ....the region is still effectively run by a small coherent and cohesive local elite. Looking across the various agencies one sees not just the same interests represented but also the same handful of names drawn

from the ranks of the 'great and the good' (Robinson and Shaw, 1991, p. 280).

We may conclude then that if there is to be a re-awakening of interest in examining the groups now dominant within British cities - their patterns of recruitment and the mechanisms through which they maintain their power - it is to the corporatist, rather than the growth coalition model, that observers should turn.

An earlier version of this chapter first appeared in the journal *Regional Studies*.

5 What's in a name? The invention of Wearside

Pete Rushton

Abstract

The re-invention of the past to aid with the redesign of the present has been one of the themes of the last decade. We are encouraged to see the past in a way that firmly commits us to the modernized future. The result is both an artificially preserved past and a present disguised by the adoption of new identities. Whereas those forced on the public by local government reorganization failed, the newly marketed local identities are designed with a view to attracting investors from outside. The new identity therefore has to be apparently apolitical, futuristic, yet garner public support through pride in a suitably sanitized past. Wearside, the poor relation of the North East, is one of the new identities through which regeneration has been attempted. The term 'Wearside' has a past association with Sunderland's football club and the River Wear, but recently it has become the watchword of a new sub-region as programmes of advertising, sloganising and hopeful campaigning have aimed to revive the area in the midst of the death of its traditional industries. Optimism is the keynote of the new identity, constructed to counter the economic decline experienced by local people.

Introduction

When was Wearside? In the 1990s it has suddenly appeared everywhere in local language and political speeches, newspaper reports and official titles. Yet few outside Roker Park in the 1930s would have called themselves 'Wearsiders', as journalists now describe everyone from Sunderland or Washington. While pride in Sunderland seems strong, a new gloss has been added to local identity, one that marks out a sub-region from the surrounding areas, above all from Teesside and Tyneside.

This is the study of this new creation.

The invention of tradition

All traditions have to be invented: sometimes they also have to be abolished and replaced (Hobsbawm and Ranger, 1983). What makes the 1980s interesting is the way these processes have occurred simultaneously. While living in a heritage safari park marked with carefully beautified items from the past, we are constantly bombarded with images of a future that invite welcome and admiration. The two are subconsciously connected, of course. The more relieved we are to have left the bad old days behind us, thankful of our freedom from the grim necessity of working in the mine/mill/shipyard that the tourist industry now charges us a fortune to visit, the more eager we are to embrace the high-tech, if rather lowly-paid, future.

These are not strikingly original observations. It has been clear to many that the political agenda in the 1980s involved a contest over the meaning of the past, and, almost equally, a war for the nature of the future. In order to reconstruct the present all the better, we have had to learn how to view our past (particularly the recent postwar past) appropriately. The nostalgic obsession of the British with their history has frequently been emphasized in diagnoses of the current malaise in our industrial society. This view has both right-wing and left-wing exponents, all forceful modernisers for whom repudiation of the mistakenly conceived past is the essential pre-condition of national economic and social revival. For example, on the right, Wiener sees historical fantasy as part of the anti-industrial culture that has since the mid-nineteenth century obstructed our development of a fully modern capitalism, and Corelli Barnett has asserted that our liberal-labour mixture of traditionalist industrial habits and utopian dreams of the future impeded success even in the national efforts of our 'finest hour', World War II (Wiener, 1982; Barnett, 1986). By rejecting historical sentimentality, especially that of working-class history and solidarity, the New Right aims to introduce a more 'realistic' modern culture. From a contrasting perspective, Wright among others has highlighted the way the heritage industry supports this new agenda by integrating icons of our history into an artificial modernity. The preserved ruins of our history offer us, at best, a local identity, but more importantly they teach us the essential lesson that the past is over (Wright, 1985; Hewison, 1987: p.141). We are prevented from using history as a critique of the present because in its preservation it has become sanitised and safe. Costume drama and re-enactment merely entertain and do not remind us of values that might disturb the current drive to 'modernisation'. Some nostalgia is permitted, of course, but if any values are retained, they are always of the 'Glory that Was Greece' variety, or more realistically 'Brideshead Revisited', reflecting a conservative longing for great days of high culture to which modern mass society cannot aspire. As Samuel points out, this tends towards a popularist form of Little Englandism, a longing for a time when supposedly neither foreigners nor rising crime nor other troublesome forces disturbed the people (Samuel, 1988; Pearson, 1985). But alternative histories - of struggle, of trade unionism, of successful rebellion (what Gramsci called 'remembrance') - are rendered obsolete by the changing context of modernity: the present does not need any items from this junk-yard, because they are no longer relevant (Kaye, 1987: p.358). It is the present to which heritage is directed, for the past is merely to be visited (Wright, 1985: pp.75, 150-1; Hewison, 1987: pp.140-3; Horne, 1984).

One consequence of this past-future nexus is that realism about the past and scepticism about the future are now often greeted by accusations of unrealism or, worse, treachery to the future (particularly to local future prospects). We must not speak of the past's gains that need to be preserved, only of the future that must be different. As Wright observes, the past is an accusation against those who refuse to change - the many recalcitrant sentimentalists who wish to preserve its (largely collectivist) achievements. While memories are to be treasured, we must look to the future. 'In the name of memory, history has been abolished' (Lefebvre, quoted by Wright, 1985: p.243). Thus the struggle over the meaning of the past is directed towards the reconstruction of the present. This is the essence of the new rationalist position, the hallmark of Wright's 'anti-traditionalist technicists' who demand discontinuity with days that were bad not because they involved suffering, but because they fostered pathetic dependent habits that no longer have a place. 'The age of ruins is past' has been the doctrine of rightwing modernists since the nineteenth century in their attempt to haul both high and low culture into the future (Disraeli, 1962: p.133).

What has made North East England so interesting over the last twenty years is that these processes can be observed almost daily. The brutal death of traditional industries has been accompanied by a fixed-smile optimism about the future. Museums and memoirs of traditional working-class life have been celebrated as a means of attracting tourists and giving the region a distinctive identity. But the aim is to recreate the present as much as pay homage to the past. The political paradox has therefore been exposed in the sight of very traditional Labour Party leaders, deriving their power from unchanged party machines, devoting their efforts both to lip-service campaigns to preserve the traditional industries and to a synthetic modernism in order to attract new ones (see Keith Shaw's analysis in this volume). No doubt these processes were replicated elsewhere in Britain. In the North East, however, there were no major refuges of traditional cultural identity to hide behind - no Welshness or Scottishness; in Sunderland they were not even Geordies. The local reputation - 'We're mak'ems and tak'ems' - was of skill and toughness, not of culture or style. If there has been a form of 'cultural localism' here in response the forces of change and external indifference, it has lacked the coherence and social commitment characteristic of the peripheral rural communities which have attracted anthropological study in Britain. Nor has there been a dominant ethnicity around which such an identity could form (A.P.Cohen, 1982: pp.5-7; Tonkin et al., 1989; A.D.Smith, 1991). Local identity once derived from the industries that made the area known to the rest of the country. The invention of a new, marketable, image has had as its aim the attraction of new industries. Now, the North East is the place of Nissan not Armstrong-Vickers: regeneration has become a matter of new brand names.

Regions, localities and localism

The dimension of space has always given sociologists and historians among others great difficulty. One problem is knowing where the boundaries of social units lie. Formal borders often have little meaning, a problem shared with official areas of administration. Many examples suggest that units of administration are frequently too large to engender cohesive loyalty. For example, in the eighteenth century many huge parishes in Durham and Northumberland dissolved into smaller units (usually called 'townships') for running the poor law, because local elites were resentful of having to pay welfare to 'strangers' a mile or two away. The unit of administration was larger than the unit of sentiment, though the feelings were expressed by the bare majority who had to pay rates (Rushton, 1989). In such examples, the boundaries and those asserting them are easily identifiable: the local loyalties are specific to small numbers in relatively self-contained areas. The situation in modern Britain is more diffuse, a vagueness reflected in the construction of the rival conceptions on offer. In recent debates, the different languages of community, locality and region have all vied for attention, both academically and politically. As Massey points out, industrial capitalism has repeatedly shifted the geographical significance of areas as some are developed (or favoured) while others are abandoned. Consequently, we need a range of concepts to deal with the constantly changing structures of spatial inequality (Massey, 1984: p.49). Put simply, where is the local, and if a local identity has been invented, who by, and who is included within it?

Historical analysis tends to rely on a straightforwardly naive geographical perspective, supplemented by a recognition of local subjective loyalties. Rowe, for example, regards the North East as a genuine region, bounded by the Pennines, the Cheviots and the sea; only the agricultural plain on the Durham-Yorkshire border makes this well-defined region fuzzy at its southern edge. Within this economically and socially diverse area, there are great emotional chasms - the Tyne that divides Newcastle from that 'dirty lane', as Gateshead was once described, leading to it. The second, of course, is the split between Newcastle and Sunderland, which has always suffered from being a 'small scale version of Newcastle', without even the grandeur of 'Tyneside Classical' architecture. (Rowe, 1990: pp.417-9; Wilkes and Dodds, 1964). We might add a comparable rift, that between Teesside and the rest - Durham having some emotional borderline drawn south of Hartlepool, thus excluding Middlesbrough, in many people's minds. Yet while this kind of analysis is attractive, the underlying assumption about 'region' is incoherent, for on this description the North East has neither the homogeneity nor the complementary self-sufficiency of inter-connected industries that have been used conventionally to define a true region (Urry, 1981: p.467). The difficulty is that '"regions" and coherent local areas are not pre-given to analysis, nor are they unchanging. They are continually reproduced in shifting form', as economic and political relations change (Massey, 1984: p.195).

Recent academic study of contemporary economic and social problems has therefore apparently moved down a level, from the region to the locality, reflecting both the intellectual problem of defining 'regions' and the waning fortunes of regional policies in an age of compulsory self-help. The predominant reason, however, is the recognition that economic decisions by large corporations and government, so essential to local developments, are influenced mainly by the character of the local labour market. Uneven spatial development is therefore occurring at a sub-regional level (Savage, 1989: p.254). The politics of local areas have changed accordingly. Once, 'regional consciousness' generated a set of political demands that found a ready reception at the national level: this was particularly evident during the 1930s and the long post-war consensus when every government had to have a regional policy of sorts (Parsons, 1988: pp.137-43). In the 1980s the bargaining unit shrank. As a result, despite objections that it is a redundant concept, 'locality' has become fashionable in academic analysis (Gregson, 1987). The shift in terminology may partly derive from the decline in regionally-specific economies: the North East no longer specializes in particular commodities that distinguishes it from other areas. All are involved in what has been called 'intra-sectoral specialization', that is, specializing in different stages of the process of accumulation within the same industrial sectors: this is frequently organised, not at the national but the international, level (Wheelock, 1990: pp.107-8; Stubbs and Wheelock, 1990). Consequently, much of the analysis has concentrated on how particular areas have made connections with global organisations through marketing their local attractions and gaining the favours of the mighty. Some of these discussions take on a messianic air. Cooke, for example, asserts that the 'locality is a concept attaching to a process characteristic of modernity namely the extension, following political struggle, of civil, political and social rights of citizenship to individuals'. It is the place where they exercise these rights, a centre for individual and social mobilization in cultural, economic and social life. 'Locality is thus a base from which subjects can exercise their capacity for pro-activity by making effective individual and collective interventions within and beyond that base' (Cooke, 1989: p.12). This is the individualistic language of empowered 'citizens' and the locality where they can make things happen (Dickens, 1990, Ch.3). Within this perspective, analysis has concentrated on the success or failure of local initiatives in the 1980s, of 'place-marketing' (the selling of a new image) and local employment policies (Cooke, 1985, and Campbell, 1990). Many studies merely engage in an empirical test of the consequences of policies at the local level (see Campbell, 1990: part 2). This approach largely accepts the agenda of self-help dominant in the 1980s, though the language of 'local social movements' among the left provides an equally optimistic scenario of local mobilization: a strategy of resistance to anonymous external forces is offered, in which the 'local' replaces 'class' interests and, through which, indeed, class divisions are submerged (Urry, 1981: pp.469-70).

The optimistic language of locality, however, misses the point that political movements on local issues usually reflect the priorities of national agendas (Pickvance, 1985). Localism - the emotional and political mobilization of sub-regional identities - was a compulsory strategy in the policies of the 1980s. As Robins points out, localism provided a broad approach to both the search for a new industrial dynamism and the attempts at regeneration of the culture of cities (Robins, 1990: p.196). As before, regional inequalities were not overcome: indeed, they became worse as the North became more dependent on manual, mostly semi-skilled, work (Wheelock, 1990). While the government repudiated any regional policy aimed at equal development, many policies continued the post-war tradition of 'a low level of intervention combined with a high level of experimental institutionalisation. Under Mrs. Thatcher agencies have proliferated as actual assistance has declined' (Parsons, 1988: p.200). The local - not the local government - was given special assistance from agencies which encouraged self-help and initiative. Perhaps in the 1980s new localities were invented because government policy demanded newness and innovation, or perhaps because there was a genuinely-held belief among local politicians that things might be made to happen.

Localism therefore became the strategy to gain the attention of national agencies and international businesses. This suited the politics of the North East in many ways. Because of the pre-existing variety and rivalries of the economic background, it could not be expected that the 'region' would act cohesively in recession (Rowe, 1990). The 'diversity in decline' that allegedly characterised Teesside has been typical of the whole north-east in that the timing of collapse has varied from place to place (Beynon et al., 1990: p.235). Yet the forces shaping the 'reconstruction' seem similar, a mixture of external, mostly international investment, attracted and supported by a powerful, apparently immovable collection of political elites. The old capital/labour consensus about economic growth, national commitment and regional development has been replaced by an equally claustrophobic consensus about the need to market ourselves to anyone who will invest. This may not be a new development - trends away from local to international capital were detectable even before World War II, but it has an added resonance when selling a region and its people involves the almost unconscious adoption of a new identity (Rowe, 1990: p.465). The mystery is how the identity developed and became dominant.

From river to region

A literal descriptiveness characterized the language of locality around Sunderland until very recently. When was 'Wearside'? There are no signs of it in the eighteenth century. Before 1800 there was some confusion in the region, for example in legal documents talking of 'Sunderland by the Sea', or in letters referring to striking miners travelling to 'the Sunderland River' (Colls, 1987: p.207). 'Wear' is common enough among Sunderland's riverside industries in the nineteenth century, in the names of glass works, breweries and other firms in the 1850s and 1860s to judge from the town's directories. In the 1890s, for example, a group of workers such as the shipwrights in Sunderland used 'Wear' in the title of their benevolent society. These usages reflect the centrality of the river in people's lives as much as anything else: the waterway provided the main cause of the town's prosperity (Rowe, 1990; Milburn and Miller, 1988).

The first usages of 'Wearside' locally date from the late nineteenth century, and may be connected with organised sport and regional rivalry. For just a year in 1886-7 a magazine called The Wearside Review was produced in Sunderland, with items of local interest vying with articles on political philosophy. The first issue carried an outline of socialism, including a reasonably clear account of Marx's theory of surplus value. Critical denunciations of Sunderland Corporation ('the most illiterate, irresolute and incompetent public body in Sunderland') were followed by a sorrowful report on Sunderland's failure to beat Newcastle (despite a replay) in the 1887 F.A. Cup. Here, the team are for the first time called Wearsiders whose 'doggedness increased with their difficulties, and after a magnificent struggle they were only beaten by a very questionable goal' (February 1887: p.512). The association of the supporters with the river and the 'Barbary Coast' adjacent to it, combined with their rivalry with the 'Tynesiders', created a fierce identity. As a literary title, however, it did not last. In March 1887 the publication changed its name to The Northern Magazine and Monthly Spectator, 'in order to appeal to a wider circle of readers'. As a result, 'Wearside' had little public life until just before World War I. Sometime between 1909 and 1911 the Wearmouth Catholic News changed its name to Wearside Catholic News. In 1913 the Wearside Furnishing Stores opened in Crowtree Road, to survive as one of the growing number of businesses to adopt the new title in the subsequent forty years. The use of 'Tyneside' in official organisations, however, was given a great boost by its use in regimental and battalian recruitment in the Great War, including ethnic divisions such as the Tyneside Irish and Tyneside Scottish battalians who served in the trenches (The Observer, 20 June 1991: p.42).

The numbers of 'Wearside' titles among local organisations grew very slowly, without official sanction - only eight by 1952, and fifteen by 1970 (listed in the various directories of the area, such as Ward's, and the local telephone books). Some of the bodies adopting the label were semi-political: the communists in the 1940s, for example, tried to lead the Wearside Apprentices Movement into wartime opposition, though without apparent success (Milburn and Miller, 1988: p.192). By the end of the 1960s there were hints of deliberate modernity in organisations such as the Wearside Trades Council and a firm called Wearside Electronics Ltd. Yet in the popular memory at this time 'Wearside' still had simple geographic connotations, referring to the riverside and its people. McCutcheon's account of the Wearmouth pit and its union still uses it in this way (McCutcheon, 1960). Only gradually has the word been applied to an area larger than the old riverside strip of industries, as these have died one by one. In the 1990s the local telephone book offers a full range of 'Wearside' identities, among businesses and local associations. Many social agencies have adopted this new local identity - the Council of Churches, the HGV Training centre, a Housing Association, and the Skills Training Agencies among others. Significantly, perhaps, the designation of the area by British Telecom changed to 'Wearside' when the new ten-figure numbers were imposed in the late 1980s. Ironically, then, as the river has ceased to matter economically, it has become the symbol of the new region.

The new locality has not had it all its own way, however: throughout the twentieth century 'Sunderland' has retained its grip on the emotions of local identity. In 1970 'Sunderland' organisations (excluding those of the borough council) outnumbered 'Wearside' four-and-a-half times, and as late as 1990 by more than three times. In many forums there was no mention of Wearside at all: as late as 1977-82 in official documents such as the council's district plans drawn up for Sunderland Town Centre the word is absent. Nor does the official history of Washington New Town (significantly called 'Quicker by Quango') use the word, probably because there is no recognition that the westward development of Sunderland upriver but away from its industries might provoke a crisis of identity in the area. (Holley, 1983; Borough of Sunderland, 1978; 1981). The abolition of Tyne and Wear Metropolitan County (in 1986) may have left a gap in the language of local identity - especially since Sunderland was not restored to its pre-1974 location, in County Durham. Yet Sunderland, alone among the towns bidding for promotion, was awarded city status in 1992, to such local delight that it reached the national press (The Guardian, 15 February 1992). Many people have thus moved location while staying in the same place - through two counties to a new city in a sub-region.

Today Wearside is everywhere - from the newspaper reports of how the 'Wearsiders' are doing at football to the Training and Enterprise Council ('Putting Enterprise into Wearside' is their slogan). The word has entered local speech, found everywhere in reports and public relations material. Only when the council speaks as SUNDERLAND City Council, in material handed out directly to its constituents, does it carefully avoid the word. The absence almost shrieks at you. Wherever 'Wearside' occurs, there is an air of bright-eyed enthusiasm about the future. Many new directions are celebrated with 'Wearside' terminology. For example, the Wearside Training and Enterprise Council has set up a Sunderland Business

Development Centre, with the words 'there has never been a better time to be thinking of setting up in business in Wearside' (Sunderland and Washington Times, 15 November 1990). Increasingly, Sunderland is the parochial, while Wearside is the local. We are gradually learning to think bigger than ourselves, but not too big.

Typical of this developing style is the local alliance of politics and business in The Wearside Opportunity,

> The Wearside Opportunity (T.W.O.) launched in January 1989 is a partnership of local Business and Public Sector leaders who came together to harness Sunderland's many attributes; in particular the skills of its people and its attractive location and lifestyle. T.W.O. has set out a vision for Wearside as the Advanced Manufacturing Centre of the North (advertisement in Adult Learning Links Summer 1990).

Clearly this alliance intends to do for Sunderland what the Tyne and Wear City Action Team and the Northern Development Company in their publications of 'Great North Prospects' (for graduates among others) are trying to do for the North as a whole. In January 1991 T.W.O. launched its 'Make it Wearside' campaign with black and red posters and stickers with the slogan distributed all over the area. Significantly, the colours are also those of Sunderland's football club. In the accompanying literature, it is claimed that,

> this major marketing initiative aims to foster a feeling of civic pride amongst the local community and raise the profile of Wearside nationally.

This kind of campaign, drawing only upon the elites of business and other local organisations, is a new development in the 1980s and 1990s, heavily influenced by the American model. T.W.O.'s retiring chief executive, on going back to a life in accountancy, prophesied that the campaign would be productive of new ideas in its future as 'a business leadership team' (Sunderland Echo, 24 January 1991: p.7). A similar gathering of 'community' leaders is Wearside Common Purpose, designed to 'bring senior managers, decision makers and potential leaders from the region up-to-date with the major issues affecting Wearside', on the pattern of the American model of community leadership schemes (Sunderland and Washington Times, 8 November 1990). Now there is a new joint initiative between the City Council and the TEC, 'Wearside into Europe' to entice European Community funds into the area more effectively.

Whatever the new identity has done for the local elite's morale, for many it has not solved the problem of local loyalty but only offered a euphemism amid confusion. People live in Sunderland or Washington, Soulgrave or Town End Farm. They are represented by MPs for Sunderland (South and North) or Washington. The language may therefore vary according to the political purpose - the rhetoric of Borough, now City, when the council is talking to its voters, of Wearside and regional need when advertising to the world at large. The rhetoric offers different possibilities of exclusion and inclusion, depending on the nature of the parochial, regional or national audience. The question arises whether a new identity can resolve the dilemma of how to be both local and national simultaneously.

The language of modern localism

The effectiveness of names is not inherent or automatic. Opposition is probably easier to identify and understand than passive acceptance: the reluctance with which the new counties of 1974 were accepted shows this clearly in recent history. We still have obdurate Yorkshire patriots using the three Ridings in postal addresses, with the acquiescence of the Post Office, and Humberside was never acceptable on either side of the Humber. Some identities are re-inventions, such as Langbaurgh in Cleveland - a former 1851 census district, which is unpronounceable (most pronounce it to rhyme with 'bar', or more rarely, 'laugh'). These kinds of local identities, conjured up for administrative convenience are 'what you get when you let a natural compromiser loose in the archives', and are unlikely to stir any loyal emotions (The Guardian, 29 April 1991: editorial). Changing names may not alter the public image: when Windscale nuclear reprocessing plant became Sellafield, the criticisms of its safety record went on unabated, and merely provoked poor jokes about the need to call Chernobyl by some other name to hide its own disaster. 'Wearside' must deliver something new if it is to become the dominant self-identity, a real prospect of change.

In the North East the way names and promises can be connected is best demonstrated by the MetroCentre in Gateshead, a place that should be prosecuted under the Trades Descriptions Act since it is not at the centre of anything, and only indirectly connected to the metro system. Yet the triumph of MetroCentre is its freedom from local ties and politics: it is the centre of itself. Amidst much theoretical debate about post-modernism and style, one thing emerges about MetroCentre: its self-enclosed identity, reflected in its architectural style (a brick shed that reveals its secrets only on entry) and the complacent arrogance of its name indicate very precisely its administrative and financial isolation from normal political and social life in the North East. This is the essence of the independent 'Big Sheds' of modern consumerism (Pawley, 1990). Only in its sources of finance (the Church Commissioners are the landlords) does MetroCentre evoke memories of earlier forces of 'improvement' in the North East (Chaney, 1990: pp.56-8). More importantly, perhaps, MetroCentre seems to reflect the blandly uniform region-less style of motorway consumerism that is everywhere. The predictability of places of consumption - the same everywhere, with the same 'style' and quality of goods - does not yet have its equivalent in conditions of production.

Sunderland and the new town of Washington, by becoming 'Wearside' seem to be trying to emulate the great rivers of the northern past by building a new identity in this stylized future. Some problems of credibility are likely, in part because of the pretension in challenging Tyneside and Teesside. In making a claim to greatness we are also challenging their pasts as much as their futures. Teesside has the administrative and emotional pull of having been a 'problem' area for nearly thirty years (the Teesside Surveys and Plans date from the mid-1960s), and gained the seal of historical approval by having a volume in a county history series along with Tyneside in the 1970s (Fraser and Emsley, 1973; Harrison n.d.). Nevertheless, there are some difficulties in official and popular consistency if not of credibility. To this day on the southern approaches to Middlesbrough along the A19, the signs by the dual carriageway initially announce the turning to 'Tees-side' airport, before confirming in a second sign that 'Teesside' is really meant. One result of the confusing double 's' is that some books are published with only one, even by reputable printers (Boyle, 1989). If the locals are confused, outsiders are going to be left helpless.

What are the chances of Wearside proving effective? Within the North East people from Washington and Sunderland may be Wearsiders: to real outsiders, from beyond the North, they would have to explain why 'Wear' does not rhyme with 'hare'. One academic study (admittedly in the middle of quoting a long political speech) overcomes the pronunciation problem of standard English by calling it 'Weirside' (Parsons, 1988: p.139). This indicates the problem of the audience for the new identities. With MetroCentre, the market is clearly wider than just the North East because the shopping centre has been marketing the 'experience' to coach parties from all over the North, thus becoming an instant tourist attraction. It is also the only piece of modernisation, apart from the Nissan factory, to figure largely in the national media (Chaney, 1990). To be convincing is therefore the primary duty of any new local identity. How is this achieved? Characteristically, all new identities are immediately celebrated by a memorial festival or series of events. Every summer Sunderland Council runs a series of events under the title the 'Wearside Festival'. Many of the activities centre on the river and have the added attraction of offering something to both tourists and potentially idle schoolchildren during the long summer holiday. This is part of the reorganisation of leisure in which consumerism and tourism are merged. People will come to celebrate the place where the Venerable Bede entered a monastery and see the only surviving colliery railway built by George Stephenson - the 'bible trains' and the train buffs together, in an eclectic trip through Wearside's past, present and future (Sunderland Star, 17 January 1991 and 7 February 1991). A rival attraction is proposed at the northern half of the joint monastery, St. Paul's Jarrow, where an Anglo-Saxon village is to be built for £2.75m, 'Bede's World', to attract tourists to the Tyne. The 'area's history is to be revived', it is alleged in reports (Sunderland Echo, 21 May 1993). These sound less bizarre than other attractions in the North East. In Hartlepool the nuclear power station draws 36,000 visitors a year, and in Middlesbrough the 'Tees Valley' offers a compilation, ranging from the football club to a soft drinks factory, in a programme called 'The Valley at Work' (The Guardian 2 January 1991). Sunderland Council's 'tourist supremo' has tried to emulate this, suggesting 'nuts and bolts' visits to local factories as a means of enhancing brand loyalty, good public relations and employee morale (Sunderland and Washington Times, 6 June 1991). No wonder those participating in this fragmented and half-understood pastiche of the local have been dubbed 'post-tourists' (Featherstone, 1990: p.102). The tendency to turn the past into entertainment, holding festivals and ceremonies in museums, has as its counterpart the creation of the instant tourist attraction in the new centres of production: both are exotic and unusual, offering different kinds of dramatic commercialisation (Robins and Webster, 1989: p.81). Whether these sales drives will be sufficient to bring the world to Wearside, Teesside and Tyneside remains to be seen.

Local thinking : thinking locally

The changing image of the local, and the carefully-constructed attempts to make that image locally and nationally plausible, demonstrate that, in the 1990s, while we are learning to think locally, we are also learning to think internationally. This is reminiscent of the slogan 'local commitment, global capacity' adopted by Nomura, the Japanese finance house (Allen, 1990: p.192). The problem of attaching the local to the global is in fact a problem for the inhabitants but not for the incoming global businesses or tourists (Robins, 1990). We are not likely to go out and conquer the world with our own resources: that belongs to the past. So the local is defined with reference to the global in a supplicant role that leaves our significance defined by outsiders. We succeed only to the extent that we attract them. But this produces a substantial readjustment in our horizons. For Japanese companies in the North East, the local can be both Wearside and Europe - the centres of current production and future consumption. We, too, must therefore 'think European' for that reason alone. Ironically, the older industries really thought in much broader terms than this when they sought a world market, as the vulnerability of NEI Parsons to crises in the Middle East like the Gulf War of 1990-91 should remind us. Our horizons may actually be narrowing as we become more 'modern', because that kind of world market is vanishing, for British-owned industry at least. The paradoxical effect of the new Wearside may be to reinforce the reduced horizons in the world that economic decline forced on Sunderland, but this time in the name of modernisation. The 'world we have lost' was global. today's world is strictly local. The best we can do is Wearside and Europe.

6 Is Andy Capp dead? The enterprise culture and household responses to economic change

Jane Wheelock

Abstract

Policy makers throughout the 1980s insisted that Britain and its regions needed an enterprise culture to ensure regional economic development and international competitiveness. In the 1990s, changes in individual values continue to be seen as an important key to indigenous growth and to reversing regional decline. Wearside has experienced dramatic economic restructuring in recent years. Have people changed the old ways of doing things? The results of two case studies of Wearside households at the margins of employment show that there have indeed been changes. Andy Capp, the north east cartoon character who fulfils so many of the stereotypes of the working class male chauvinist, is not representative of some of the new gender roles being adopted. However, the changes found did not fit well with the demands of an enterprise culture, which requires people to respond to economic incentives. Households who were able to avoid dependence on benefits were instead adopting a culture of survival with dignity, based on a domestically oriented value system.

Introduction: the effects of livelihoods on lives

Faced with the consequences of dramatic change in regional and local economies, governments during the 1980s placed increasing emphasis on the need for changes in values and attitudes as a solution to the problems of contraction and closure of local industries, and widespread redundancies and unemployment. The New Right has had both pragmatic and ideological reasons for arguing that it is not the role of government to intervene in regional problems (Michie, 1992). Governments faced with rapidly rising levels of public expenditure at the start of two successive decades, have argued the need to cut back on spending programmes. And at an ideological level it is argued that the beneficial characteristics of the market mean that it is thoroughly desirable for governments to withdraw from economic interventionism in any case (Hahn, 1988; Gamble, 1986). It is indigenous growth and self reliance that will ensure regional or local economic development, with the operation of market forces in turn ensuring competitiveness in the international economy (Young, 1991).

As governments abrogate responsibility for the economic fate of their people by emphasising the role that markets play, the individual is magically transformed into the culprit. It is the citizen's responsibility to get out there in the market place, respond to opportunities and incentives, and make things happen. This needs a change in the attitudes of individuals. The language of economic liberalism was indeed rediscovered during the eighties, as a recent volume on the enterprise culture argues,

> But this programme has increasingly also come to be represented in "cultural" terms, as concerned with the attitudes, values and forms of self-understanding embedded in both individual and institutional activities (Keat and Abercrombie, 1991; 1).

It is here that governments have deigned to be proactive, and policy makers throughout the eighties insisted that what Britain and its regions needed was an enterprise culture. Fortunately public relations campaigns are relatively cheap, and make it easy to devolve blame on to the individual citizen for not being enterprising enough. Government promotion of the enterprise culture was very largely a matter of exhortation, with an emphasis on changing individual values, and getting rid of old ways of doing things. This included what was seen as the 'culture of dependency' on the welfare state. Yet the rhetoric of the enterprise culture was at variance with the reality of labour market policies which were carefully promoting distinctly old ways of working - withdrawal of employment protection for young people, restriction and then abolition of wages councils, privatisation of central and local government services which meant that low paid workers were re-employed at even lower wages, and so on.

This chapter asks whether the old ways of doing things have changed in a locality which has experienced just the sort of dramatic economic change for which the adoption of an enterprise culture should provide some solution. It is argued that evidence must be drawn from households as institutions, rather than from individuals, and uses two case studies. The first set of households consisted of men who had become unemployed, but whose wives continued to work. The second group had set up in business or become self employed during the 1980s. They were households which had been at the receiving end of the dramatic structural change described elsewhere in this volume. The effects of these changes on the lives and livelihoods of these households at the margins of employment were investigated using tape recorded, qualitative interviews. This meant that it was possible to get at what made people in these households tick; how their attitudes and values were formed. It proved that changes in the ways of doing things had indeed taken place, particularly with respect to gender roles.

But were they the sorts of changes advocated by proponents of the enterprise culture? Certainly, a strong set of values came through from the households interviewed, but there are three problems in trying to link the behaviour of these households with any kind of enterprise culture, which will be demonstrated in the course of the chapter. Firstly, the values were not predominantly individual values, but collective ones, linked in particular to the household. Related to this, and in the second place, economic rationality proved to be only a part of what motivated households. The enterprise culture argues that people respond to economic incentives, but my studies show that even households with low levels of income, for whom economic factors would seem to be of particular importance, operate from a variety of motivations, including a desire for dignity and self respect (see Wheelock, 1990; 1992a). Where does dignity or self respect fit in to an enterprise economy?

Thirdly however, households face serious tensions arising from the strategies they can adopt in order to maintain that self respect. I will argue that these tensions can only be understood if they are set in the context of a process of economic change which has led to a return to old ways of working, embracing low pay or long hours, or both. Labour market policies since 1979 have consistently encouraged the use of extensive rather than intensive ways of working; in Marxist terminology, a reliance on absolute rather than relative surplus value. Cheap labour does not encourage capital intensity or innovation in an economy. Other chapters in this volume examine the accepted wisdom about new ways of working in the high tech sectors of the economy. Here, I am primarily examining the interrelations between low income employment, self employment, being on benefit and doing unpaid work, for those at the bottom of the income scale. The result, I would argue, is that those who have been able to avoid dependence on benefits, have adopted a culture of survival with dignity, a culture that is at odds with the enterprise culture in crucial respects.

So what are the effects of the recent dramatic structural economic change on the lives and livelihoods of people in households at the margins of employment? The case studies are of two kinds of household whose sources of livelihood have changed in all too typical a way during the 1980s. The first study, undertaken in the mid 1980s, was of households where husbands had become unemployed, but where wives continued to work. Small business or self employed households, interviewed in 1990/91 made up the second group. At first sight, the results of these studies seem to indicate a new social dawn for the north east. Contrary to the conventional stereotype of the Wearside household economy, the first study found that men were taking on housework and child care tasks when they were not in the labour market. There were also fewer gender divisions in business families than indicated in other British studies, and it was unexpected to find how extensive family involvement in these urban small business undertakings proved to be. Both studies, in other words, showed that household work strategies were in some degree responsive to the large scale economic restructuring that had taken place in the Wearside economy over the decade. Can this be taken as evidence that north east households are becoming more entrepreneurial in their attitude or are they simply making flexible and adaptable adjustments to economic change? To reach a judgement it is vital to look more precisely at the pressures for such change, and at the social costs involved.

Examination of the motivations within households shows that in a local economy subject to economic restructuring, there is a pincer movement at work on family lives which operates from several different directions. The first contradiction that households face is that whilst the market forces involved in male job loss push women into employment, the historical development of the gender division of labour ensures them low wages. But household work strategies are also negotiated in response to traditional views of the division of labour between men and women which tend to be reinforced by the benefit system. For a number of the households with unemployed husbands, it was not even economically rational for wives to work, given the combination of benefit rules and low pay. Further, the slack labour market had, throughout the decade, pushed both men and women into self employment or starting up a business. Again, for many households, the economic rewards were extremely meagre, and in a number of cases no better than being on state benefit.

It appeared that in both the case studies, households were seeking self respect or dignity, and avoiding alienation, by undertaking meaningful work where possible. Families were both insulating themselves from the economic rationality inherent in the market, and from dependence on state benefits. Yet the decade was dominated by a Thatcherite economic ideology based on the pursuit of economic self interest. Effectively, the market mechanism and the economic individualism of the New Right interact to ensure that any individuals or families who base their decision making on self respect will at best be taken for granted, at worst taken advantage of or exploited by the economic system within which they find themselves. The presence of varied motivations will tend to focus economic and social conflict inside the household. To start the story of how changing livelihoods influence lives and attitudes, the next section provides more background for the case studies.

Changing livelihoods

On Wearside, as with other peripheral local economies, it is very clear that a process of social, or class, and gender recomposition of the labour force has gone on alongside the process of economic restructuring. The two empirical projects undertaken provide typical case studies of such a recomposition. Households with wives continuing to work while their husbands are no longer in the labour market are relatively few in the population as a whole. Indeed, at the time of this study, only 22% of wives with unemployed husbands were active in the labour market, in contrast with 62% of wives of employed husbands (General Household Survey, 1985). Yet such households were representative of the Wearside situation at the time of the study in a double sense. Employment opportunities for male manual workers had declined, and by the mid-eighties unemployment had reached an all time post war high, having remained at almost twice the national average since 1971. The prospects for low paid women workers had however remained relatively buoyant - despite traditionally low levels of female employment, by 1984 women made up 47.5% of the Wearside work force compared with a regional proportion of 42% and a national one of 43%. Thus, while male employment on Wearside declined by 9.3% between 1981 and 1984, female employment rose by 2.4% (Stone and Stevens, 1986).

The number of households relying on small business or self employment rose dramatically during the 1980s. At the same time, governments saw indigenous growth based on new small firms as the solution to those problems of economic restructuring and employment decline so typical of Wearside. The rise in new firm formation was seen as significant evidence of the growth of an enterprise economy. Unfortunately, academic commentators point out that much of this rise can be put down to the relative decline of large scale enterprise which has been part and parcel of British de-industrialisation. Indeed, on Wearside, net employment loss from plants with above 500 employees accounted for virtually all the net loss in manufacturing employment between 1973 and 1987, which suffered a 43% fall over the period (Stone, 1993). True, since 1986, as with other regions, the differential between Wearside and national rates of unemployment had declined: they were 11.9% compared with 7.4% nationally in 1991 (Employment Department, 1991). However, evidence of a regional enterprise culture was far from encouraging. Taking the rate of new firm formation as an indicator, Daly's Employment Gazette articles (1990, 1991) show that the Northern region performance is either near to, or at the bottom of the league table with respect to VAT registrations and self employment data. And whilst the number of VAT registrations grew substantially in all regions during the eighties, the North was second lowest at a 19.2% rate of growth, and from a low base, with the South East as the highest at 40%. My research set out to find whether extant Wearside small firms - and the families who were involved - had any characteristics which might compensate for this gloomy picture.

The 1990s seem to indicate that government policy has proved very effective in intensifying competition and worsening conditions in the labour market, but that this has not solved the problems of the overall competitiveness of the British economy. Indeed, fourteen years on, the policy has still failed to keep British wage increases below the rate of inflation, though encouragingly, the gap has recently narrowed. Britain seems set in a pattern of high unemployment rates, particularly for men, while small businesses have seen unprecedented rates of failure. Self employment and small business formation are continuing at historically high rates, though they are unlikely to increase as much as during the previous decade. As political ideology and the unsolved problems of the national economy still exercise the government, the policy of indigenous economic growth is likely to remain the only strategy for the regions. Although we may not have heard so much about the rhetoric of the enterprise culture since Mrs Thatcher was replaced by Mr Major, policy is still based on individual success in a market economy. The lives and livelihoods of households with females employed and males unemployed, and households reliant on small businesses, will thus continue to be representative of the economic structure of the 1990s too. It is time to turn to the stories of these households. These stories show flexibility in paid and unpaid work roles within the household based on value systems relating to household independence. Yet this is found alongside an exploitation based upon a recrudescence of old ways of working involving low pay and insecurity of employment.

Flexibility and exploitation in families with working wives and non-working husbands

The sample of thirty families with children was obtained from a project examining employment potential in Sunderland, which involved a questionnaire interview with a 7 per cent sample of households in selected areas of the city of Sunderland The aim of the study was to look at how changes in the division of domestic labour took place in a situation where it was likely that there would be some change, namely in households with high levels of domestic responsibility, yet where wives were also active in the labour market. The sample was less homogenous than originally intended in two respects. Firstly, families with adult children still living at home were included, and secondly families with non-employed men below the retirement age of 65. This was justified on the grounds that as job opportunities decline and long term unemployment grows, definitions of unemployment for men become less clear; in particular, men who are sick, but not incapable of work, may become discouraged workers and give up seeking work in the face of poor prospects.

I have described the analytical starting point for the study elsewhere (see Wheelock, forthcoming). Four categories of organisation of domestic work were distinguished: traditional rigid, traditional flexible, sharing, and exchanged role. In the traditional rigid form of organisation, the husband performs almost no domestic tasks apart from some predominantly male minor tasks such as mowing the lawn. In the traditional flexible household, the wife may still be busy at the weekend or regularly do housework before or after going to work, but her husband will undertake some non-traditionally male minor tasks, as well as, perhaps, washing up, a major gender-neutral task. In the case of sharing households, a range of tasks including some of the five major tasks (vacuuming, washing up, making the main meal, washing and ironing) are shared between husband and wife, or may even be done by the husband. The sharing household often has an ideology of mutual support and company.

In exchanged roles, the husband does a substantial range of tasks, either alone or shared with his wife, whilst she is either the family breadwinner or has more or less full-time employment. Whilst the wife may have little to say about domestic matters, her husband may well describe his household routine in some detail, and will have substantial responsibility for the household, at least through the week. Although this form of organisation involves a much looser gender segregation than the others, there will still be residual elements of tradition. An exchanged role organisation implies just that; there has been some exchange of roles between husband and wife, but there is certainly not complete role reversal (for further details see Wheelock, 1990).

When husbands became unemployed, there had been some change in organisation of domestic work in nearly half the families (8 from a traditional rigid to a traditional flexible form of organisation, 5 from traditional flexible to sharing), and there was substantial change in a further 6 families, with 3 families moving from traditional flexible to exchange roles and 2 from traditional rigid. In other words, 20 families (nearly 70 per cent of the sample) underwent change towards a less rigid division of labour within the household, while only 7 families (less than a quarter) did not. (Three families couldn't be assessed, either because they had been unemployed for such a prolonged period, or because they had only recently married.) This is a striking indication of the responsiveness of the gender organisation of households to the non-employment of husbands, although it must be kept in mind that even the change to exchanged roles means that there is still a core of household and child care tasks undertaken by the wife. It is nevertheless a far cry from the Andy Capp image of the north east household.

Pahl and Wallace (1985; p. 218) talk of a process of polarisation between busy households with many workers who are employed, do domestic tasks, own homes and cars and have money to maintain them, and unemployed households. In contrast, despite the men being out of work in the Wearside sample, families were participating in the social (unpaid) economy to a considerable extent. Thus rather more extra self consumption activities were undertaken, with men and women doing work in the household that could have been provided through the market. Households also undertook work for other households, collecting rent or visiting neighbours in hospital for example. The evidence pointed to a lack of gender differentiation in this involvement, although there was some gender division in the type of work done.

Where wives work then, it would seem that families are able to avoid some of the most debilitating features of the unemployed household. Taking their involvement in the social economy together with the gender shift in housework and child care already mentioned, it would seem that men on Wearside who have no employment are being responsive to a total household work strategy within which their wives have taken on paid work. Is such behaviour enterprising? Certainly, if enterprise is seen as the polar opposite of dependency, it might be. Those concerned with feminist and gender issues within the welfare state have highlighted the way that policy makers have ignored that the price of women having others depend on them is their own financial dependency (see for example, Wyn, 1991). Unemployed men in this sample were actually taking on the unpaid caring roles of their spouses, so avoiding some of this dependency. But when have policy makers ever taken unpaid work into account in their formulations (see Waring, 1989)?

The flexibility and adaptability shown by the men in the sample seemed primarily based on a pragmatic response to practical circumstances; in general it was practical circumstances that led to change rather than abstract attitudes to roles. Men had a strong sense of what it was fair that they should do around the house when they were at home and their wives were out at work. Nevertheless there could be serious conflict between traditional, patriarchal attitudes, and practice; in which case the gender division of labour actually adopted within the household tended to be less gender segregated than attitudes. Now of course the Wearside families studied were in circumstances which negated much of the basis for a patriarchal attitude: none of the husbands were in employment, and unemployment makes a nonsense of ideas of a male breadwinner and a family wage. Indeed, particularly wives in full-time employment, were often regarded as the breadwinner, whilst a substantial proportion of husbands were taking on more domestic work than previously. Negotiations over the gender division of labour within and outside the household were thus subject to a conflict between the traditional, or patriarchal model and the rationality, or maximisation of economic interests model. (See Yeandle, 1984)

The state exacerbates this possibility for conflict within the family in two ways. Firstly, there is the gender bias in the benefits system which derives from the assumptions underlying the Beveridge system, which in any case no longer correspond to the structural realities of the British economy. Though the research was undertaken before the reform of the benefit system, many of these problems remain. Thus paid employment no longer prevents financial poverty. Female heads of household in particular are likely to be low paid; full-time work is no longer the norm, again predominantly for women; full employment for men is no longer proving feasible, particularly in the regions; and finally, married women who undertake paid employment are no longer appropriately regarded as financial appendages of their husbands or cohabitees. Secondly, many of the families in the Wearside sample were subject to the 'poverty trap' - or more specifically the 'unemployment trap'. It is the combination of the unemployment trap with women's low pay which undermines the incentive for families to move towards role reversal as a response to male unemployment, and encourages the polarisation of households into those where husbands and wives are both in employment, and households where neither are in employment (see Morris, 1990).

The Wearside sample was surprising in two respects. Firstly, women did work despite the restrictions of the benefit system and their own low earnings. Secondly, the number of hours that some women were prepared to work was unexpectedly high. The popular conception of low paid female workers is that they are uncommitted to the labour market. This was certainly not the case for the majority of women in the sample: not merely were many prepared to work despite the disincentives of the benefit system and of low pay, but also hours worked and length of time in current job indicated a substantial commitment to the labour market. Such commitment is confirmed by Stubbs and Wheelock's (1990) study of women's employment potential on Wearside.

This empirical evidence suggests a third model for negotiations over the gender division of household work strategies in addition to the traditional and the economic rationality models: a model of dignity or self respect, or avoiding the alienation of not being employed. (Though the term 'negotiation' should not be taken to imply a reasoned dialogue between couples.) In a substantial proportion of the sample - some 10 families in all - wives continued to work despite the fact that the family was at best only very marginally better off, and in some cases was actually worse off as a result. The concern for self-respect, in some of the sample families at least, was sufficiently strong to overcome both economic rationality and traditional attitudes. The potential for conflict within families where husbands are not working and their wives are in low paid work is thus high.

Not merely are households the arena within which the gender conflict between the economic rationality demands of capitalism and the traditional demands of a patriarchal rationality is playing itself out; the household is also the focus for resolving the conflict between market rationality and the urge towards self reliance and independence from the state. Self reliance and independence are key words in the rhetoric of the enterprise culture, yet here they are at loggerheads with market motivations. In households where men have become unemployed, it is wives who hold the key to the self respect which the family can obtain by irrationally working in the labour market in order to avoid dependence on the welfare system, whilst also flouting traditional views of the gender division of labour. Despite Wearside men taking on new roles which by no means correspond to traditional stereotypes, then, adjustment to non-employment is not easy, since the potential for conflict within the household is large. But are such changes representative of a new enterprise culture? Before drawing any conclusions, let me consider the case of small business households.

Flexibility and exploitation in small business families

Small business households are popularly regarded as the mainstay of the enterprise culture. If we look for the key feature of small businesses, labour is generally seen as the major resource at their disposal, while for the self employed, their capacity to work is usually their sole resource. This analytical starting point has also been described elsewhere (see Wheelock, forthcoming). In the second study, the families of 24 small businesses set up during the 1980s were interviewed, including 8 female headed and 8 male headed businesses, 7 husband and wife partnerships and one family (initially, father-daughter) partnership. The study posited that small businesses and the self employed would be likely to be able to make use of the labour of other family members in addition to that of the proprietors themselves, and that this might provide the business with an important element of flexibility. But members of a family do not just have one work role. Any family unit combines work performed to earn income, unpaid work done domestically or work for self consumption, as well as unpaid work outside the household unit such as voluntary work. Work for self consumption includes all domestic tasks, as well as care of the young, the sick and the elderly. It is worth bearing in mind the part that families play in providing the next generation of the work force: their role in the reproduction of labour. Unpaid work is not purely private and personal.

In the 'entrepreneurial family', as we might provisionally label it, it is therefore possible that three work roles are being fulfilled: a full time or part time job in the formal economy, work in the business, and unpaid work in the complementary economy. Individual families need to combine work for self consumption with work for income, taking account of the fact that the work they do in the social economy is unpaid. Family work strategies will change, not only with the family life cycle stage, but also in response to changes in the economy. In the case of small businesses, they may also change in response to the life cycle, or stage of development of the business.

Given the predominance of labour as a factor of production within small scale enterprise, flexibility in the use of family labour provides a key to understanding the overall flexibility of such enterprises. In the entrepreneurial family, work for the business unit and work for the family unit are closely interrelated, so that the work strategies adopted justify the use of the term 'family economic unit' (see Lowe, 1988). We can in fact look at the monetarily rewarded aspects of the family's work (business and employment) and at its unpaid work (domestic and caring roles) and develop a model of the internal flexibility of the small firm (for details, see Wheelock, 1992b).

The research showed that the family economic unit is able to make use of a wide range of strategies to ensure flexibility in the performance both of direct business tasks and of indirect enabling work. What comes out of the Wearside study is that family and business needs are integrated with each other in the 'entrepreneurial' family. Like their unemployed counterparts considered in the last section, Wearside 'entrepreneurial' families were adopting a more or less 'domesticated' set of values, although in this case these derived from family involvement in the business project of the family, both directly and indirectly. This meant a particularly intense form of domestic value system. It also places the family economic unit at the meeting point of the complementary and the formal economies, and integrates private family roles and public business roles. It is in this integration that the heart of the satisfactions of running a small business are to be found.

It is worth noting that for rather more than a third of those interviewed, being part of a small business family gave husbands the opportunity to take a role with child care which they might otherwise not have had the opportunity for. For several of the families interviewed, one of the positive aspects of running a small business was that it provided both spouses with the opportunity of participating in domestic and family life. Indeed, in as many as 11 of the 24 business households, the domestic division of labour was a sharing one, although as indicated in the previous section, this does not mean an equal sharing of domestic chores between husband and wife. It is also interesting that these domestic arrangements appeared to pre-date setting up in business. Is a relatively sharing practice in the division of domestic labour a pre-disposing factor in setting up in business?

When the costs and benefits for the small business family are examined, the family economic unit is not entirely economically rational, and it is precisely this domestic orientation of the entrepreneurial way of life that constitutes its appeal. Whatever the debate over flexibility as a novel development in the labour process and industrial organisation, it seems widely accepted that the intensity of work has increased, and the study sample of small businesses on Wearside were no exception. There was an almost universal feeling amongst the sample families that hours are either long, or very long, when you set up in business. These findings confirm Rainbird's (1991) study where many of her (also qualitative) interviewees reported working over 50 hours a week and up to 60 or 70 hours in some cases. Work time can impinge particularly severely on the family when it is located at home, as was the case for well over half the sample when the business was set up.

Yet there were some non-monetary rewards for the patterns of work involved. For nearly half the sample, running a business meant that husband and wife could spend more time with each other, in some cases because they work with each other in the business. It could also mean more time with the family. When examining how family and personal lives get structured by entrepreneurial work strategies, Finch's (1983) observation of family life as a series of overlapping and interacting timetables is a useful one. Thus, it is the flexibility of business hours that may allow proprietors more time with children or spouses, or to cope with illness for example.

What of monetary rewards? During the 1980s policy makers have seen the material rewards for business ownership as of supreme importance, concerning themselves with creating a system of incentives that will ensure profits. Such incentives have been seen as an essential ingredient of the enterprise culture. Yet in the Wearside sample, only 5 families saw themselves as distinctly better off as a result of being in business, with a further 6 marginally so. Even when looking at this group it is worth realising that some were on benefit beforehand, so that income levels were still not high. Seven families were actually worse off than they had been, with 4 having about the same income level. Levels of income were such that a number of business families were entitled to draw benefits, including family credit, free school meals or prescription charges and housing benefit. For a number of businesses, a further enabling income coming into the house was essential. It is worth noting however, that a likely contributor to low incomes, particularly at the outset, was that nearly half of the sample stated that they were avoiding borrowing for the business; for many this meant reinvesting a substantial proportion of takings, and restricting what they took out of the business.

It is apparent then, that even modest income rewards were comparatively rare for the families in the sample. It seems that the small business proprietor (and family members) must work ceaselessly to obtain an often meagre financial reward. Why then are families prepared to do this, and should such small businesses be seen as part of an enterprise culture? True, there are financial features of business life which help to make the business feel like 'ours' for the families concerned, as Rainbird (1991) also found. Fringe benefits, such as a car or a telephone paid for by the business, can help to identify the business with the household. More significantly, the business has assets held on behalf of the family, and some families identify the business as a form of security for their children.

Essentially, the rewards derive from the way of life, which, while demanding, is intrinsically satisfying for most families, despite its problems and pressures in terms of hours of work or uncertain financial rewards. It is a lifestyle that integrates family and business satisfactions and values. Personal satisfaction is gained from being in control of doing a good job, providing a quality service, with the hope of economic rewards, but with the reality of sheer survival as a base line. Largely, however, motivations are not individually based, but derive from a focus on the domestic values of the family economic unit.

New forms of individual enterprise or old familiar ways of working?

These two studies have shown how important it is to examine the economic character of households, and not just to look at isolated individuals, if we are to see how people's lives change in response to changes in their means of livelihood. Yet policy makers and academic commentators alike have tended to emphasise the importance of the individual. This is not surprising, given the dominance of New Right ideology in Britain since 1979. At a time of rapid economic change, policy makers have increasingly abdicated economic responsibility to the impersonal market mechanism as the only means of ensuring social harmony. As Polanyi pointed out in *The Great Transformation* (1946), the market economy derives from the expectation that individuals will behave to maximise their economic gain. Economists have always put themselves forward as the discipline which analyses and explains the market system, and they too have a long tradition of starting from the individual who is assumed to behave as a 'rational economic man' (sic). As I have argued elsewhere (Wheelock, 1992a), even those economists who do start from the household and the family, namely the new household economists who follow Becker (1965), persist in positing that individual household members are economic maximisers. Both in policy terms, and in the academic debate therefore, the individual has generally been the starting point. In Mrs Thatcher's well known phrase, 'there is no such thing as society'. During the 1980s it became morally acceptable for people to pursue their own self interest in an enterprise economy, which would, so it was asserted, restore British competitiveness and ensure trickle down benefits for those at the bottom of the income scale.

These case studies have shown that if we start by looking at people where they live, in households, market motivations are not the only ones at work. In looking at the economic character of households, it becomes apparent that non-economic motivation may be as important as economic rationality. People living in households want a way of livelihood that ensures self respect and dignity for the family. Indeed, both families with unemployed husbands and small business families are prepared to modify traditional patriarchal rationality, and to fly in the face of economic rationality in order to achieve this. Although Andy Capp may not be dead, he and his wife have seriously modified their characters. And they are prepared to pay a price as well: the exploitation of low pay and low monetary rewards for this modicum of freedom from conventional gender roles.

So, this perceptible post industrial shift in roles within and outside the household has gone along with a return to old ways of working in the labour market. The survival of the small business families interviewed, is a survival on the margin between the formal and the informal or complementary economy, based as it is on the flexibility of the family economic unit and the intensification of its labour. There are some interesting parallels with Gudeman and Rivera's (1990) study of the house economy in rural Colombia. Like the peasant house, the family based small business is confined to the periphery of competition, and persists where the corporation cannot. Many of these small businesses are operating at the margin of profit, and beyond the production possibility frontier. Indeed, few of the Wearside businesses introduced any form of innovation to survive. Their functioning relied on the value produced by labour. Similarly, the working wives of unemployed men were involved in low tech, low wage, 'women's work', such as home helps, canteen workers or shop assistants. Their husbands had lost jobs representative of the structure of the local economy in the late 1960s, together with the skills of shipbuilding, mining and engineering.

Individual and family or business survival, then, are bound up together through the continuing use of old ways of working, forms which rely on intensifying work, yet which combine the growth of underemployment and unemployment. This suggests a 'culture of survival' which is quite distinct from the enterprise culture of politicians and policy makers. Certainly in Britain, governments have orchestrated an ideology of an enterprise culture which provides a justifying language of social integration for a world of economic insecurity, emphasising the importance of qualities like individualism, independence, self help and anti-collectivism (Burrows, 1991). In contrast to government revivalism, John Ritchie (1991) suggests that a pragmatic 'doing the business' typifies the enterprise culture of the subject, the business person him or her self. But it is important to go further than this to understand how the values of dignity and self respect coexist with the exploitation derived from old ways of working. It is survival that is crucial for the small business proprietor in an increasingly insecure labour market. The key lies in values that are ignored by politicians who trumpet the individualism of the enterprise culture or economists who assume the individualism of a 'rational economic man'. These are the values of reciprocity as an irreducible feature of human life.

Following Polanyi and Sahlins, Gudeman and Rivera (1990) see reciprocity as the obligation to give, receive and return as a mode of integrating the inherent opposition between the self and the other. The predominant stream of thought in economics follows Smith in seeing the 'propensity to truck, barter and exchange' as a basic economic motivation, with the conflicting interests of self seeking individuals harmonised through the market mechanism. Reflections on the contradictory outcome of economic change highlight that the importance of the household is not sufficiently recognised by policy makers. To reduce conflict within the family and to harness people's sense of self respect, economic rationality and dignity need to be brought into line with each other in a humanised incentive system, one which does not simply rely on selfish monetary rewards, as the enterprise culture posits.

This could be done by a concerted effort to make institutional changes to reduce the conflict introduced by low pay, by the state benefit system, by the taxation system and by owner occupation. The impact of patriarchal rationality also needs to be reduced, bringing economic rationality for men and women into line with each other. Proper consideration needs to be given to a total work strategy which takes account of all forms of work, and not just reasonably paid male work. In times of persistent high unemployment it is unrealistic to advocate redistribution of income to ensure social justice, nor does such a policy satisfy people's need to contribute to the wider society through participation in paid work (see Jahoda, 1982). If individual households are to have a genuine choice of work strategy, there must be more equitable sharing of decently paid employment between men and women, and between regions. This would mean reducing the hours of paid work for some, particularly men. This would in turn facilitate more equitable sharing of unpaid caring and domestic work.

The alternative, household survival relying on the destablilising effect of low wage competition in a region in economic decline, is not viable in the long term. How long before the sorts of households whose story has been told here sink into dependency on what is left of the welfare state? The changes in attitudes that have been described here are changes that have taken place despite the policy context, not because of it. They have been changes that are subtly, but significantly, out of line with the values of the enterprise culture. They are changes which try in some degree to buck the market, to escape individualism and to modify sharp gender divisions inside and outside the home. Yet they are not the direct product of any new social movement, and the husbands interviewed were certainly not Guardian reading new men. Is anyone in politics prepared to pick up on these currents for social change amongst those at the lower end of the income scale, and abandon twentieth century versions of Samuel Smiles' *Self Help* market individualism once and for all? Dependency, as Williams (1991) points out, has important positive attributes, and the social interdependence demonstrated in these households is a powerful cohesive force which not only deserves to fostered, but which politicians ignore at our peril.

Note

I would like to thank the Equal Opportunities Commission for the grant which made the earlier study possible, and the Economic and Social Research Council (award no. R000 23 2524) for their support for the small business family research. My thanks also go to the Wearside families who so kindly agreed to be interviewed.

The empirical material described in the central body of this chapter has also been used to support a further argument on 'Household responses to urban change: the clash between incentives and values' in Wheelock (forthcoming).

7 Back to the future? Preparing young adults for the post-industrial Wearside economy

Bob Hollands

Abstract

The primary aim of this chapter is to evaluate the vocational preparation and labour market position of young adults in Wearside within the context of what has been referred to as the 'post-industrial thesis'. The main argument hinges around 'going back' to re-interpret changes in the local labour market as viewed within the limited confines of post-industrialism, in order to understand how the debate about young adults and vocational training can progress 'into the future'. To fulfil this aim the chapter is divided into three parts. First, the idea of a post-industrial society is subject to critique and its relationship with vocational training is explored. Second, the chapter turns to an examination of the Wearside economy and demonstrates how this has affected young adults labour market and training experiences. Finally, in conclusion, it is argued that if there is to be an economic future for young adults on Wearside, then it is imperative to widen the terms of the debate beyond the idea of a post-industrialism and develop policies based on more explanatory paradigms and theories.

Introduction

...To begin with, the society that is now emerging is in no sense 'post-industrial'. Indeed, in its increasingly advanced technologies, it is a specific and probably absolute climax of industrialism itself. What is often loosely meant is the declining relative importance of manufacturing, which is due to follow agriculture into being a small minority sector of employment...Yet at this stage it is necessary to insist that a decline in manufacturing is not a decline in 'industrialism', and certainly not in industrial capitalism. The system of rationalised production by increasing applications of technology, within a system of regular wage-labour hired by the owners of the means of production, is not weakened but in its immediate terms strengthened when smaller and smaller workers are required to operate it. Moreover, service employment of a related kind, in distribution and checking, including the distribution and checking of information, is itself caught up in the same process...

Raymond Williams (1983)

I want to suggest that the new approach and emphasis given to 'skilling' in both the secondary school curriculum and 16-19 training provision, is primarily about the inculcation of social discipline; but this is no simple harking back to 'Victorian values'; on the contrary, it represents an attempt to construct a more mobile form of self-discipline, adapted to changing technologies of production and consumption, and to link this to a modern version of self-improvement aimed at the reserve army of youth labour.

Philip Cohen (1984)

Two of the fundamental aspects in the debate about post-industrial work are changing employment patterns and the re-definition of skills and attitudes in relation to these supposedly new forms of labour. Nowhere is the confluence of these two ideas more evident than in the debate about the vocational preparation of young people for employment. Vocational training has played a key ideological role in supporting the argument about the need for a new 'flexible' workforce necessary for a rapidly changing post-industrial economy.

This chapter attempts to examine and evaluate the validity of the 'post-industrial thesis', in light of a case study focusing in on the preparation and training of young adults for the Wearside(1) economy. The use of this locality as a specific case is particularly pertinent because the North East region is generally recognised as having experienced a dramatic reduction in the primary and manufacturing sectors of the economy. It also has the highest percentage of school leavers in training in England, Wales and Northern Ireland. As such, it offers up an interesting challenge to those who popularly apply variants of the post-industrial scenario in a positive manner in terms of evaluating the economic future of the area.(2) My main argument here is that it is imperative to 'go back' and re-examine changes in the economy and the labour market as viewed through the post-industrial lens and begin to re-interpret this recent history, if we are to seriously take the debate about young adults and vocational training 'into the future'.

To this end, the chapter is divided into three sections. First, I provide a background context by briefly analysing the concept of post-industrialism and assessing its relationship to vocationalism and the preparation of youth labour. Second, I turn to an examination of the Wearside economy and demonstrate how it has influenced young people's labour market prospects and training experiences. Finally, in conclusion, I discuss current economic and vocational training trends in the area and provide some political and policy-oriented interpretations and critiques surrounding the notion of training for a post-industrial society.

Vocationalism and the construction of 'Post-Industrialism'

To begin, it is essential to examine the connection between vocationalism and the general argument concerning the movement towards a post-industrial economy. This entails first, looking briefly into what is implied by the term post-industrialism, and second, examining the particular role vocationalism and youth training play in this scenario. The point is not to deny some of the changes that have taken place in our society, but rather to challenge dominant ideological interpretations of these transformations.

The debate about post-industrial society has its roots in conflicting sociological perspectives on the nature of modern society- namely theories of industrial society versus theories of capitalist society (Giddens, 1986).(3) Central to this former approach is the notion that industrialisation (in the form of new technology and an increasingly complex division of labour) is the driving force in the movement from traditional to modern societies and that such a transition represents a fundamentally progressive historical trend. The extension of this thesis occurred amongst certain theorist in the 1950s and 60s, who argued that 20th century industrialism was developing to such an extent that it was already beginning to create a new and different post-industrial order (Bell, 1962; 1974).

While such analyses were guarded, the main elements of such a prospective society and economy were fairly clear. First, proponents highlighted the well recognised economic trend away from manufacturing towards service employment, particularly those concerned with providing information (Bell, 1980). Second, in conjunction with this economic change, there was to be a political change in class power- for instance the transcendence of class and class-based parties based on the control/ or lack of control of the means of production in manufacturing, with the rise of a so-called 'professional/technical' classes who control the means of information in society (Bell, 1974). Finally, as Swingewood (1977) argues, post- industrial theorists also highlighted some of the cultural changes such a society would bring about, like increased leisure and a pluralistic/ democratic assertion of tastes and activities.

An underlying critique of post-industrialism then lies in the problematic theory of industrial society itself. The idea that there was a mechanical transition from traditional to modern society (fuelled by new technology and a complex division of labour) is only one theory of social and economic development. Alternatively, the Marxist position continues to stress the importance of class, class conflict and capital as the main structuring influences on the shape of modern work and society (Miliband, 1969; Braverman, 1974; Meikisins-Wood, 1986). According to this perspective, new technology and increasingly sophisticated production techniques are utilised by the capitalist class to subordinate workers in new ways and to ensure the continued extraction of surplus value.

Capitalism as an economic system is largely hidden from view in the post-industrial thesis. Part of the problem lies in the unhelpful separation of the technical 'forces of production' from the 'social relations of production'. As Raymond Williams has argued,

> ...it is a very weak kind of thinking to abstract the technical and technological changes and to explain the widespread social, economic and cultural changes as determined by them. This error, now identified as 'technological determinism', bears with particular weight on interpretation of all the later stages of industrialisation. It is especially misleading in descriptions and predictions of a 'post-industrial' society.
>
> (Williams, 1983, p 84).

Despite wide-ranging changes in our society, Williams argues our economy is still driven by the needs of capital to expand and much work continues to be characterised by rationalised forms of production and an unequal wage-labour relationship between capital and labour.

Williams' (1983, p. 87) goes on to make a number of other significant criticisms of post-industrialism which are relevant for the case study to follow. In particular he draws attention to the fact that the tripartite division of labour markets (into primary, secondary and tertiary sectors), masks the interdependent nature of work and plays down the supporting function that service sector employment has for manufacturing (eg. the role education and health play in training and restoring workers). Williams also questions the notion of service sector employment arguing that figures are often inflated and anyway such work is subject to exactly the same processes of capital intensity and labour-saving devices as the manufacturing sector. Finally, there is the whole issue of skill classification in the capitalist economy. While there indeed may be the need for a small, highly skilled technical and professional band of workers, a general process of deskilling across whole sectors of the economy has actually occurred (Williams, 1983, p. 87; also see Braverman, 1974; Wood et al, 1989).

Vocationalism in general, and the youth training curriculum in particular, have been partly constructed within the context of this post-industrial scenario and similarly have actively been used to support the notion that we are moving rapidly towards a new and different type of economy. It is important to note here that while the training debate has included the whole of the workforce, young people in particular have been singled out as a special segment of the labour market. Part of this response was motivated by unacceptably high levels of youth unemployment. Additionally, employers have continued to see school leavers as malleable and not yet socialised into 'inappropriate' work cultures (Metcalfe, 1988). Central to this argument was a decline in the need for out-dated craft skills training and the development of new vocational skills and attitudes necessary for the growing technical, professional and service occupations (Cohen, 1982; Green, 1983; Cohen, 1984; Finn, 1987; Hollands, 1990). As such, the government quango responsible for training in the 1970s and 80s, the Manpower Services Commission (MSC), generated a great deal of material on the need for a national youth training strategy designed to develop new 'flexible' and 'transferable' skills for a changing economy (MSC, 1976; 1977; 1981; 1982).

Much of the groundwork here was laid through a redefinition of the concepts of skill and vocation by policy-makers, professional trainers and government ideologues- a configuration which came to be called the 'new vocationalism' (Cohen, 1984). In so called industrial society, vocation referred primarily to the notion of an occupational 'calling', based upon an individual's adoption and mastery of a specific array of skills (usually over a lengthy period of time). In working class terms, vocation was specifically tied to the inheritance of a particular set of manual or domestic skills- a kind of cultural apprenticeship (Cohen, 1983). As Cohen (1982, p 46) explains: 'Under the old system, vocational courses were a misnomer for quite specialised training in practical skills for a particular trade or occupation, in other words a form of apprenticeship'.

Yet under the rubric of post-industrialism, the term vocation is recast in a new form, and refers to broad-based, transferable, non-job specific sets of skills. The grouping of skills in youth training into Occupational Training Families (OTFs) was not intended to '...incorporate job elements specific to the task or the employer, or specific technical skills', instead, 'the focus is on effective and appropriate performance rather than skills' (Farley quoted in Finn, 1987). Importantly, within the new vocationalism, skill begins to become redefined as 'performance', or more generally as a particular set of mental attitudes and approaches to working life (hence the use of such terms as 'personal effectiveness', 'life-skills' and 'impression management'). What is 'new' about the new vocationalism is that it promises to churn out a whole new generation of young workers who transcend narrow and restrictive craft practices, who are highly flexible and adaptable and who have the 'right' mental attitude towards their work (Cohen, 1984, p 107).

Not surprisingly, all this fits very neatly into, and indeed helps to drive the post-industrial merry-go-round. In particular, the new vocationalism and youth training schemes have aided the demise of and lowered the level of craft skills in manufacturing. This has occurred partly through the assertion that Britain no longer needs such skills and partly through the absorption and watering down of existing craft training by its incorporation into official government schemes (Finn, 1987).

Similarly, the new vocationalists have heavily promoted the idea that youth training schemes can provide a step up the ladder to career opportunities in the new technical, professional and service industries. Much has been made over the introduction of 'information technology' and 'computer literacy' components of the training curriculum (MSC, 1983), despite numerous criticisms that neither the quality nor the quantity is sufficient to meet the needs of a modern economy (YTS Monitoring Unit, 1985; Copsey and Hollands, 1988). The ideology of professionalism and career advancement has similarly been played out through an aggressive advertising campaign, which attempted to portray the image that young people could easily move into professional careers through youth training. Finally, case studies of the vocational curriculum on the Youth Training Scheme (YTS) in particular, have demonstrated a consistent theme of self-improvement, entrepreneurship and career advancement in redefined service occupations (Hollands, 1990). Much of this redefinition has occurred within those service industries traditionally characterised by female labour (i.e. child care, hairdressing and beauty therapy, retail and secretarial labour). The attempt has been made to recast traditional skills under the rhetoric of the new vocationalism and locate training within an imaginary promotional and/ or self-employment frame of reference (Hollands, 1991b, p 180-2; Cohen, 1984, pp. 106, 149-153; Cockburn, 1987).

There are clear parallels between the rationale of the new vocationalism and the movement towards a post-industrial economy. This is not to argue that young people have automatically accepted such a scenario as inevitable. Indeed as the Wearside case study of training and the labour market in the next section demonstrates, there are many contradictory tendencies created out of the clash between local cultures of work and the reality of the local labour market, and the modernising thrust of the new vocationalism and the post-industrial dream.

Preparing for the Wearside economy: training and the youth labour market

In this section I look at training and the youth labour market in Wearside as a case study for critically assessing the notion of post-industrialism. This necessitates two things. First, there is a need to provide a brief picture of changes in the Wearside economy and locate the position of young adults within this. Second, I want to look more specifically at the structure and organisation of training and work preparation schemes for young people in the area, and situate this whole discussion in the wider context of the debate about 'post-industrial Wearside'.

Young adults and the Wearside economy

Dramatic changes in the North East and Wearside labour markets have been closely tied up with the long-term decline of the British economy (Gamble, 1981). The concentration of primary industries and manufacturing in hinterland regions, has meant that the most significant job losses and de-industrialisation have occurred in the North (see Massey and Meegan, 1984; Martin and Rowthorne, 1986; Robinson et al, 1988). Also central to this decline has been the effect of the political-economic programme of 'Thatcherism' or more correctly the 'New Right' throughout the 1980s (Hall et al, 1983; Jessop et al, 1988). For example, in the U.K. numbers in manufacturing employment fell from 8.7 million in 1966 to 5.4

million by 1984, with over half this loss occurring since the election victory of the Conservatives in 1979 (Rowthorne, 1986).

The precise impact these economic and political trends have had on Wearside industrial and domestic life have been well documented (Stone and Stevens, 1985/6; Milburn and Miller, 1988; Wheelock, 1990; Stubbs and Wheelock, 1990). The most well publicised declines have occurred in the traditional primary industries like coal and shipbuilding. Employment in coal mining for instance declined from 18,000 in 1960 to 3,500 by 1985 and ten times as many were employed in shipbuilding in the mid-sixties as there were in the mid-eighties (Milburn and Miller, 1988, p. 201). The percentage of the workforce in the primary sector stood at less than 5% in 1987 (Training Agency, 1990, p 6). Overshadowing these figures has been the more recent closure of North East Shipbuilders Limited in 1989, with an estimated loss of 2,200 jobs and a further 4,000 in related industries (The Guardian 24.1.89).

Less well publicised have been more general declines in basic manufacturing and construction throughout the 1980s. A Training Agency document analysing the local labour market showed a continuing decline in employment in the manufacturing and construction sectors (down 11.2% and 7.3% respectively between 1984-87). This has occurred despite the movement of a number of Japanese branch plants into the area, most notably Nissan.(4) The percentage of workers engaged in manufacturing has shrunk consistently throughout the 60s and 70s and by 1987 made up only 23.6% of the workforce. If we group together primary industries, manufacturing and construction, the area experienced an overall loss of some 7,400 jobs between 1981 and 1987 (Training Agency, 1990, p.6).

The key problem for the Wearside economy has been that it has been largely unable to compensate for job loss in the primary and secondary sectors, with new employment opportunities in the tertiary sector (i.e. service industries). Although this latter economic sector has grown from 42% of the workforce in 1971 to nearly 67% in 1987, the main problem has been one of 'rate of growth'. While 4,406 new jobs were created in the service sector between 1984-7, the corresponding loss in the remaining sectors resulted in an overall loss of 1.8% over this period (Training Agency, 1990, p. 6).

For many analysts however the problem runs deeper than just sheer numbers. First, some commentators have been sceptical about the reclassification of jobs once thought to be manual labour, as new service occupations (Huws, 1981). Second, there is a problem with equating jobs numbers created in the service sector with those in the primary or secondary sectors. For example, the majority of primary and manufacturing jobs were long-term, while service sector jobs may be short-lived as the domestic economy fluctuates. Similarly service jobs are more likely to be taken up by women and are part-time and low-paid, rather than full-time employment. This general pattern is evident in Wearside where it has been shown that the number of part-time employees increased by 9% from 1984 to 1987 and encompassed 27% of all jobs in the region (Training Agency, 1990, p. 7).

Due to these imbalances and structural weaknesses in the economy, Wearside has remained high in the national and regional league tables for unemployment rates. In the depths of the 1980s recession and manufacturing 'shake-out', Sunderland experienced some of the worst unemployment rates in the country. Unemployment rose by 100% between 1979-85 and by January 1986 the rate for the town was 22.7% as opposed to the national average of 13.9% (Milburn and Miller, 1988, p. 206). While these figures have fallen consistently since the mid-80s (never reaching pre-1979 levels however), the region is still relatively worse off than many areas in the country, including its position relative to other North East cities and towns. This history of changes in the Wearside economy calls into question some of the rosier aspects of the supposed move towards a post-industrial economy. Unemployment has had a devastating effect on the region and has not been reduced to acceptable levels in real terms. The decline of admittedly back-breaking and dangerous work in the primary industries and monotonous assembly line jobs has not been matched by a corresponding increase in numbers or of comparable kinds of employment in the service sector (i.e. comparable conditions of service). As such, it may be more realistic to speak about 'de-industrialisation' rather than post-industrialism. It might also be argued that very few of the new jobs in the service area contain or require high levels of training and skills and as I will go on to argue, the quality of training provision on government schemes has, if anything, actually contributed to this process of deskilling.

All of these general features of the Wearside economy will have a particular bearing on the youth labour market. Youth unemployment and school 'staying on' rates, the changing nature of employment patterns and the prospects for work for young adults, as well as the development of new training and work preparation schemes, are all effected by these elements of the local economy (Aston et al, 1988; MacDonald, 1991; Coffield et al, 1986). Despite much public debate about a declining youth population(5) young adults still form an important segment of the local labour market. The latest available figures for Wearside (1989) show that approximately 42,500 young adults fall into the 16-24 year old band. This represents 14.3% of the total population and 30.2% of the population deemed 'economically active' (Training Agency, 1990, p. 9). Within this overall figure, the actual number of school leavers in 1989 was 4,253, which represents about 10% of the 16-24 year old cohort and approximately 1.5% of the total population. Changes in the destination figures of successive cohorts of school leavers provides an important monitor of changes in young people's economic prospects.

The first and most obvious influence a changing Wearside economy has had for young people, is in the area of unemployment. The issue of unemployment is an often neglected feature of the post-industrial thesis. The assumption is that the move from manufacturing to a service sector economy will be relatively smooth, new technology will create jobs and increased training and education opportunities will moderate the demand for work. As we have seen neither of these post-industrial assumptions are borne out in an area like Wearside and this is particularly the case for young people in the area. Over the last decade unemployment amongst Sunderland's youth rose dramatically until the mid 80s, before falling more slowly over the second half of this period. By 1985 the 16-24 year old cohort made up nearly 40% of the total unemployed (while only making up 22% of the population). In some electoral wards (i.e. Town End Farm/Downhill and Hendon) the percentage of this age group out of work reached 58.8% and 54.5% respectively (Howard et al, 1986). Similarly, the percentage of school-leavers becoming unemployed remained consistently over 20% in the early 80s, reaching a high of 25%.4 in 1986, before falling more slowly during the remainder of the decade.(6)

Optimists would quickly point to a steady drop in unemployment figures for the youth population in particular and more generally through the population as a whole. This temporary 'hiccup' in the economy was, the argument goes, the result of over-employment in manufacturing and slower than expected growth in the service sector. However, the Unemployment Unit, an independent research institute, has vigorously maintained that the figures have been artificially reduced due to the vast number of changes in the Government's mode of calculation (some thirty changes since 1979). This point is especially significant for young people. First, the rise of youth and then young adult training schemes have mopped up a significant number of those who would have once been classed as unemployed. Second, social security legislation has resulted in 16-17 years olds becoming ineligible to claim income support (unless in exceptional circumstances). The point is that over the last decade of so called post-industrial change, a majority of Wearside school leavers have faced a bleak future characterised by long bouts of unemployment, interrupted by either short-term work or temporary work preparation/ training schemes.

Employment opportunities for the youth cohort, particularly for school leavers, have fallen over this same period and one might be tempted to explain such changes in terms of an increase in training and education options. However, there is evidence to suggest that many working class school leavers actually prefer a job to training, education and of course unemployment (Hollands, 1990; Willis, 1985; Finn, 1984). Employment opportunities for Wearside youngsters have consistently shrunk in real terms, despite the fact that levels of qualification have actually risen over the years. For example, an analysis of a Career Service report of 20 years ago, when levels of qualifications were not as high as today, shows that over 90% of those who left school were placed in work (Sunderland Borough Council, 1969/70). Similarly, an ethnographic study of 58 Wearside women (in the 25-44 age range) showed that only one person was unemployed after leaving school, despite the fact that only about one-third of the respondents had gained some kind of educational qualification before leaving (Stubbs and Wheelock, 1990). In the last decade, the percentage of school leavers in the area finding work has fallen from 23.4% in 1981 to 14.4% by 1990.(7)

One of the explanations often given for this drop in youth employment is that jobs today require significantly more training than those in the past. What kind of evidence exists which appears to support or refute this statement? What kind of jobs did youngsters of twenty years ago go into and how do they compare to the types of employment school leavers can expect to obtain today?

Historically, we do have some idea about the types of employment school leavers in this area used to enter. A Career Service report of job placements over 20 year ago show a mixture of manufacturing and service sector jobs being taken up (Sunderland Borough Council, 1969/70). Out of a total of 2,248 school leavers in 1970 who found employment, 533 (or 23.7%) were placed in the wholesale and retail sector, while 496 (or 22.1%) found general factory work. Of course significant gender differences exist within these categories and a closer analysis reveals quite different patterns of employment. For young men the single largest category of employment surprisingly was in the wholesale and retail field (28.5%), followed closely by general factory work (24.7%). Just over 14% were placed in engineering and allied trades and approximately 4% obtained jobs in shipbuilding. The largest single occupational category for young women school leavers was the clerical/professional field (38.2%), followed by general factory work (19.2%) and wholesale and retail (18.6%). Research by Stubbs and Wheelock (1990, p. 64) supports this gender pattern. Over a quarter of their female sample started work as shop assistants, just over 20% started as office juniors and nearly 30% entered the clothing trade.

How then do these previous employment patterns for school leavers compare with those of today? While there is little current data which is directly comparable with these historical sources, there is evidence of some general trends. The Assistant Careers Officer in the borough has been quoted as saying that the majority of jobs for school leavers today are in the clerical field/ service industries with small companies (The Guardian 24.1.91). The point is, as we have seen, that growth in the service sector has not been enough to offset declines in manufacturing and traditional industries. There has been a substantial drop in apprenticeships in engineering and shipbuilding, as well as a general decline in factory work (Copsey and Hollands, 1988; Stubbs and Wheelock, 1990). Young people have lost opportunities in traditional employment, while gaining only a limited number of jobs in the tertiary sector.

A final avenue of employment for young people in the borough is in the setting up of small businesses. Self-employment, of course, has been a cornerstone of the Conservative government's attempt to construct an 'enterprise culture' spirit amongst the population and the effort has not been spared on the young. Enterprise training in schools, on youth training schemes and through special programmes such as the Enterprise Allowance Scheme (EAS), have all sought to instill the virtues of small business into young people. The problem however, has been that in areas like Wearside neither the local work culture nor the economic climate are conducive to the spirit of entrepreneurship, particularly amongst young people who have few or no resources. Available figures suggest that self-employment is not that popular amongst the young. In the 1985 Sunderland Household Survey, researchers found that only 12.1% of those classed as self-employed were from the 16-24 year old group (Howard, et al, 1986). The popularity and indeed success of the EAS programme has been flagging with a 40% business failure rate immediately after finishing the scheme and a declining number of people taking part (numbers declined from 522 in May 1990 to 365 by March 1991). In-depth research in the neighbouring borough of Cleveland, has shown youth enterprise and self-employment to be a 'risky business'- characterised by a high failure rate, low pay, long hours and personal and financial bankruptcy (MacDonald and Coffield, 1991).

A final test of the post-industrial thesis, and an important factor affecting the local youth labour market, is revealed through looking at staying-on rates in education. The general idea is that an increased need for professional and technical staff will result in higher participation rates in continuing education. Part of the problem here is that this aspect of post-industrialism is more applicable to North American society which has always had higher staying on-rates and a higher percentage of young people in further/higher education. England, on the other hand, continues to have one of the worst staying on rates amongst its major economic competitors (Green, 1990) despite recent improvements.

The latest regional figure for staying-on rates in education for the North was 44% in 1991, the lowest in England and Wales (Guardian 26.4.91). In Wearside the latest figure available (1990) stood below this at 39.1%, an improvement on figures from 1989 (36%) and 1981 (30.8%). While this rather modest increase in staying-on is to be welcomed, it is hardly surprising considering the scarcity of jobs available, as well as numerous national and local attempts to vocationalise and make 'relevant' the educational curriculum.(8) Importantly, a significant number of Wearside youth continue to reject furthering their education for a stab at the world of work, which as we have seen is at least partly understood to be jobs in traditional industries.

All of these factors then, a history of traditional primary and manufacturing industry, slow growth of the service sector, class cultural dispositions towards work and education and high rates of unemployment, have had a specific impact on the post-industrial dream in Wearside and on the employment possibilities for young adults. When confronted by this array of contradictory results, proponents of the post-industrial vision often point towards the rise of training to support their assertion that we are indeed moving (perhaps more slowly) towards a post-industrial economy. Particularly important here has been the growth and development of various youth and young adult training and work preparation schemes designed not only to smooth the transition from school to work, but in the government's own terms, to 'retrain the workers of the future'. The key question is, how do the schemes in this area attempt to bridge the gap between the professed need for a post-industrial labour supply and the economic realities of Wearside?

Preparing for 'Post-Industrialism'?: training schemes for young adults in Wearside

The rise of training has become one of the most significant factors affecting young working class people's transitions into work in the post war period (Cohen, 1983; 1984; Green, 1983; Finn, 1987; Hollands, 1990). At the last count no less than seventeen employment and training initiatives have been launched since the creation of the original MSC. While not all these programmes have been exclusively aimed at the youth population, it is clear that they are viewed as an important target group. Nationally, numbers in youth training grew four-fold from 1979 to 1988 (Department of Employment, 1988) and the Unemployment Unit calculated that by May 1988, 70% of 16 year old school leavers and 25% of 17 year olds were joining YTS (Unemployment Unit, 1988). The development of the adult scheme, Employment Training (ET) in 1988, which was in reality targeted at the 18-24 year old group, initially was projected to cater for 600,000 participants although actual numbers on the scheme were significantly lower than this, due in no small part, to its unpopularity. Most significant however are the successive cohorts of young people who have been through one or more training schemes in the past decade and a half.

While training has been a national initiative, there have been some significant local variations. In the North there is a clear regional pattern, influenced in no small way by a declining industrial and manufacturing base. It is not surprising to find that the Northern region had the highest percentage of school leavers in training in England, Wales and Northern Ireland in 1990 (The Guardian, 24.6.91). Wearside is no exception to this regional trend. The percentage of school leavers in training (excluding those staying on in school) grew from 45% in 1981 to a high of 63.8% in 1989, before dipping just below 60% in 1990. If we add 17 and 18 year olds in training (i.e. those on second year YTS and 18 years olds on Community Industry) to the raw numbers of school leavers, there were well over 4,000 participants in youth training during 1988-9. Additionally, while age related figures for schemes like ET do not exist, one can assume that because young adults are a target group, they form a significant percentage of the cohort on this programmes as well (there were over 3,000 participants on ET in March 1990). It is clear that a majority of working class school leavers of the last decade have experienced at least one, if not more than one government training scheme in their attempted transition into work and adulthood in Wearside.

There are a number of other regional factors which besides affecting training rates, may influence both the quality and type of training undertaken in the area. For example, Wearside Training and Enterprise Council (TEC) figures show that the local economy is characterised by a handful of big corporations and a large number of small businesses. It is estimated that 88% of the labour force works for businesses employing less than 25 people (Training Agency, 1990). National studies of training providers have shown that small employers (particularly in a recession) are often reluctant to be directly involved in training due to problems of resources, administration and a fear of trained workers being 'poached' by rival employers (YTS Monitoring Unit, 1985). As such, the organisation of training by Managing Agents is often left to major employers, community and voluntary groups or more significantly Private Training Agencies

(PTAs see below), with small companies being utilised as 'work experience' providers (Finn, 1987; Hollands, 1990).

Local statistics from the Careers Service show that just over half of the training providers in youth training in Sunderland are what are referred to as 'employer-led' (the rest being categorised as community-based/ workshop/ college-based). Yet the employer-led category does not readily distinguish between 'genuine' employers and PTAs. The distinction between genuine employer-led schemes and private trainers is that while both are private sector agents, the latter are in the business of training for a profit, not for the needs of their own workforce. While there exists a lack of information on Wearside, an analysis of a neighbouring borough, which shares some of the same training agencies as Sunderland, has shown that over one-third of the total number of young people in training were with PTAs (TUSIU, 1988).

The presence of PTAs has been shown to have a significant impact on the type and quality of training. First, because profit margins in training are small, PTAs tend to be large schemes (sometimes processing 200 to 300 trainees per year), which concentrate in low capital cost types of training (i.e. secretarial/ clerical/ retail). Second, they characteristically provide much of the off-the-job training on a rotational basis, while contracting trainees out to smaller employers for their work experience. These two factors, mean that a high incidence of PTAs in an area can skew training towards particular service occupations, as well as raise major questions about training quality, financial stability and proper monitoring of work placements (YTS Monitoring Unit, 1985; YTURC, 1985; Finn, 1987; Hollands, 1990).

While all of these factors may have an influence on training provision in a locality, there is a further need to investigate the relationship between work preparation and the demands of the local economy. One method of going about this is to compare numbers in training by occupational category, with trends and developments in the local labour market. Information provided by Wearside TEC on numbers in training on Youth Training (YT) and Employment Training (ET) by Standard Occupational Category (SOC) for 1990 can be found in Table One.

While Table One highlights differences in numbers of trainees in specific occupational categories (which I refer to later), the data are not grouped together in such a way as to make wider judgements about total numbers in training according to post-industrial theories of the labour market. Table Two is an attempt to group together and present the raw data in such a way as to evaluate this thesis. As such, I have constructed three main categories of training in relation to the labour market. First, a Professional/ Managerial/ Technical sector which represents training in occupational areas most representative of those characterising a post-industrial economy (SOC categories 01-07; for example, managers, professionals and various technical occupations). Second, a Service category encompassing training in a variety of service jobs (SOC numbers 08-09; 16-21; such as secretarial and clerical occupations, health and childcare, personal services and sales). Finally, I have included a Manual sector, which is broken up into skilled (SOC 10-11- i.e. skilled construction and engineering), semi-skilled (SOC 12-15- i.e. welding, vehicle trades, textiles, and craft) and unskilled (22-25- i.e. operators/ assemblers; transport; agriculture and other elementary occupations) sub-categories. (See Table Three).

Taken together Table One and Two reveal some interesting and perhaps unexpected patterns. First, Table Two clearly suggests that training in professional/ managerial/ technical occupational classifications (01-07) is not very prevalent on Wearside. Just over ten percent of trainees are undergoing training in what we might vaguely call post-industrial type occupations. Table One provides a further breakdown of this grouping by SOC for both training schemes. The largest occupational categories making up this sector for ET and YT together are Science and Engineering Associate Professions (04), followed by Literary, Artistic and Sport Professions (07) and Corporate Managers/ Administrators (01).

This closer look at these occupational categories raises a number of issues. First, one needs to seriously question the academic and vocational level of training provided on ET and YT in such areas as science and engineering, computer programming and management. Numerous studies have questioned the level of skills training provided in these areas (see NEDC/ MSC, 1984; Finn, 1987; Copsey and Hollands, 1988). Second, one would be hard pressed to believe that even a fraction of young people currently training in these categories would be able to compete in the labour market with those graduates from further and higher education. Because YT and ET are unlikely to lead to further training and education and due to the questionable skill levels attainable on these programmes, it would be fair to say that young adults hoping to progress to a professional career through this route will be disappointed. Taking into account these points, it could be argued that not only are numbers in training in this sector small, but overall this category is generally overstated.

The second major point which Table Two reveals is the relatively high number of young people training in what we might call the service industries. Over 40% of those in training fall into this category. While this phenomenon would appear to support the move towards a service-led post-industrial type economy, it is important to exercise caution in interpreting these general figures. Table One again provides a further breakdown of this service grouping by providing exact numbers in training on ET and YT by occupational grouping. By far and away the most significant categories within this sector are (SOC 08-09) Secretarial and Clerical Occupations (1,169 trainees) and (SOC 18) Health, Childcare and Related Occupations (656 trainees). Taken together, numbers in training in secretarial and clerical occupations make up 46.5% of the entire service category. Health, Childcare and Related Occupations make up another 26% of the service total and consist of training in such areas as nursing, care assistants, nurseries and play groups.

The bulk of training in the service sector appears to be in traditionally female occupations such as secretarial/ clerical work and the caring field and this mirrors national trends with respect to gender (see Cockburn, 1987; Fawcett Society, 1985; Hollands, 1990). Training in service sector jobs like these is not anything particularly new or representative of the coming of a post-industrial economy. Careers Service reports of twenty years ago show a similar number of young people (primarily young women) training in the secretarial/ clerical field. While one of the arguments might be that skill levels in this occupational category have increased (hence the need for training), numerous studies have demonstrated that if anything clerical labour may have become increasingly 'deskilled' (eg Braverman, 1974; Downing, 1981). Similarly, research into training for 'caring' and 'personal services' (i.e. hairdressing/ beauty therapy etc) occupations also hints at a low level of skills transmission and assumptions about young women's 'natural' aptitude for this type of work (Attwood and Hatton, 1983; Hollands, 1990; Cockburn, 1987). Excerpts from a booklet produced in Sunderland outlining young people's views of their YTS experience (SYEP, 1984), appears to raise at least questions about the skill component of training in these two areas,

Julie

...On my YTS I worked in an office. Everytime someone wanted something it was always "Julie go to the shops for me" or "Julie make me a cup of coffee". I mean just because you are YTS they all think that it's your job...

Sue

...I then went to a nursery and they make you do everything. They treat you like shit as if you were a kid yourself. The kids get on your nerves screaming all day long and all they want you to do is sit and play, but when you do sit and play you get told off by the supervisors as they tell you to get all the mess cleared up...

Increased numbers training in the service sector do not necessarily support post-industrial assumptions about new types of work or the need for increased training in these occupations.

Finally, the third and perhaps the most surprising major finding evident from Table Two, is the continuing significance of training for manual jobs. Nearly 47% of the total number in training on ET and YT could be said to be preparing for manual occupations. Within this general sector, Table Three (on the same page) provides a further breakdown of numbers in training into 'skilled' (SOC 10-11), 'semi-skilled' (SOC 12-15) and 'unskilled' (SOC 22-25) categories. Of those training in the manual sector, just under 30% fell into the skilled category, 42% into the semi-skilled band and just under 29% in the unskilled category.

Under the post-industrial scenario this is precisely the kind of training that is no longer required for the economy. Not only are there significant numbers training in this general sector, but over two-thirds are training for semi or unskilled occupations. Table One presents a further breakdown of this manual sector again by occupation. The largest single SOC occupational category is number (25) Other Elementary Occupations (21% of the total), followed by (15) Craft Occupations (20%), (10) Skilled Construction (19.8%) and (13) Vehicle Trades (14.6%). Skilled Engineering/ Electrical/ Electronic Trades, by contrast makes up only 9.7% of the total. Ironically, the largest single category, Other Elementary Occupations, includes training in traditional occupations such as mining and docking, as well as other unskilled labour such as cleaners, road sweepers, refuse collectors and porters.

Once again, one might want to call into question the skill levels obtained on YT and ET in occupations such as engineering and construction, by comparing them with those obtained under the apprenticeship system of the past. Research conducted on YTS has seriously called into question the levels of skill training gained in the manual trades through the MSC's preoccupation with 'broad-based' and 'transferable' skills, as well as questionable work experience in these fields (Hollands, 1990). A local example (SYEP, 1984) of a trainees' experience of manual skills training on YTS supports these wider findings,

PW

> I was on YTS for a year. It was so boring in some ways like you had to do what they wanted you to do. You had no option what you wanted to

do because I took construction. I wanted to do bricklaying and I did plumbing, plastering, basic skills, joinery, painting and decorating. I thought it was a bore because you did not take any notice of anything. If you had a chance of doing something that you wanted to do you would enjoy your work and take interest...

Overall, the main finding here is that significant numbers of young adults in the area are continuing to choose to train in occupational categories supposedly no longer required by a post-industrial economy. Second, skill levels gained must be questioned and there should be concern over the fact that much of this training is for semi or unskilled work.

One might be tempted to make the argument that these figures provide only a rough indication of types of occupational training and anyway such preparation is always somewhat out of phase with the wider needs of the economy. However, Wearside Tec also attempts to match up numbers in training by occupational area with local data it has collected on labour demand (Training Agency, 1990). For example, it has noted that much of the demand in manufacturing/ engineering and construction is not in terms of sheer numbers, but rather a modest demand for highly skilled labour. For those training in construction the local TEC admits that 'placing rates for YTS are poor' and that for both construction and engineering demand is towards the 'higher skill levels' (p. 11). On the service sector side, the TEC justifies the high numbers training in office work citing continued growth, while being slightly more cautious about job prospects in the health/ childcare sector.

A final way to assess the performance of training and work preparation for both the economy and trainees themselves is to look at the job success rate at the end of schemes. This is not to fall into the vocationalists' grand delusion that it is possible to perfectly match up training to job placement. The quality of the young person's experience and skills/ qualifications gained should also be accounted for in any evaluation of training success. However, job placement rates do give some indication of the quality and applicability of training in meeting the needs of the economy, as well as contributing to young people's perceptions about the usefulness of schemes.

Not surprisingly, considering what has been said about the Wearside economy, job take up rates following training are less than favourable. Sunderland Careers Service figures for YTS (November 1988) showed that only 37% went into a job or another scheme, 1.5% went into FE, with 60% becoming unemployed. Recent national figures, which provide regional variations, claim that the jobless rate for YT leavers in the North rose by 26% from November of last year (The Guardian 3.2.92). Local figures for job success following ET were even worse with only 20% finding work after leaving the scheme (1991 figures). Data obtained from Wearside TEC show slightly more optimistic figures of 55-60% for YT and 30% for ET gaining jobs for that cohort who completed their training programme. Whatever figures one is to believe, it is clear that for a significant proportion of young adults, training schemes have not been a particularly successful avenue into the local labour market.

This section has sought to examine young people's relationship to the Wearside labour market and has particularly concentrated on the role training has played in their preparation for work. A close examination of a range of data reveals that the post-industrial scenario does not readily explain nor help us to understand either the training and labour market experiences of young adults, or changes within the Wearside economy. In the final concluding section I consider some of the political and policy implications which arise out of the post-industrial training debate.

Back to the future?: Politics and policy in 'Post-Industrial' training

This chapter has sought to evaluate the vocational preparation and labour market position of young adults in Wearside within the context of what has been referred to as the 'post-industrial thesis'. While there have been substantial shifts in the local economy over the last couple of decades, it is clear that not all such changes can be accounted for by this
model. The main argument made here has been the necessity of going back and reviewing more closely some of the fundamental contradictions inherent in the use of the post-industrial framework for understanding the state of region's youth training and labour market. In order to face the future and take the vocational argument forward, it has been necessary to contrast the realities of the Wearside economy, with some of the ideals and projections assumed by the post-industrial thesis.

At the most general economic level, it is true that Wearside has witnessed a very real decline in employment in the primary and manufacturing industries. This trend has often been interpreted in a positive light as an inevitable facet of the movement towards a new post-industrial type economy. Additionally, much has been made of the fact that many of the jobs in the primary sector were both hard and dangerous, and that the region is better off divesting itself of this type of employment. However, there is much less discussion and commentary concerning the replacement of jobs in traditional industries, with developments in the tertiary or service sector of the economy. The fact is that while service employment has grown, it has neither grown fast enough to absorb the jobless, nor has it provided comparable employment in terms of wages, skill levels, collective representation or job security.

With regard to vocational training and the youth labour market, the post-industrial thesis appears equally fragile in its analysis. This is so despite the fact that the 'new vocationalism' has fundamentally sought to redefine occupational skills, shift the balance from manufacturing to service sector employment and re-shape young worker's orientations and attitudes to supposedly new types of work. The fact is that young adults in areas like Wearside have largely borne the brunt of the gap between the rhetoric of post-industrialism and the realities of the Wearside economy. Instead of a bright new future, they have more likely experienced unemployment, punctuated only by low quality training schemes and/ or short-term, low skilled and often part-time work. Despite the vocationalisation of the school and F.E. curriculum, class cultural dispositions to formal education and the lack of any real progression between training and further/ higher education have meant that very few young working class Wearsiders have been able to take advantage of educational routes through the system.

The lot of the vast number of Wearside post-school leavers has been vocational training. One might have believed, through all the 'modernising' discourse, that investment in training and foresight of a changing labour market would lead to new opportunities and creative futures for young adults. Yet again, the reality of vocational training is out of step with the stated projections of the post-industrial dream. For instance, the North's number one position as having the highest percentage of school leavers in training, has more to do with weaknesses in the local economy than it does with any real vocational commitment. Similarly, a lack of training in professional/ managerial/ technical occupations, an over-abundance of trainees in the clerical, secretarial and caring side of the service industry category, as well as a significant majority continuing to train in manual trades, all appear to question rather than support any kind of post-industrial scenario.

As Wearside TEC's own figures show just over 10% of YT and ET participants are gaining training in those occupational categories relevant to a post-industrial economy. Of those training in this area, there are very real questions to be asked about levels of skill/ qualifications gained and the quality of training in general. Additionally, the government's reputation for promoting information technology and high-tech training has been tarnished by the fact that nationally it has closed a significant number of IT centres in the 1990's (The Guardian 5.11.91).

The reality of training for service sector occupations has also been shown to be problematic. Locally, nearly three-quarters of young adults training in the service area are limited to two occupational categories;

clerical/secretarial and the caring professions. Again questions concerning the quality of training, not to mention gender segregation, need to be raised. Clearly, increased training in these fields does not support the idea that a post-industrial labour market is just around the corner.

Finally, there is evidence to support the view that a majority of young adults are continuing to train for manual occupations, jobs which supposedly are to become redundant in the not too distant future. For those few jobs remaining in engineering and construction, emphasis is on the upper end of the skill hierarchy and there is justification to argue that training on YT and ET is nowhere near the quality required. Instead, over two-thirds of trainees could be said to be receiving training in either semi or unskilled occupational categories.

What kind of conclusions can be drawn from this analysis? One inference might be that it is no longer acceptable to keep shouting about a post-industrial miracle when it has not happened or is not about to happen in the foreseeable future. Without accepting and addressing many of the contradictions and problems raised, it is simply wishful thinking to believe that somehow the local economy will transform itself through inevitable technological change. The same can be said for the training debate. The rhetoric of the new vocationalism will not in itself transform the British economy into a post-industrial paradise. What is required is a real debate about training and the economy- a broadening of ideas and solutions beyond ideological rhetoric and glib phrases.

For example, we need to move away from the 'New Right' view that economic development, and more specifically educational and vocational preparation for the economy, can simply be left to employers, industry and the marketplace (Education Group, 1991). Historical evidence has shown that employers have traditionally paid lip service to training in this country, both in financial as well as ideological terms. Investment has been patchy, training needs have often been short-term and technical/ craft and professional training (eg. management in particular) have been less than adequate. Recent government policy appears to have ignored this history. Financial cutbacks in the overall training budget (there has been talk of slashing some £1 billion off the training budget, some of which would be in the high technology area - The Guardian 24.10.91), and the shifting of power and responsibility for training onto employers through the Tecs, will result in lower quality and more poorly monitored training provision.

What in fact is required is a sound financial commitment, national monitoring and a much wider partnership of participants in the organisation and delivery of training. This is not an argument for a revamped MSC or a return to the old corporatist structure of government, trade unions and business. Some kind of national structure may be necessary to coordinate policy and set national or indeed European standards. Yet one of the positive aspects of the TEC structure is that within financial limits it has had some local autonomy. The problem however is one of financial resources and the lack of an equal partnership between employers and other constituencies concerned with training including local authorities, trade unions, community groups, educational establishments and young adults themselves. It remains to be seen how far the Labour Party's training strategy can begin to respond to these issues (Hollands, 1991a).

A second problem concerns the historical separation between vocational training and the education or schooling system. England in particular, continues to possess one of the most exclusive, class-ridden education systems in the world (Green, 1990). Working class resistance to formal schooling has a long historical basis (i.e. Humphries, 1981; Willis, 1977; Hollands, 1990) and is reflected in high truancy rates, disruptions in the classroom and one of the highest early leaving rates amongst its economic competitors. The separation of vocationalism, particularly in the form of on-the-job training, from formal schooling and the persistence of a divisive examination system, has led to a three tier system of education and training, with little or no connection between these levels. Again, relatively successful economies like Germany possess a system which does not so readily distinguish between education and training and through which a higher percentage of school leavers gain qualifications and go on to further education and/ or training. In summary what is required is an entire overhaul and reform of the 16-19 education/ training structure and beyond.

None of this is an argument for going back to a mythical past. Rather, it is a call for re-opening the debate about the economy and the role training and education play in relation to social and economic development. I have attempted to show that the post-industrial scenario, in its haste to confirm its own predictions, has failed to analyze the internal realities of the Wearside labour market. Additionally, the rhetoric of the new vocationalism has also contributed to muddying the waters sufficiently and has stultified the wider debate about training and education. If there is to be a economic future for young adults in Wearside, and the Northern region as a whole, then it is essential to widen the terms of the debate beyond the idea of post-industrialism and develop policies based on more explanatory paradigms, theories and local case studies.

Notes

1. It is important to make clear my use of terminology here. First, I use the term 'Wearside' purely as a term of geographical boundary-making, including the now city of Sunderland and the towns of Washington and Houghton le Spring. For a historical discussion of the origins and socio-political use of the term see the article by Pete Rushton in this volume. Second, the term 'young adults' is utilised here primarily to account for the expansion of Government training schemes for school leavers (i.e. Youth Training or YT) to those in the 18-24 range in the form of Employment Training or ET. Young adults will generally denote the 16-24 year old group unless otherwise specified.

2. I am referring primarily here to those individuals and agencies in the region whose job it is to extol the virtues of the area to inward investors, companies relocating, the general public etc (i.e. what came to be called 'The Great North Debate'- also see Fred Robinson's chapter in this volume).

3. The former position derives largely from Durkheim, while the latter perspective is decidedly Marxist in orientation. However, there have been some curious exceptions to this general classification. Ralf Darendorf's (1959) reinterpretation of Marxian theories of class and class conflict was an early example of a 'radical' version of an industrial society thesis. This concern with the changing nature of class and class consciousness was later taken up radical theorists of new social movements (Touraine, 1974), those emphasising the decline of the working class (i.e. Gorz, 1982), as well as varieties of post-modernist thought (i.e. Laclau, 1987). For a critique of this latter perspective see Meikisins-Woods (1986). Giddens (1990) has more recently distinguished between theories of post-industrialism and those of 'post-modernity' and provides a clear and accessible route through some of these complex debates.

4. For a discussion of Nissan see the chapter by Philip Garrahan and Paul Stewart in this volume. For a more extended discussion see Garrahan and Stewart (1992).

5. Much has been made in recent years of the fact that the youth population is declining. The general argument has been that this group is no longer a 'problem' or priority of government training policy and that this demographic miracle will effectively solve youth employment

prospects. For a through-going critique of this argument see Hollands (1991a).

6. The figures quoted here exclude those who have stayed on in education. I use this mode of calculation consistently, unless otherwise noted. Much of the information on school leaver destination figures come from Careers Service Minutes from the respective years. Unfortunately many of the minutes are not properly dated and are hence difficult to reference accurately.

7. The figures quoted here come from Sunderland Careers Service Sub-committee Minutes from the respective years (see note 6).

8. For a discussion of the vocationalisation of the school curriculum see Dale et al (1991) and Bates et al (1984).

Table 1: Numbers in training by standard occupational category (SOC), employment training (ET) and youth training (YT)

SOC Group and Category	ET	YT	Total
01 Corporate Managers/Administrators	120	9	129 (2.2)
02 Managers/ Proprietors	7	10	17 (0.3)
03 Professional Occupations	1	27	28 (0.5)
04 Science and Engineering Professions	28	155	183 (3.1)
05 Health Associate Professions	12	0	12 (0.2)
06 Legal, Business, Social Welfare and Other Associate Professions	107	0	107 (1.8)
07 Literary, Artistic and Sports Professionals	139	13	152 (2.6)
08 Clerical Occupations	271	260	531 (9.0)
09 Secretarial Occupations	409	229	638 (10.8)
10 Skilled Construction	427	122	549 (9.3)
11 Skilled Engineering, Electrical and Electronic Trades	56	214	270 (4.6)
12 Metal Forming/ Welding Trades	77	16	93 (1.6)
13 Vehicle Trades	129	277	406 (4.6)
14 Textile Trades	38	68	106 (1.8)
15 Craft and Related Occupations*	438	119	557 (9.4)
16 Protective Service Occupations	14	0	14 (0.2)
17 Catering/ Waiting/ Travel	108	67	175 (3.0)
18 Health/ Childcare/ Related Occupations	345	311	656 (11.1)
19 Personal Service Occupations**	27	134	161 (2.7)
20 Buyers and Sales Reps	0	127	127 (2.1)
21 Sales Assistants/ Other Sales Occupations	49	165	214 (3.6)
22 Industrial Plant Machine Operators/ Assemblers	36	35	71 (1.2)
23 Transport Operatives/ Drivers	133	0	133 (2.2)
24 Agriculture, Forestry and Fishing Occupations	8	0	8 (0.1)
25 Other Elementary Occupations	69	513	582 (9.8)
TOTAL	**3048**	**2871**	**5919 (100)**

Source: Wearside Training and Enterprise Council (1991 figures). For further details about occupations within each SOC see OPCS (1990).
* Includes Printing, Woodwork, Food Preparation, Horticultural and other Craft Related Occupations
** Includes Hairdressers, Beauticians, Domestic Staff and other Personal Service Occupations

Table 2: Numbers in training by labour market sector (Percentages in brackets)

	Professional/ Technical/ Managerial(1)	Service(2)	Manual(3)	Total
ET	414 (13.6)	1223 (40.1)	1411 (46.3)	3048 (100)
YT	214 (7.5)	1293 (45.0)	1364 (47.5)	2871 (100)
TOTAL	**628 (10.6)**	**2516 (42.5)**	**2775 (46.9)**	**5919 (100)**

1. Professional/Technical/Managerial Sector includes SOC 01-07
2. Service Sector includes SOC 08-09; 16-21
3. Manual Sector includes SOC 10-11; 22-25

Table 3: Numbers in training in manual sector by skill categorisation (Percentages in Brackets)

	Skilled(1)	Semi-skilled(2)	Unskilled(3)	Total
ET	483 (34.2)	682 (48.3)	246 (17.5)	1411 (100)
YT	336 (24.6)	480 (35.2)	548 (40.2)	1364 (100)
TOTAL	**819 (29.5)**	**1162 (41.9)**	**794 (28.6)**	**2775 (100)**

1. Skilled category includes SOC 10-11
2. Semi-skilled category includes SOC 12-15
3. Unskilled category includes SOC 22-25

8 Transnational corporations, human resource management and regional regeneration

John Knell

Abstract

This chapter examines how inward investors, pursuing human resource management(HRM) strategies, affect the character of the local economy and labour pools in which they locate. Specifically, it assesses the extent to which their activities upgrade labour force skills and restructure local labour markets within the locality in question. It argues that the local labour market impact of an inward investment cannot be read off from a consideration of its skill requirements and wage levels. The nature of the incoming firm's work organisation and labour process, and the specificities of a particular region, in terms of the existing traditions within local and regional labour pools and the configuration of institutional forces, all have an important influence on the emergent character of HRM strategies and their impact on labour force skills. In particular, the study suggests that the character of the existing stock of skills within a locality exerts a powerful influence on the ongoing nature of indigenous and inward investment. The implications of these arguments for the formulation of regional regeneration strategies are then explored.

Introduction

A policy consensus, which emphasises the pivotal role of inward investment in regenerating the UK economy, has emerged at both the national and local levels. With respect to the quality of labour force skills in Britain, it is commonly asserted that inward investors have had a major positive impact. The Government in particular, has been keen to stress the beneficial impact of such investments, associating them with positive skill upgrading and employment effects and, particularly in the case of Japanese inward investors, 'best-practice' management techniques and 'progressive' industrial relations practices. In light of these claims, the concern of this chapter is to explore how inward investors, pursuing HRM strategies, affect the character of the local labour pools and economy in which they locate. How pronounced are the differences between these inward investors and indigenous firms in terms of their strategies towards the recruitment and development of human capital? The empirical research reported below focuses on two MNCs which claim to have well formulated HRM strategies. The research reveals that their labour management policies were consistent with their broader business strategies. However, the character of this 'fit' between their business and labour use strategies did not generate an upgrading of labour force skills.

The next section will briefly set out the theoretical framework informing this paper's assessment of these issues. This is followed by an examination of empirical evidence from a study of the human resource management strategies of two multinationals in a mature industrial region undergoing structural change. The concluding sections discuss the implications of the findings for HRM research, for the relationship between inward investors and regional economies, and for the character of regional regeneration strategies.

TNCs, HRM and regional regeneration.

A focus on the activities of TNCs within a local economy offers insights into the impact of the growing internationalisation of capital on that economy, and on the degree to which 'space' exists for actors to affect meaningful transformations at the regional level. If it is the case that the fortunes of regional economies increasingly depend upon the processes of globalisation and the decisions of economic actors outside of their boundaries, to what extent should we perceive regions to have a measure of autonomy? For Castells(1985) the answer would seem to be fairly clear cut,

> ... perhaps the most striking effect of the new international economy on cities and regions is the loss of their autonomy vis-a-vis the world-wide economic actors that control their activities in terms of a global logic largely ignored and uncontrolled by local and regional societies.

Although commentators differ on the extent to which they would support Castells position (cf. Hirst and Thompson, 1992), there is a growing recognition that the pattern and nature of foreign direct investment(FDI) is a key causal influence on regional development and that these investment flows are in turn shaped by the character of the international division of labour(INDL). Different national economies are inserted into the INDL in ways which reflect the historically determined character of their economic and social relations(Knell, 1993).

The result, as noted by Amin and Malmberg, is that,

> . . . uneven spatial development is less a matter of interregional competition than a question concerning the impact on local economies of the uneven spatial distribution of tasks within [an]. . . integrated corporate production system. The consequence of this process is the sacrifice of local territorial integrity as regions come to play fragmented roles in a global system.(1992:p.411)

There is a danger that such arguments lead to an assumption that the character of regional and national economies can then be 'read off' from their place within the international division of labour(cf. Sayer, 1985). This runs the risk of compressing the actual specificities of particular regions, or of ignoring the ongoing relevance of such specificities in mediating the forces of global restructuring. A more satisfactory approach is to locate analysis of the activities of inward investors in a particular structural and institutional context. The advantage of such a focus is that it affords the opportunity to integrate such an analysis with an historical perspective on the changing nature of economic and social relations within a locality, bringing with it a number of benefits. For example, as Pollard notes, ". a region is normally the store-house not just of one skill, but of a range of complimentary skills, built up labouriously over a long period of time and not easily replicated"(1991:p.41). This raises the important question of the extent to which the inherited stock of skills within a region might have a significant conditioning effect on the ongoing pattern of investment within it?

The strength of such an approach is underlined by the fact that it is at the level of the local labour market that the effects of uneven spatial development manifest themselves most clearly. As Dicken notes in this regard,

> What is often overlooked in the debate on the effects of TNCs is the spatial unevenness of their impact on the local scale. Beneath national

aggregates of balance of payments figures, trade statistics and national employment totals, the real impact of the TNC is felt in specific localities. It is at this scale that the real problems of adjustment occur.(1988:p.388)

These observations serve to emphasise the distinction between choices made by firms to either restructure in place (i.e. through in situ adjustments), or restructure through space(i.e. through physical relocation)"(cf. Peck, 1993:p.4). Within the economic geography literature the latter has received more attention than the former. In light of the arguments presented here, we would endorse Peck's proposition that more emphasis should be placed upon ". mechanisms of local labour market adjustment and their relationships with processes of industrial restructuring."(ibid., p.15) These issues will be explored further in the case-studies.

The impact of FDI on a local economy: two case-studies

The case-study research focused on the Metropolitan District of Wakefield in West Yorkshire, which is a mature industrial region undergoing major structural change. Currently the locality is suffering the effects of long-term structural unemployment, directly and indirectly associated with the continued decline of the coal industry and related sectors. Reflecting this, unemployment rates within the locality have continued to remain above the national average figure. In January of this year, unemployment in the locality was at 13.1% compared to a national average figure of 12.5%(Department of Employment Gazette, 1993). Against this backdrop, the area has in recent years been the recipient of increasing flows of FDI. New FDI into the district in 1991 totalled seventeen million pounds, creating an estimated 586 jobs, 60% of which are in industrial manufacture (unpublished Local Authority figures). Recently developed industrial estates, such as 'Junction 41', have proved the favoured location of these new industries for they offer easy access to the national motorway network. This underlines the external orientations of many of the new firms, and serves to emphasise both the growing extent to which the local economy is becoming integrated into the national and international economies, and the increasing diversification of the local economy alongside the traditional sectors of coal and textiles.

Our exploration of the HRM implications of these structural changes will be based upon an investigation of the labour utilisation and recruitment strategies of the two largest examples of inward investment in the region, and their impact on the local labour market. The case-study material was generated from primary source documentation, and through interviews with senior management, shop-stewards, regional trade union officials, and senior officers in the Local Authority's Economic Development Department(EDD). In Company X, a soft drinks manufacturer, interviews were conducted with the Human Resources manager, and a number of Shift managers, whilst in Company Y, a major Japanese electronics manufacturer, interviews were conducted with managers at the directorial level. In both plants, interviews were carried out with a number of shop-stewards, and with those regional union officials who had formal responsibilities for the union members in the respective companies. The research examined, for each company, the nature of the production system and work organisation, industrial relations and personnel practices, recruitment and training, and the skill composition of the workforce.

The case studies themselves have two characteristics which locate them firmly within the recent empirical agendas of the HRM literature. Firstly, they are both 'greenfield site' developments, and as such conform with some of Guest's (1989) preconditions for the successful articulation of HRM policies, namely a 'greenfield' site with a carefully selected 'green' labour force. Secondly, one of the firms is Japanese and the other American. Firms from these countries of origin have often been presented as being at the forefront of new HRM practices.

The labour market of Wakefield.

The Wakefield Employment Skills Survey (WESS) (Policy Research Unit, 1989) revealed that 60 % of the population within the locality did not possess any formal qualifications, compared to a national figure of 36 %. Reflecting these low levels of attainment, a more recent analysis (Faulder, 1992) has confirmed that the Wakefield District has a high proportion of semi/unskilled manual workers and a low proportion of managerial and professional workers, the figures being consistent with (and slightly worse than) those for Great Britain as a whole.

In addition to the deficit in formal skills identified above, there is evidence of important skill mismatches with the skill profile of the locality being more suited to the now declining industries than newer developing ones. In part, this reflects the traditionally dominant role of the coal industry which, in the case of Wakefield, has resulted in an inherited stock of skills developed from industrial experience which is inappropriate to the needs of new industries (WESS, 1989).

This discussion should not be taken to imply the acceptance of either 'skill' or the 'local labour market'(LLM) as unproblematic concepts. For the purposes of this discussion, it would be useful to briefly highlight a number of issues in this regard.

A number of officers within the EDD suggested that both an ideological and social construction of skill underpins much management recruitment practice in the locality. These more traditional patterns of labour market segmentation are augmented by spatial processes which serve to underline that Wakefield does not possess a coherent LLM. For example, not only has the demand for skilled labour displayed a tendency to transcend the limitations and potentialities of the LLM, but there is an uneven spatial differentiation of employment opportunities across the district. Indeed, the locality is characterised by discrete pockets of very high unemployment. Inward investors may view these as 'captive labour pools.'

The case-studies sought to discover whether these characteristics of the local labour pool (cf. Peck and Lloyd, 1989), and deficiencies in the quality of the District labour force, discouraged skill up-grading investments by the firms in question; and the specific ways in which their activities were restructuring local labour markets.

Company Y

In 1991, a major Japanese electronics manufacturer, Company Y, invested twenty million pounds in a new audio-visual equipment manufacturing plant within the locality which currently employs 300 staff.

The plant is a manufacturing facility organised on a traditional flow-line assembly basis. Each line sustains approximately thirty workers working on long production runs of relatively standardised goods. Company Y has not as yet confirmed any intentions to locate more technologically complex component production, or research and development (R&D) activities, at the Wakefield site. The geographical separation of these activities from each other, and in turn from the final assembly of the product that takes place in Wakefield, conforms to the classic model of a 'branch-plant' operation (see Massey, 1984).

In terms of the company's human resource/industrial relations policies, in common with many other Japanese investors, the plant operates with a 'single status' philosophy and facilities. The payment system is organised on a traditional salaried basis, with the workforce paid monthly.

With regard to union recognition, after an initial 'beauty contest' featuring five unions, the company signed a single-union deal with the EEPTU. Such an outcome is consistent with other studies (see Morgan and Sayer's (1988) study of the electronics sector in Wales) which revealed the preference of inward investors, particularly Japanese companies, for single union deals with 'responsible' trade unions. The company has proved keen to encourage membership, with levels currently standing at between seventy and eighty percent of the workforce.

In interviews, senior management stressed that they had attempted to create, in their view successfully, a work culture that made the workers feel 'secure', and which fostered a good team spirit. Introducing techniques which would stimulate participation by the workforce was seen as an important part of this process. In this regard, whilst they acknowledged that the nature of production organisation placed limits on the extent to which 'team-working' could be easily implemented, they stressed the importance of the daily line meetings in uniting the workers and management over issues such as production quality and information sharing.

However, the extent to which these employee involvement techniques had impacted positively on the motivation of employees, and their perception of worker - management relations, was thrown into question by the shop stewards in the plant. For example, with regard to the daily line meetings, these took place every morning at ten to eight. A significant proportion of the workforce did not attend them because this was viewed as unpaid time, the shift commencing at eight. This fairly rigid attitude was a reflection of the fact that the workforce felt that the 'line pushed them very hard,' without compensating them with bonus payments. Importantly, these attitudes were a direct reflection of the workforce's past work experiences. Given that a large number of the women working in the plant had previously worked in the textile industry, in jobs in which they could more effectively control their output and earnings, they felt that they had suffered a relative loss of control and discretion in Company Y. Perhaps reflecting these feelings, absenteeism levels surged after the initial intake of workers had passed through their probationary period. The levels were such that it forced the company to introduce a verbal and written warning system as an attempt to tighten their control of medically uncertified absenteeism. All this suggests the workers perceived and experienced the production process in ways that induced scepticism with regard to the genuineness of the company's broadly articulated company culture.

Additionally, the company had shown resistance to the union's demands that they make a commitment to an agreement on the continuous upgrading of the labour forces' skills. This in turn weakened the company's message with regard to the secure nature of employment, or any stated commitment to employee development.

In terms of the skill and personnel composition of the workforce, all but one of the senior managerial positions are filled by Japanese expatriates from the company's home operations, and the one UK director was already employed by Company Y in Britain. This suggests that little transfer of skills is taking place in the high level management positions. Middle management, comprising of line supervisors/ managers, constitutes seven percent of the work force. These are predominantly graduate engineers, and are recruited from the national rather than the local labour market. This group is the one section of the workforce receiving intensive training to develop firm specific expertise and skills. Much of their training takes place in sub-contracting factories in Japan, working exclusively for Company Y. Finally, ninety percent of the total work force is categorised as un-skilled. A senior Director revealed that these workers receive only rudimentary 'on-the-job' training. Such limited training was considered suitable preparation for the routine tasks which characterise the traditional flow-line assembly production process. In line with earlier studies (Hakim, 1979; Morgan and Sayer, 1984; Pearson, 1989) which pointed to the feminisation of low-grade assembly work within foreign TNCs operating in the UK electronic sector, it is almost exclusively women that fill these positions.

Company Y reported that it had been able to recruit suitable female applicants from the local labour market, many of whom came from the textile industry with skills well suited to the demands of assembly-line production. Senior management indicated that they were very satisfied with their capacity to 'learn quickly' and that they had proved 'easy to train'. Such claims notwithstanding, the limits to the company's human resource policies were reflected in the management's decision to class these women as 'unskilled' workers, demonstrating their reluctance to formally recognise the full extent of their skills. In common with many other employers, Company Y derives economic benefits from the social construction of skill, which allows for the definition of these women's skills as a distinct category from semi or skilled labour in general, thereby denying that these workers possess a degree of skill which justifies greater recognition and remuneration.

In terms of the Company's relationship to and impact on the local economy, it is evident that Company Y's decision to locate production in Wakefield was not motivated by a desire to access a highly skilled local labour force. Indeed, the company was more concerned to establish that a captive local labour pool existed before making its decision to invest. As we have seen, however, this has brought with it certain problems associated with the specificities of this labour pool; i.e. levels and patterns of absenteeism commonly associated with the coalfield areas; the tradition amongst textile workers to move fairly frequently from job to job; and the negative attitude of a number of these ex-textile workers to the labour process at the Company. These observations suggest that it is difficult to isolate the influence of historically forged 'external' conditions, as opposed to immediate managerial policy and practice, in shaping the attitudes of workers to the company.

Company X

The other major inward investor, Company X, a soft drinks manufacturer, set up a manufacturing, filling, packing, and distribution facility in the locality in 1989. It has invested sixty five million pounds in the operation, making it Europe's largest soft drinks manufacturing plant, currently employing 280 staff. The processing, bottling, canning, and packing of the product is fully automated, with CAD/CAM, JIT, and robotisation all featuring within the production line process. Production is characterised by very long runs of standardised products. The workforce is organised into teams around these main production processes. There are six processing teams, eight bottling teams, and two canning teams. The plant runs on a twelve hour Continental Shift pattern (i.e., three days on, then three days off), with individual teams having to be self-relieving whilst on shift.

In terms of the skill and personnel composition of the workforce, senior management represent 8% of the workforce. A few were already employed by Company X, with the remainder recruited from the national labour market, many of them being existing factory managers. Office staff constitute 7% of the workforce, the remaining 85 % being classified as technicians. In contrast to Company Y, the majority of the 257 full-time employees are men, reflecting the gendered division of traditional skills, and the incompatibility of the company's continental shift pattern and the domestic duties frequently shouldered by women.

The company has a clearly articulated human resource development strategy, exposing the centrality of multi-skilling. To quote their Factory manager: "Multi-skilling is a feature of our factory philosophy with staff training in cross craft skills enabling full flexibility.

Secondly, it has defined very clearly the company culture, which is encapsulated in various phrases and policies. In this regard the company talks about 'the pursuit of excellence by individuals,' and that "better people equals faster people equals fewer people equals excellence." These messages are reinforced in team briefings, which take place at all levels within the organisation. The company sees these meetings as vitally important in ensuring that employees develop a broad loyalty to the plant, in addition to their more narrowly focused commitment to their teams, which the company suggests is high and tangible. At the heart of the company's message is the idea that in the event of any problems emerging within the production process, they should be treated not as a particular team's problem but as a 'Wakefield problem'. In addition to these group based employee involvement techniques, the company runs an individualised Performance Development Appraisal programme, in which all staff participate in order to identify their objectives, personal achievements, and training needs.

With regard to union recognition, Company X negotiated a single union deal with the AEU, and membership levels have reached about fifty percent of the workforce. The company has recently set up a Site Council, stipulating that union and non-union representation on the council should broadly reflect shop-floor allegiances. The last round of pay negotiations took place within this forum.

The company operates a traditional salaried system, but does not make any over-time payments, instead offering time off-in-lieu. Apart from at the senior management grades, there has been no movement to individualised performance related pay(PRP). In recent negotiations, the Site Council felt that individual PRP was contrary to the effective operation of team working. It put forward an alternative bonus scheme - a 'leading edge award' package - with payments to be triggered by the reduction of material and usage wastage across the whole factory.

What emerged from the interviews with the shop stewards, is that the harmonious and transformative picture of worker-management relations presented by the company, diverged somewhat from workers own experiences. In many respects, the pattern of development of employee perceptions has reflected the observations that Newell(1991) amongst others has made, that the company unrealistically heightened employees' expectations through methods of selection, and 'hype' about the need for self-motivated, multi-skilled, flexible employees. Workers' actual experience of work has confounded these expectations. In this regard, let us examine the success of the company's initial intention to develop a 'multi-skilled' and 'flexible' workforce.

As part of this strategy, it sought to recruit 'greenfield people' to complement the 'greenfield site', that is people without direct experience and thus preconceptions of the soft-drinks industry. It was thought that such candidates would be more likely to possess the key characteristics sought by the company, in particular a 'willingness to accept new methods' and an 'ability to work successfully in a team'.

In practice, however, Company X has found it difficult to achieve these intentions. Despite the 'catch-all' nature of the 'technician' category, it is made up of several distinct grades and skill levels. Three grades fall within the 'technician' category, namely Supervisor/Team Leader, Senior Technical Operator(STO), and Technical Operator(TO), and these grades reflect the skill requirements of the production teams into which the workforce is organised. Each team consists of eight personnel, made up of one Team Leader, one STO, and then six TO's. Team Leaders and STO's are usually highly qualified engineers or electricians. They are expected to develop a full working knowledge of all of the production process and machinery on a line, and carry out, and lead all maintenance work. The central difference between Team Leaders and STO's is that the former are expected to demonstrate greater employee-management skills. Beneath these two grades come the TO's who are less well qualified and would be expected to develop mastery of only a particular part of the production process, or a specific piece of machinery on the line.

Despite the company's commitment to full flexibility and multi-skilling, the highly automated flow-line nature of the production system has diminished the need for such a highly skilled workforce. An interview with the Human Resources Manager revealed that a number of the original recruitment in-take, mainly at the TO level, have since left the company because their initial expectations with regard to the level of training that they would receive had not been met. Moreover, they felt that their existing skill levels were being diluted. It was suggested that such feelings were due, at least in part, to the highly automated nature of production, as a consequence of which much of a shift pattern can be rendered relatively mundane. Additionally, these workers found it difficult to adapt to the expectation that team members should be prepared to do anything, including sweeping the floor if required. In direct response to these difficulties, Company X has recently introduced a new semi-skilled Operator grade to carry out the more mundane tasks so that the skilled employees do not feel they are being de-skilled by the production process within the company.

Reflecting these developments, training plans for the twelve months from September 1991 were suspended despite the fact that the company had already made budgetary provisions for them. These experiences, and the emergence of other grievances (over staffing levels, holiday shifts etc.), have impacted directly on the conduct of industrial relations in the plant. Workers have become increasingly aware of gaps in the single union agreement, which the company has been able to interpret to its own advantage. As a consequence, the composition and impact of the Site Council has changed. Initially, upon the company's insistence, membership of the council was split fifty/fifty in terms of union/non-union representation. Moreover, the initial cohort of representatives were hand-picked by the company. Now, the council is entirely populated by union members, including some stewards, who have been directly elected by the workforce. Given that the District Secretary of the then AEU, had suggested that the original balance of the site council was an attempt by the company to effectively 'recognise two unions', this development can be seen as being at odds with the company's overall policy of recognising, but carefully circumscribing, the union's role within the plant.

In terms of the impact of the Company on the local economy, two points emerge from the above findings. Firstly, Company X's impact on the stock of skills in the Wakefield Metropolitan District has been mixed. Team Leaders and STO's, already highly skilled individuals before they entered the company, have been en-skilled. Grades below this level however have had a different experience in that many of them have not acquired new skills as such, nor developed new competencies. Rather they have had to accept the centrality of the team concept to Company X, and adopt a positive attitude to this and other specific aspects of the company's production process.

Secondly, the uneven nature of Company X's impact on human capital formation is underlined by its recruitment strategies, which have also fallen someway short of the company's original intentions. In particular, notwithstanding the company's stated objective of not recruiting people with previous experience of the soft drinks industry, they have poached a significant number of workers from indigenous firms involved in the food processing industry. Company X has done so by paying premium wage rates, their Human Resources Manager confirming that they are 'one of the top six payers in the region.' As a consequence, not only is it directly commensurate industries, such as food processing, that have lost employees to company X, but also a significant number of regional engineering firms. This policy reflects the Company's need to shorten the lead times before the plant was fully productive.

Local labour market impacts: 'Global firms, 'local' practices?'

The two companies displayed much more developed HRM strategies than their indigenous counterparts. However, the differences between these companies and indigenous firms become markedly less pronounced when their impact on the local labour market and labour force skills is considered. In this regard, the two companies acted remarkably like indigenous firms interacting with the existing local and regional labour market in very similar ways but, due to their greater resources, with extended reach, impact, and sophistication. Firstly, both companies have displayed considerable sophistication with regard to their recruitment practices, taking great care in assembling their workforces. Company Y for example, carried out extensive aptitude and spatial awareness testing on its prospective applicants, and was aided by the Local Authority which helped sift the LLM for these purposes. Company X subjected all prospective employees to skill and psychometric tests, and carried out four thousand interviews for the two hundred vacancies initially available in the plant.

With regard to their reach and impact, for most grades of employee the relevant 'local' labour market for Company X, with its higher skilled labour requirements than Company Y, has been the region, and not Wakefield and its surrounding areas, with the Travel-To-Work-Areas (TTWA) for the site extending some 25-30 miles. The Company has been able to draw relatively freely on the regional labour market for its higher skilled labour requirements because of its ability to distort existing local wage structures, and attract workers from other firms. The Company's dependence on the regional (and to a more limited extent the national) labour market for its higher skilled labour requirements, suggests that the skill profile of Wakefield's local labour market was a low order factor in Company X's decision to base production in the locality . It is likely its activities in this regard will have adversely affected those indigenous firms who have been forced into competition with Company X for key skills, thus offsetting some of the positive impact that the company has had on the broad process of human capital formation. Company X's impact would have been still more significant, but for the nature of production organisation at the plant. The continental shift pattern was the main reason workers did not choose to apply for a job within the company, or left soon after recruitment. A number of local firms initially lost skilled labour to Company X, who then subsequently returned to them having experienced the disruption to their lives caused by the shift pattern.

Company Y has also had a significant impact, but within a more localised labour pool, and on a narrower set of indigenous employers. For example, a significant number of textile companies complained to the Local Authority that they had lost workers to Company Y. Taken together, the two companies have tended to reinforce and augment the existing ideological, social and spatial forces contributing to the segmentation and fragmentation of the local labour pool that were identified earlier. As such these findings would support the suggestion by Cooke that,

> ...new and more highly differentiated local labour markets come into existence because of the ways in which the production process in large corporate organisations is decomposed or fragmented in ways which take advantage of the size, skills and level of organisation of local labour markets."(1983:p.222)

One central implication of the analysis then, is that the local labour market impact of an inward investment cannot be read off from a consideration of its skill requirements and wage levels. The nature and character of the incoming firm's work organisation and labour process, and the existing traditions within local and regional labour pools, all have an important influence on the ways in which existing and prospective employees respond to these sorts of labour market opportunities.

TNCs and HRM: towards a new research agenda

These case-studies raise a series of important issues with regard to the assessment and impact of HRM developments. Firstly, the studies revealed there are problems with employer-derived accounts of HRM, in that there is often a gap between espoused theory and theory in use (Storey, 1987). There is a need to focus explicitly on how workers themselves perceive and experience HRM initiatives. The contradictions of HRM are most apparent at the level of actual practice, and concrete management-worker relations (cf. Blyton and Turnbull, 1992:p.11). In our studies for example, the ways in which workers viewed the nature and organisation of production, the intensity of effort demanded from it and the character of competing labour market opportunities, were central in shaping their attitudes to the wider HRM policies of management.

Moreover, in terms of underlining the importance of detailed case-study analysis, as Peck and Stone (1993:pp.62-63) have recently revealed, survey findings may actually reveal little about concrete practices, because of the substantive contrasts in the meaning associated with HRM practices in different plants and still less about the extent to which the existence of HRM strategies necessarily implies an upgrading of labour force skills. Hard human resource management, and soft human resource management may be useful conceptual markers, but in empirical contexts it becomes difficult to discern with any certainty their particular forms, or the character of the relationship, if any, between them.

Turning to the issue of whether HRM is a useful tool of analysis in attempting to unravel the current developments within the management of the employment relationship, one implication of the work is to cast doubt on the adequacy of much recent empirical research which has tended to measure labour management policies of firms against some abstract model of HRM practice. The problem with this approach is that it operates with an abstract model of ideal practice and then seeks to account for deviations from this ideal in practice.

A more satisfactory approach is to examine how labour management policies are being implemented in a particular structural and institutional context. A comparative international focus in this regard, focusing on how

TNCs and multinationals segment their activities across different nation states, reflecting in turn differences between systems of labour regulation, local labour pools, and specific configurations of local, regional, and national institutional forces, would allow an exploration of the extent to which the character of human resource management policies may have a distinct spatial dimension. The issue here is do different geographies of HRM exist?

In this regard, in terms of the relationship between inward investors and the local economy, the impact of inward investment is both complex and spatially differentiated. The labour recruitment and utilisation strategies of the inward investors in our study reflected and conditioned the character of local labour pools. The two companies have accommodated themselves to the region's existing human resource endowments, and in so doing consolidated the prevailing conditions under which labour is recruited and utilised within local labour markets. For indigenous firms, as indicated above, the effects of the policies of these companies were felt in terms of increased competition for key skills and commensurate increases in local wage rates.

Regional regeneration strategies

What are the implications of these arguments for the conduct of state policy, both at local and national levels? At the local level, the Wakefield Metropolitan District Council formed the EDD in 1987 to spearhead the economic and social regeneration of the District in response to the rapid disintegration of the locality's coal industry. A key element in its strategy has been the attraction of inward investment in high value-added production and skilled labour processes, associated with good training provision.

The EDD has succeeded in bringing new jobs to the locality, but its objective of securing a general upgrading of the skills of the labour force has been less successful. As our analysis has revealed, its aspirations in this regard have been blunted by the adaptive policies of inward investors. In the case of Company Y, for example, the basic assembly-line production process has been matched with a relatively low skilled labour input. In the absence of further investment, bringing more technologically advanced component production to the site, there seems to be little remaining potential to significantly upgrade the skills of the current workforce. In Company X, a highly automated production process has in fact necessitated the downgrading of the labour force's overall skill profile. The workforce has been restructured via the creation of a new semi/unskilled operator grade in recognition of the fact that : (1) the skills of certain sections of the workforce were being diluted; and (2) that the production process required a lower-skilled labour input than initially envisaged. Thus both Company X and Company Y exemplify the process by which production technologies associated with their particular sectors, and the concomitant form of work organisation, may place limits on the character of HRD policies, and on the positive impact of such investments on the stock of human capital within a given local labour market.

In addition, and relatedly, the studies suggest that the character of the existing stock of skills within a locality exerts a powerful influence on the ongoing nature of indigenous and inward investment. The bias towards relatively low-value added production activities has tended to reflect inherited weaknesses in the local labour force (see Knell, 1992). In turn, it seems likely that skill deficits in the local labour supply will diminish the extent to which any positive job creation effects arising from FDI are felt within, rather than without, the locality.

This analysis indicates the difficulties involved in pursuing upgrading strategies within the UK economy. Local authorities have had to formulate their initiatives in an unfavourable historically forged structural and institutional context, which has been reinforced by national government policies which have sought to consolidate Britain's specialised position within the advanced capitalist economies as a relatively low wage, low skill production centre. Such a national policy framework has encouraged inward investors to adapt their production operations in ways that reflect and reproduce the inherited weaknesses of the British economy and their manifestations in particular regional and local contexts.

In short, local economic regeneration strategies which are heavily reliant upon inward investment flows, may do little to alter the current developmental trajectories of less developed regions.

9 Foreign direct investment and local economic recovery

Philip Garrahan and Paul Stewart

Abstract

Japanese auto transplants have figured strongly in the UK's policy of encouraging foreign direct investment to promote local economic regeneration. Associated with this trend in the auto industry is the notion of 'lean production', according to which labour works not harder, but smarter. Heightened skills, flexible working, and team organisations at the shopfloor level form the core of this new management practice. Yet, little attention has been paid to the real effects this has on training. In this chapter, the opportunity is taken to conceptualise training in the Japanese auto transplant factory as largely company-specific. The analysis is critical of the (often exaggerated) claims made on behalf of foreign direct investment as a major part of the solution to the problem of local training needs. This is especially true in places such as North East England where long-term economic decline has highlighted the failure of policy remedies designed to boost training and capitalise on new investment.

Introduction

Foreign direct investment (FDI) by multinational companies is currently credited with significant effects on industrial location, employment, training, and the culture and organisation of work. This is especially the case in places which are the object of interest in this book because they are aiming for economic regeneration following a period of decline. In the leading edge instance of the auto industry most of the effects, assumed to be positive, are associated with the notion of lean or waste-free production. Williams et. al. (1992) have drawn attention to the wide ranging reference to lean production. Of all the fashionable notions in debates about post- industrial, post-Fordist, or post-modern society, it is lean production which is entering into popular (i.e. journalistic) as well as academic usage. (See for example, Garrahan and Stewart, 1991). Against the notion of lean production, other concepts such as flexible specialisation or 'just-in-time' manufacturing have a more restricted appeal in the burgeoning debate about the future of the UK economy. This is so in particular with reference to the understanding of contemporary industrial change. The profusion of conceptual labels stems from a genuine difficulty in distinguishing short term shifts from the long term restructuring of industry which the UK has experienced.

Making sense of this change has often meant brutal dichotomies: in the case of FDI in the auto industry in North East England, we have remarked how policy makers denounced a past represented by old, inefficient, and heavily subsidised smoke-stack industries. At the same time they heralded the new, competitive, and market driven auto industry which would revive the urban manufacturing economy of a declining industrial region. (Garrahan and Stewart, 1992) The convenience of this dichotomy for the proponents of the industrial change that is under way is that it permits no questioning of the present, since to do so is to be accused of defending the past. In like manner, the conceptualisation of industrial change on a national or global scale refers to '...the bad old paradigm and the good new paradigm of business organisation which in this case means mass production versus lean production.' (Williams et. al., 1992) Critical examination of the grounds for these dichotomies inevitably finds them lacking. In this chapter we aim to contribute both to the assessment of the specific case of the Japanese auto transplant, and to the more generalised argument about the conclusions which can be drawn from this for urban economic recovery.

Evaluating the economic impact of FDI on training

During the post-1945 period, training has the been at the forefront of government concerns as a range of attempts were made to remedy Britain's failing economic performance. This modern period saw training initially as the preserve of the private sector. Subsequently, government took on an interventionist role through the Industrial Training Boards in the 1960s, and the Manpower Services Comission in the 1970s. Since the advent of Thatcherism, there has been a continual move away from direct public responsibility for training and a shift back to making this the responsibility of the private sector. This involved firstly the emergence of the Training Agency as a substitute for the more corporatist Manpower Services Commission, and then in the 1990s the establishment of local Training and Enterprise Councils run largely by local employers. This shifting of ground by policy-makers has been likened to a cycle of change in which, '...Britain has now come full circle in its training decisions, moving from laissez-faire, to centralisation, decentralisation, and now returning to employer-led initiatives.' (Crosbie and Morgan, 1993: p.89) None of this, however, has made a substantial difference and the gloomy picture persists that the inadequacies of Britain's vocational and educational training system play a major part in the country's relative economic decline. A singularly important dimension of this decline has been the transition to a low skill, low wage economy, leading to the view that the interface with global investors puts the British economy very much at a disadvantage. (Finegold and Soskice, 1988; Nolan and O'Donnell, 1991)

Against this background in the mid-1980s, new investment from Japan in an auto industry for North East England was declared by the companies involved, local authorities, unions and government alike to be a much needed boost to the local economy. However, this was mirrored by significant job losses in other local industries, notably shipbuilding, coal, and steel/heavy engineering. While the Nissan plant in Sunderland will employ four thousand people directly and lead to a further thousand jobs in local supplier firms, the closure of the Sunderland shipyard alone, North East Shipbuilders, made two thousand people redundant. Extremely high local levels of unemployment are vividly illustrated by the thirty eight claimants recently registered as unemployed for each job vacancy. There is little doubt that the region's new investment in auto assembly has brought much needed employment to the area, but in view of the pessimistic picture painted above more critical attention needs to be focused on the contribution this has made to training as a spur to local economic regeneration. An essential part of this exercise is the assessment of the impact of the new inward investment on the local labour market and the local skills base.

Several features were stressed as conducive to regenerating the local economy over and above the creation of direct employment in auto assembly and the manufacture of components by local and regional suppliers. Firstly, the North East's economy would become involved in the supply of goods, and services which were needed for the final assembly process. It was claimed that this was occurring as the new plant stepped up production and press coverage made much of the positive reaction of the British and EC components industry, claiming that local components suppliers were benefitting vrom the new business opportunities. Nevertheless, a closer examination of the evidence about the geographical location of auto components suppliers in 1988 showed that only two of Nissan's UK based suppliers (then numbering fifty-eight) were located in the Borough of Sunderland. Only six out of the fifty eight were from the North of England. This suggested that, other than the direct employment in the plant itself, the local economy was being left out of the wider additional benefits resulting from having a major auto assembly firm in the area. Although there were some signs of supplier firms moving into the local economy, these always constituted only a small proportion of the total.

By 1993 FDI in the North East's auto sector will lead to the expenditure of some £850 million on components, which is double the value of components purchased in 1991. But where is this expenditure on components directed? It can, of course, hardly be expected that most of this will be spent in the North of England, a region with no tradition of volume production in the modern auto industry. Inevitably, the greater proportion of this stimulus to the components industry will benefit external economies with an existing manufacturing base in the automotive supply sector. By 1993 there were over two hundred components suppliers based in Europe, of which - consistent with the original pessimistic picture above for the local economy - fewer than forty are in the northern region of England. But much more significant than the low proportion of auto components suppliers in this region is the sort of production activities in which they are engaged. Importantly, they are mostly engaged in low value-added activities which contribute little extra demand for a skilled and highly paid workforce.

Those suppliers accessible to a local workforce are summarised in Table 1, where the evidence shows a further worrying sign. The Japanese transplants were justified by the British government on the grounds that further investment would be attracted into the UK auto components industry. In North East England, at least, a great deal of the new investment turns out to be via acquisitions which have low multiplier effects and may even result in a net loss of employment. Acquisitions can amount less to a change of ownership, and more to a re-orientation in the extent of high value-added work while not creating increased opportunities for employment except in the low value-added end of the range. (Smith, 1986) Additionally, the trend towards joint ventures indicates that components firms can rely on sourcing from outside of the UK and where feasible will continue to locate their high value-added production abroad.

This is made more likely whenever the joint ventures are with Japanese firms linked globally into the Nissan network of companies (or keiretsu).

Table 1: Auto industry investments in North East England, 1986-1993

A   British Owned:
- seven firms supplying plastic trim, paint, fastners, door handles, and small engineering components.

B   Acquisitions:
- nine former British firms supplying chemicals, seat belts, gaskets, pipes, plastic mouldings, and selected suspension and chassis components.

C   Foreign Owned:
- twelve suppliers (in nine of which Japanese firms have sole or joint ownership) making body pressings, pneumatic and exhaust systems, switches, steering columns, and seats.

FDI in the new auto industry was on the understanding that there would be substantial benefits for local economic recovery. Under a bilateral agreement with the British government, Nissan cars will achieve 80% 'local content', but with 'local' interpreted as from any of the member states of the European Community. The practice of requiring a high 'local' content was intended to hamper Japanese firms with typical European costs, which would consequently reduce their commercial lead. (National Consumer Council, 1990) However, this is judged to be insufficient to protect existing EC-based firms from the extensive productivity lead said to be enjoyed by Japanese transplants. Even without this point, we suggest that the 80% 'local content' myth should be buried and forgotten once and for all. It is widely acknowledged that the measure used (i.e the percentage of the ex-works value) is inappropriate since it includes labour costs, as well as other costs such as factory maintenance, product marketing, and so on. To establish the degree to which FDI stimulates the components industry - local, national, or EC - we need to know the value and country of origin of all components in a vehicle which is locally assembled in the North East.

EC member states with the most threatened indigenous car firms (France and Italy) have argued that the transplanting of production from Japan to the UK does not make Nissan, Toyota or Honda's vehicles European within the EC's agreed definition. While an interim agreement has been negotiated, the political difficulties of achieving a single European car market have been considerable. These have stimulated support for economic nationalism - hardly in the spirit of EC92 - as in the example of the French minister for European affairs who spoke of a flood of Japanese cars which, '...could destroy the European car industry', by which he meant important elements of the French car industry. (The Guardian, 7 March 1990) While the EC is prevented from instituting Community-wide regulations on 'local content' by the General Agreement on Tariffs and Trade (National Consumer Council, 1990: pp.20-21), this has not deterred direct campaigns by leading European manufacturers. For example, Fiat recently denounced the Nissan Bluebird model (now replaced by the Primera) as containing only 20% of its parts which were clearly of European production; a further 32% of parts could not be given a clear place of origin; but the remainder were definitely not of European origin. (Financial Times, 13 October 1990)

The assessment of the country of origin of the components in Japanese cars made in the UK is thus highly politically and commercially sensitive. It is deliberately obscured by the inclusion of other costs. There is reason to suggest this is because the cars made in Japanese transplants in the UK continue to depend on a very high level of components and sub-assemblies imported from Japan. If this is so, then the Conservative government's policy to revive car manufacturing in the UK by encouraging and assisting Japanese investment is having the effect of distorting the industrial base. Some idea of the scale of this distortion can be gauged by examining increases in automotive imports from Japan.

In the second half of the 1980s and in to the beginning of the 1990s, when Nissan's UK output of cars rose significantly, so did Japanese imports of vehicle parts. Between 1986 and 1993 there was a dramatic increase in particular in the total of imported high value-added parts, namely precision engineered gearboxes and engine components. Gearboxes imported to the UK from Japan shot up from £157,000 in 1986 to over £130 million in 1993. Similarly, engine components witnessed a sharp increase from below £10 million in 1986 to in excess of £80 million in 1993 (Source: Business Monitor Overseas Trade Statistics of the UK (CSO), various years). Commercial confidentiality prevents us from establishing a direct link between these high value-added imported goods and their probable destination for the assembly of vehicles at Japanese transplants in the UK. However, all the available evidence pointing in this direction confirms the worst fears about Japanese auto transplants. Their benefits of direct employment in assembly are offset by a system of tied imports. This is reflected in the increase in the trade of semi-manufactured auto components. The trade is one way and is dominated by components at the higher end of the value-added scale.

For local economic regeneration in the North East to become a reality as a result of initiating a new car industry, there would have to be much more investment in high valued-added activities, thus producing substantial technological advances. Also required would be more indication of re-training across a wide range of skills, especially for high-skill based employment in the local economy. Recent research into these aspects of economic development and the comparative disadvantage still suffered by the North East points to quite opposite outcomes (see the chapter by Robinson in this volume). In the absence of any evidence for a sustained economic recovery in the area, a more pessimistic conclusion is that the skills in this new regional auto industry tend to be company specific. We have argued that the skills used in the new auto industry rather than in Sunderland's now defunct shipbuilding industry are considerably more company specific. (Garrahan and Stewart, 1992b) The diverse shipbuilding industry in the North East in the past boasted several companies, and the skills they employed could be used in other areas of heavy engineering in the local economy. A narrower range of skills can be said to be evolving with the expansion of the region's auto assembly industry and these skills are not as easily transferable to other industrial activities.

The popular reputation of Japanese auto transplants is as employers with high technology manufacturing systems, but this is another aspect of the image generated by FDI about which a degree of scepticism is justified. One of our interviewees summed up the experience of working for Nissan as a high-tech company with the colourful local phrase, '...it's a case for all fur coat and no knickers'. Volume production of motor vehicles using assembly-line methods is now widely considered to have reached a plateau in terms of substantial productivity increases to be gained by extra automation. The basis of the productivity lead held by Japanese companies now rests as much with the social organisation of production as with its technological sophistication and attention has been drawn to the essentially unskilled or semi-skilled nature of much of the work done in an auto assembly plant. (Garrahan and Stewart, 1992c)

A further comment on the missing growth trajectory must be to lament the absence of attendent higher order skills. Here, the requirements of a company building cars are most likely to be in research and design for new product development, but also there are the many professional contributions associated with large corporations, such as computing, accounting, advertising, marketing, and so on. Given the option of situating its European Technology Centre (ETC) near the Sunderland plant, Nissan has chosen to divide it between the North East and Cranfield in Bedfordshire, with the emphasis very much on Cranfield. The original attraction for Nissan of the Sunderland site was partly about the availability of land (Crowther and Garrahan, 1988), and partly about access to a local labour market characterised by high levels of unemployment and low pay. The company's placing of its ETC in a part of the country already heavily populated with higher order activities of the type described above means that the Sunderland plant is essentially about making and assembling motor vehicles in an inexpensive location with a workforce threatened by high levels of local unemployment and a marginalised trade union movement. It is unconvincing to persist with the claims that FDI in auto transplants will act as a magnet to pull many high-tech operations into the local economy.

Thus, the contribution of this FDI to local economic recovery is bound to remain contentious, since even with the agreed 80% 'local' content, there are very limited benefits to the North East in general and Sunderland in particular in terms of employment creation across the whole spectrum of production related activities. Notwithstanding the direct employment created, we can conclude that there are few positive signs about the real benefit to the local economy. The predicted growth trajectory following on the development by Nissan of its Sunderland plant is not yet supported by the available evidence. However, even if it were to be hypothesised that economic regeneration might come on the back of the new auto industry, this nevertheless may be hazardous in the sense of being excessively dependent on a single major manufacturer. This scenario is exacerbated when account is taken of the disadvantages to the local economy of one of the most highly profiled virtues associated with Japanese auto transplants, namely the practice of single- sourcing of components. As one commentary argues,

> Because Japanese style production techniques demand a very close working relationship between core producer and supplier, often as the only purchaser, this can have a serious debilitating effect on the general industrial infrastructure. While small subcontractors may acquire expertise in limited areas of technology and quality control, they will not develop the kind of all-round marketing and design skills of the more traditional type, and within the new relationship they will tend to be much more vulnerable to contraction or closure by the core producer. For this reason, the sources of autonomous industrial growth within the indigenous economy are likely to be significantly weakened. (Foster and Woolfson, 1989: p.59)

The lessons of this observation may soon be learnt the hard way, as the general recessionary situation at the end of 1993 has seen Nissan announce falling output and hence cuts in the numbers of shifts worked, with the possibility of workforce reductions to follow. The impact on the local supplier base, such that it is, will be immediate.

A new agenda for industrial change

In the Sunderland area new employment opportunities are being tied increasingly to a single giant car firm. The local labour market is not being revived by substantial inward investment sufficiently tied to higher value added functions for there to be much room for optimism. There is little regeneration of the local manufacturing economy resulting from the development of a new auto assembly operation in the region. Here we stress the distinction between the assembly of vehicles from components largely imported from outside of the region, and indeed of the UK, as opposed to the promoting of their manufacture within it. There is even more cause for concern in view of the continuing recession and associated dimunition of the regional manufacturing base, the absence of any diversification of new investment, and the emerging environmental politics about the dangers of unlimited production and use of motor vehicles. It is hard in these circumstances not to sympathise with the growing sense of 'deja vu' in the local economy. During the last three decades British governments and the private sector many times set out to rescue the North East from its long term economic decline. This decline had been accentuated by the heavy redundancies following closure of much of the Durham and Northumberland coalfields and, as now, multinational companies claimed to have a solution. Then it was a matter of diversifying the local economy to avoid being dependent on inefficient and uncompetitive traditional industries. The incoming multinationals identified a large reserve of relatively cheap labour which, together with government and local authority financial subsidies, made the area an attractive one for foreign direct investment. With the end of the long postwar boom after 1973 and the onset of economic stagnation and recession, many of these multinationals quickly left. (Hudson, 1989) This helps to explain why the new FDI in an auto assembly industry, so welcome in terms of the direct employment effects, is also suspected as yet another symptom of the branch plant economy syndrome.

It would seem only prudent in the light of this experience to keep an open mind about the extent to which a local economy can be rescued by new inward investment. In the decades prior to the 1980s, especially when genuinely footloose capital investment was in more supply, British governments used regional policy as an incentive for industrial location in economically peripheral areas. Thus, the public policy stance was primarily about the creation of new jobs in the old industrial regions. (Balchin, 1989). However, a marked change has occurred during the 1980s and 1990s. The present round of inward investment into the North East, dominated by more than forty new Japanese companies in the last decade, carries an extra message to local labour markets and local communities. It is that the whole approach to industry is to be transformed from within, beginning with the individual employee who must place commitments to quality and to the company above all else; and then re-constituting the organisation of work such that people's efforts are rewarded best by combining in teams which abandon traditional job distinctions and capitalise on flexible working practices.

During the 1980s British government policies aimed to radically reform the traditions and expectations of much of the country's manufacturing base. State intervention under Thatcherism took the form of privatisation of any potentially profitable, publicly owned utilities such as the energy industries. At the same time, nationalised sectors of the economy deemed unprofitable such as mining or shipbuilding were run down and sometimes closed. The North East of England is the region of the UK which had previously been the most heavily dependent (as a result of previous postwar government policy) on nationalised industry. Added to the newly introduced strain of market liberalism in the 1980s, government fiscal policy produced rising unemployment to keep down inflation. The result for many regions like the North East was an accelerating de-industrialisation of the spatial economy. Together with other large parts of the British economy, the North East became even more attractive to foreign capital in search of cheap labour and a plentiful supply of land. The Thatcher governments' pursed the related ideological goal of eliminating as far as possible the influence of trade unions. For market liberalism to succeed, the Thatcher governments insisted on organised labour carrying much of the blame for having participated in the failed tripartite or corporatist economic planning of the 1960s and 1970s. The Thatcherite anti-union laws found a ready empathy among Japanese transplants, many of which opted for single union agreements, minimising traditional areas of union shopfloor activity. Although there is a recognised union at the Sunderland Nissan plant, this exists in name only and in exchange for its recognition the AEU has bartered almost all of the rights to collective organisation which define autonomous trade unionism. (Garrahan and Stewart, 1992)

The transplanting of Japanese auto production systems to the UK economy will come to fruition by the mid-1990s with the UK's revived position as a net exporter of cars. On this account government policies will be declared to have realised their goal, even if the economic reality is that employment in the existing UK car industry contracts as a result of Japanese investment, so that in net terms the industry ends up with fewer jobs. (Williams et. al. 1992b) Gains on Britain's balance of trade figures will have to be assessed in this light. Foreign direct investment in a depressed area like Sunderland creates some work, but as we have contested, a substantial regeneration of the local economy as a whole is another matter entirely. In fact the economic gains from this inward investment will have to be measured more than ever before against the losses: state policy in the 1980s could well be regarded as having finished off the indigenous British auto industry (vehicle assembly and components manufacturing) as a major contributor to the economy, both as the main supplier for UK-based firms and as a successful exporting industry. (Amin and Smith, 1990)

In the light of these critical perspectives on the external environment, the agenda for change within companies needs specific contextualised analysis. Once the external elements were put in place, the British car industry was expected to adapt to the demands of 'lean' methods of production. The Thatcherite path to heightened productivity then came to depend on the successful implementation of new management initiatives. Nissan, commonly held to have succeeded in this respect, also came to be known as Mrs Thatcher's favourite firm. Key elements in determining the appropriate external environment for this project to achieve a revision of industrial attitudes are: market liberalism's preference for private sector remedies for economic problems; the cancelling of public spending on the now denigrated 'smokestack' industries and nationalised industries; the promotion of unemployment via tight budgets and monetary control; and new laws to severely limit the freedoms of trade unions. In a form consistent with the ideological underpinning for all of these elements, state policy was justified all along by reconstructing reality. Thus, Nissan's choice of Sunderland was depicted as a hugely successful private sector initiative to rescue the local economy, with little mention of the £120 million plus of state support it received. Such reconstruction of the reality also happens in the case of the internal environment at Nissan.

Occupation specific and firm specific training

The agenda for change in the internal life of companies committed to new forms of management and industrial relations practices must of necessity be top down. As we have pointed out, the necessity for higher order skills is not a requirement for employment at an auto assembly plant which amounts to a final assembler of mostly imported components. So, training needs to be linked to what in effect are relatively uncomplicated assembly tasks and then the knowledge acquired in training tends towards task accretion rather than multi-skilling. Commenting on how one employee perceived his task skills at Nissan while engaging in the company philosophy, Phillipa Jones wrote that,

> Mr X, who has worked at Nissan for five years, still called himself an "unskilled worker", despite insisting how much he felt a part of the company. (The Sunday Telegraph, 21 June 1992)

This is not to say that training does not encourage, or depend upon, skill. It is sufficient for present purposes to emphasise that training is tied to the more limited skills needed to perform specific factory and company-specific tasks. This is opposed to a broader view of occupational training which allows for the development of greater employee autonomy in the labour market. Of course, the cultural and ethical aspects of the training process are important in the construction of a new model employee and this a significant issue to which we shall turn presently. But even here it needs to be emphasised how much of the values of work in Japanese transplants are indeed company-specific. This is so even though these values provide for a familiarisation with the kinds of institutional and organisational artifacts which are increasingly necessary for all model employees in all lean production enterprises. As such, it has to be said that company-specific acculturation is the key aspect in the training process and well accounts for, and justifies, the greater part of the cost of training. It is the latter which provides the rationale for higher than average spending on personnel training by comparison with other UK and UK based automotive manufacturers.

This aspect of the training process is largely supportive of research into the Japanese consumer electronics industry in Wales conducted by Morris, Mundy and Wilkinson (1992) and of their indicative findings. However, Oliver and Wilkinson (1988 and 1992) go further in elaborating the centrality of the acculturation process at Japanese FDI in the UK. (pp.186-187). It is, therefore, important to remember that the cost of training is always tied to the company's own requirements for acculturation and control. By contrast, the kind of training which is essential for local economic recovery around a broad range of occupationally based skills is unnecessary. Occupationally specific skills would allow for greater employee geographical mobility. Thus for two reasons in this situation the skills developed need not be occupation specific. Firstly, there is no need in the local economy for the narrow range of skills developed by Nissan since there is no automotive manufacturing industry in the North-East. Secondly, there are no companies in the North-East which have a manufacturing and labour process anything like Nissan's.

Nevertheless, what may be generalised is the cultural training process epitomised by company institutions. These include teamwork (including 'kaizen' or continuous improvement) and commitment to corporate goals (zero-defects) which is dependent upon individualised collectivism as a seemingly paradoxical response to management-by-stress. (Parker and Slaughter 1988) A key example of the operation of what we term individualised collectivism is where for example, in the labour process, teams of individuals learn to think of the 'downstream process as a customer'. Yet logically, how can a process be a customer? In the same way that a team can be a person - 'I am the team and the team is me - we are all one'. Or, to paraphrase the company's view: Kaizen meetings create a synergy wherein teams are worth more than the sum of their individual parts. Individuals clearly do matter, but only in their collective endeavour to further group or team interests as sanctioned by the company. Group solidarity, trade union style, is something else.

The need to secure this system, whereby the individual is subordinated to the corporate process, is not unique to Japanese auto transplants. Our preliminary research of other key players in the automotive sector suggests the development and elaboration of similar trends elsewhere. But Japanese transplants exemplify the kind of work organisation changes which Rover, GM and Ford are embarking upon. At the level of the labour process and the work organisation, these changes depend upon, inter alia, the rearticulation of collectivism-as-consumption from employee solidarism in the production process, to collectivism-as-consumption in the market place. Hence the rationale in the mantra "...process as customer" serves to individualise the result of group activity. Although this is not unusual in assembly-line routines based upon lean production methods it needs to be remembered that individual feelings about responsibility can be seen to be on a spectrum at one end of which are group centred commitments. The selection, recruitment and development training processes are oriented such that individualism (in contrast to individuality) becomes the dominant optic through which responsibility is to be judged.

In a recruitment campaign initiated before the effects were felt of the recession in 1992/93, Nissan received 24,000 applicants for 1,000 jobs. This is a significant indicator of the labour resource base in the external labour market upon which recruitment campaigns are founded. It should be emphasised that this has become a semi-permanent feature of the recruitment environment and between 1989 and the end of 1991, the annual rate of applications had risen to around 40,000. Each potential manufacturing employee begins the first stage of the induction with a minimum of six hours of tests and interviews. Such assessments are designed to determine basic cognitive skills involving literacy, numeracy and mechanical aptitudes and these are woven into leadership aptitude tests. The importance of this induction programme is that is is the start of a training system costing each year around £600 per employee. Importantly, the induction lays down a marker for the later 'kaizen' process of continuous improvement, and thus the delivery and elaboration of employee know-how is assumed as an everyday expectation.

Although philosophically there is no distinction between the training expectations of manufacturing staff and engineers (Nissan's two categories of shopfloor employees) within the bounds of company-specific competency, in practice expectations are profound. In the case of manufacturing staff, preliminary training amounts to: 'a minimum of one month of 1,500 job cycles under the supervision of the team leader, while multi-skilled maintenance technicians may be under a training programme lasting up to four years.' (Nissan, 1991: p.6) Contemporaneous to this is a high profile social and psychological education and training itinerary designed to instil the company philosophy into all employees in up to 1,200 staff development programmes. The central tenets of the 'Nissan Way' feature as pillars to 'on and off-job training' (Nissan, 1991, p7) and so there is a concern with the development of an overall philosophy of teamworking, quality consciousness and flexibility combined with giving people added responsibility to enhance the status and authority of production management. This can be distinguished from, though it is still important in, the maintenance of a deeper ideological and political core in the 'Nissan Way'. In terms of basic training, technicians are sponsored on engineering courses at a local university and around 90 manufacturing staff are 'trained to work' at a local college. The final area of commitment to training for manufacturing staff and technicians involves sponsorship of trainee technicians at another local college. There are other formal training programmes at local colleges for administrative staff.

The training of engineers allows for the scope of engineers to develop in the context of specific individual commitment to the company's interests. Thus,

> We believe that [success] is the result of each employee's gifted individuality and therefore it comes in building up unique vehicles. Individual's strong characteristics and a sense of independancy will result in a unique line up [like other Japanese auto manufacturers]...

For this reason, we emphasise, as the basic to respect each engineer's individuality, to grant heterogeneity among people, and to encourage each other in enhancing ourselves. Although this [could undermine] standardisation, systematic action and coordination of thoughts... it is also the source of Nissan's energy.. (Nissan , nd: Corporate Philosophy: p.5)

In other words, engineers' energies are harnessed in a necessary synergy which in spite of possible drawbacks allows for the development of an elite cadre at the heart of the production system. This stretches from the core R&D functions through to supervisor and teamleader (the ratio of team leader to production worker is 1:12). Supervisors and teamleaders acquire full knowledge of their subordinates tasks and the role of the latter includes participation in the initial appointment procedure. But the key feature of the training process in the case of all job grades is immersion in the acculturation process right from the intial interview stage:

It is the Supervisor who phones the successful applicant to offer the job and who then meets the applicant to talk through the job and his expectations of the new employee. This has two significant effects: it makes the supervisor committed to his staff - if there are problems he has only himself to blame and will work harder to rectify the situation. Second, it starts the bond between the employee and the supervisor - at the very least he respects the Supervisor's judgement. There can be no better way of starting the teambuilding process. (Wickens, 1987: p.91)

Personnel development in the training process: training for what?

As the quotation above emphasises, the significant aspects of training and development rely upon the pursuit of company specific knowledge(s). These are articulated in the procedures which constitute the basis of the three legs of the 'Nissan Way' - quality, flexibility and teamwork- and the three legs of the tripod need to be understood in the unity and coherence their mutual association sustains. However, as we have argued (Garrahan and Stewart,1992 and 1992b) it is teamworking which provides the lynchpin for organisational coherence and this is reinforced (aside from the cultural acclimatisation of the external social and political environment) both in the disciplines of line working and in 'kaizen' meetings. (We are not here discussing the specific acculturation of team leaders who regularly attend seven day training events at Keilder Forest in Northumberland, which form part of the wider portfolio discussed previously).

It is the development and training for production workers in performance appraisal which provides the key to the link between pay, performance and promotion. Because it is expected that all employees will perform to 'standard specifications' both on and off the line, payment by results cannot - nor was it ever intended that it should - be used as an index of employee performance. In other words, it is appraisal by performance to company norms, as opposed to appraisal of employee productivity which holds the key to the elaborate character of the appraisal system. This assumes, as the company makes clear, a constant training-for-behaviour process in which employees can be monitored in self-certified annual appraisal interviews. Progress on the pay scale is dependent on satisfactorily achieved objectives determined in advance in discussion with one's team leader. Employees are required to state their desired goals, overall objectives and training needs to ensure current and prospective development. This continual appraisal process is designed to link employees' perceptions of self-worth to pay progression and performance at the level of employee behaviour. This is the main function of kaizen meetings where employee commitment to quality and quality performance - the supply of ideas for process enhancement (Tomaney, 1990) - rather than product development explains why the appraisal norms are bound to employee behaviour.

The expectation therefore is that employees will be committed to achieve and improve upon process developments which enhance quality, flexibility and teamwork. In this sense, training is properly understood as training for the 'Nissan Way'. The company's training can be defined as job specific where task performance is concerned and company-centred where employee attitudes and behaviour are emphasised. The latter is less straightforward in so far as the 'Nissan Way' is an ideology of control and subordination sui generis, derived from employee self-involvement and commitment to a self-certified appraisal scheme. Although significantly dependent upon mutually agreed priorities, they nevertheless derive legitimacy because employees agree to their efficacy. However, this approach to training is clearly linked to the development of the so-called New Model Worker. In this respect, Nissan is not alone in its attempt to promote high loyalty from the creation of a set of ideological work practices which attempt to factor out one of the most insecure aspects of the production process - employee autonomy. Where autonomy might prevail, it needs to be defined within very strict limits or it may lead to dissent. This dissent may not lead to particularly profound forms of disruption. But too much autonomy weakens the chain of management control and it is this systemic insecurity that requires careful process monitoring. All automotive manufactures are attempting to introduce this close social and cultural work and management system but of course none has Nissan's advantages of greenfield site and virgin workforce. Nevertheless, the orientation to training programmes whose itinerary, in terms of social and cultural effects, is of greater importance than mere training for the job, is at the top of the agenda of all the leading players in the sector. It is to the creation of a novel kind of consensus that the new appraisal and performance of staff in training (both on and off site) is geared.

Conclusion

In the introduction to this chapter we alluded to the policy changes coming full circle in relation to matters of training and development. We acknowledge that the current representation of training policy as employer-led deserves a less sanguine interpretation especially since government sponsored training schemes are not central to the needs of major FDI in the region. The essence of these training schemes in a place like north east England, while not contradictory per se to the requirements of FDI, sustains a complemenetary though linked logic. Regional industrial restructuring and the consequent downgrading of the skills base is not in itself problematical for large multinational companies since, as we have shown above, Japanese transplants are capable of tailoring company training programmes to suit their own specifications. Thus, government policy in the UK has been to open regional economies to foreign competition, while de-regulating labour markets and fettering trade unions, rendering North East England an attractive proposition to FDI seeking low wage labour markets for low-skilled activities.

We have argued that the auto industry well illustrates the transition to new management styles and 'lean' systems of production, and then have taken a specific look at a Japanese transplant in the context of evaluating the impact of FDI on local training needs. Studies which focus on a single company or on a particular local economy offer an essential degree of empirical evidence for understanding the changing agenda of industrial policy and the contribution made by public policy. Nissan is one of a select few among automotive firms that maintains global production. Only Japanese auto firms currently come into the category of accessing the three major world markets, the USA, the EC, and Japan, by engaging in each of these in mass production operations. This globalisation of auto manufacturing and the concentration of ownership is heightened with the increasing numbers of mergers and takeovers among the world's car firms. Yet, the effect of these trends is evidenced most dramatically in the economies of depressed urban areas like Sunderland and, as we have shown in the case of the UK, the state's public policy has an influential effect on local developments. The concentration of ownership and subsequent domination of markets by an increasingly small number of globally organised firms should encourage critical social science to examine the local consequences on a case by case basis.

This case by case approach reveals that something very interesting is taking place at the level of skills training in the local labour market. In the case of Nissan in North East England, it is clear that skills are indeed company specific, claims to the contrary by the Nissan and local boosterists notwithstanding. From an estimation of the company's own itinerary and an assessment of the needs of the production process, including the character of local manufacturing needs, it is clear that any localisation of auto manufacturing skills in the North East local economy is unnecessary. Thus, to reiterate the point made earlier, the skills developed at Nissan are company specific because a) there is no auto manufacturing industry in the North East so that the skills created at Nissan could not be generalised even if they were occupational rather than job specific - which they are not, and b) there is no other manufacturing process in the local economy which works in the same way as Nissan's. Skills, in other words, are clearly are not transferable.

However, this is only part of the reason for the interest in training issues where companies specialising in lean production methods are concerned. If new companies are indeed seen to be purveyors of new skills bases in declining regions, how is this mission to be achieved? The answer, or perhaps the beginning of one, lies in the nature of the training process. We can see in terms of skills for doing the job, that skills are neither increased nor transferable. But as we have argued, there is also another type of skills training and that is training to work for one company only. Indeed, given the considerable time and cost of training for the 'Nissan Way', it would surely be absurd if the organisation felt it was also training employees so that they could quickly take these skills elsewhere. Training for the 'Nissan Way' - the rather more ideological side of the training and development process which begins from induction (instilling a particular set of nostrums about quality, flexibility and teamwork) - is fundamental to the overall process of acculturation. Much more needs to be understood about the concerns and expectations of inward investors, carrying the banner of lean production methods, before we can feel sanguine about the prospects for improved training and development. In the end, we need to keep posing the simple questions: 'training for whom?' and 'training for what?'

Note: This chapter draws on material in a paper presented to the Vocational Education and Training Forum Conference, University of Warwick, June 1992

10 Condemnation and closure: The Wear shipyards

Ian Roberts

Abstract

The chapter details the changes in the labour process in the Wearside shipbuilding industry during the years of rapid decline, redundancies and eventual closure in 1988. In a context in which the trade unions seemed powerless the workers struggled to defend their integrity within the changing division of labour. It is suggested that throughout this period, either as a result of conspiracy or cockup the changes at the point of production were nevertheless experienced by the workers as an attempt to secure 'voluntary' redundancies. If the logic of collective action seemed inappropriate in such an environment this did not lead to passive acquiescence, but rather individual expressions of conflict were accentuated with workers displaying a state of desubordination in relation to management. Such resistance continued in the Wear yards right up to the closure, if the changes in the labour process increasingly deskilled the work this did not produce an automatic reflex of a deskilled workforce.

Introduction

The shutdown of all shipbuilding activity on the Wear in December 1988 seemed, almost more than any other single event in the town, to symbolise the spirit of the 1980s. The rundown of traditional industries such as shipbuilding ensured the conscription of the platoons of the 'new society' variously interpreted as post-industrial, post-fordist or post-modernist.

The changes in the industrial base were seen to indicate associated changes in the quintessential essence of the working class, gone were the traditions of solidaristic collectivism and in its stead were workers who, 'began to think and act like capitalists and the values of acquisitiveness became almost universal' (Taylor, 1982, p.48). To some people this seemed a reasonable summation as to what happened on Wearside. It was certainly the case that throughout the 1980s division and dissent were more characteristic features than unity in relation to both the workers and the community during this period of the accelerating run down.

The British shipbuilding industry had experienced relative decline in terms of world market share since the early years of the twentieth century. However, it was during the 1970s and 80s, in the wake of the collapse of the long-boom of the post war years, that relative decline became absolute and closure and redundancy became increasingly common. For most people including those working in the industry a problem was identified only when absolute decline became apparent, beginning in the 1970s. An important point, however, is that the rate of relative decline was never faster than throughout the boom years of the 1950s and 60s. But of course this was hidden to most of the workers at individual yards where the unprecedented position of full order books was seen as evidence of success, not decline in competitiveness. Such an understanding was to prove divisive within the local community.

For the management the solution to the emerging problem was sought through decreasing labour costs, redundancy and the use of non-standard forms of labour contract in order to enhance numerical flexibility on the one hand. On the other hand functional flexibility was sought through an attack on the craft division of labour, interchangeability, composite work groups, computerised stock control and energy monitoring. The objectives of these two strategies were not always distinct and certainly workers experienced changing work practices and the way these were introduced as a managerial attempt not to increase productivity but rather as a way of producing enough voluntary redundancies. The attempt to introduce radical change to the labour process was never going to be enough to save an industry in which, '.... nearly two thirds of the final costs of a ship represent bought in materials and components.' (Brown & Brannen, 1970: p.197) As such the closures should have issued a dire warning about the general state of British industry and the underlying potential for a long term process of deindustrialisation. Instead the workers themselves were seen to have caused many of the problems. A view heard not only from government, but sadly one which found a resonance even in the local community.

On 5 February 1981 at the beginning of the job losses the Secretary of the Wear Confederation of Shipbuilding and Engineering Unions (C.S.E.U.) Henry Wilkinson, boldly announced that, 'there should be no doubt in anybody's mind that the River Wear as well as the rest of the country will combat any enforced redundancies.' (Spence, 1987: p.97) The question of enforced redundancies never arose, for as the Sunderland Echo of 28 February pointed out, More than 700 men have indicated a readiness to accept redundancy even in an area of 17% unemployment. (Ibid)

The Regional Organiser of the General and Municipal Workers' Union resigned in disgust saying,

> They are betraying their forefathers, throwing away - for short-sighted and selfish reasons - job opportunities for the young and putting shackles on their trade union negotiators .... I say the shipyard workers on the Tyne and Wear need a bit of fight in their bellies like the miners. Do they not realise we are a maritime nation and as such shipbuilding in this country could never be finished. (Ibid)

Was this a fair comment? Were the motives for taking voluntary redundancy simply reducible to 'Short-sighted and selfish reasons?' At a deeper level did the willingness to 'sell ones'job' indicate a change in the quintessential nature of the traditional working class? There were those who thought so,

> It has always been the Left's critique of capitalism that it must hide its true purposes from the people who, if they recognised its true nature, would rise up against it. It was Mrs. Thatcher's privilege to shout its true nature from the housetops to the plaudits of the people who, far from rising up, inclined themselves to its will. As industry after industry shrank in the early 1980s - steel, shipbuilding, engineering, cars, chemicals, construction - the workers accepted the common sense of capitalism, took their redundancy payments and were glad. (Blackwell and Seabrook, 1985: p.151)

The reality of the redundancy issue on the Wear is perhaps more complicated than either a lack of moral fibre or a 'lack of fight in their bellies' of the workforce. This issue has to be seen directly in the context of the changing nature of working practices and the wider political environment. If such an analysis is forthcoming, it is at least as easy to argue the case that the ease with which the 'voluntary' redundancies were achieved on the Wear was in part due to the high level of the struggle within the yards rather than the opposite. A point forthcoming from Wear workers when discussing the redundancy situation on the Wear in the first half of the 1980s was that,

> The old time stewards were the first, they got out 'cause they knew what we were in for. (Plater)

A change of attitude began to manifest itself in the form of a tightening of control over work allocation and time. Gradually the job content in the 'job and knock' (i.e. job and finish) negotiations assumed a larger proportion. These processes occurred unevenly between locations and shifts. The traditionally looser form of direct control on night shift remained, but even here men complained of not being able to 'get their head down' as much as they used to. Similarly, control in 'shops' tightened up more appreciably than on the ship. This meant that simultaneously there existed different forms of the effort bargain at different locations within the same yard. Thus on a night shift in the Deptford yard in 1982 whilst one group of plumbers on the ship were still negotiating 'job and knock', another section of plumbers in the 'group shop' were working for almost the full ten hours. The work pace differed accordingly in the two locations. On the ship a hectic pace was the norm in order to finish as soon as possible, whereas in the "shop" the pace was more sedate,

> I don't hurry at all, I just plod because you know when one job is finished there's always another one. (Plumber)

An interesting feature of this period was the lack of resistance offered by the workforce to this increase in managerial control. The attitude was that there was an inevitability about this tightening up. Whilst these moves were not particularly welcomed, they were seen to some extent as legitimate, given that by their own standards things had previously begun to get 'too bad'. However as time passed the managerial offensive continued until it started to encroach on areas clearly deemed illegitimate by the workforce. Thus even on night shift the foreman announced that men would not be allowed out (of the plumbers shop) twenty minutes before knocking off time to turn their cars around 'for a quick getaway', as had traditionally been the practice. This was seen as going 'a bit far' by the men. During this period discussions of the changes usually included comments upon the extent to which foremen appeared to be living in fear, and much sympathy was evident for their predicament.

However, as the tightening up continued that sympathy began to wane as frustration built up. The position in which some men could get away with more than others continued however, and could be a source of light relief at times.   One incident recalled fondly at Deptford involved a foremen trying to prevent workers leaving a ship some twenty minutes before 'knocking off' time. One man, a plumber called Gordon, came down the plank first. The foreman said,

> I'm sorry Gordon, but if you leave the boat I'll have to put your name in the book (for a written warning). The reply was to the point, You put my name in that book and I'll rip your fucking spine out. (Plumber)

He then pushed past the foreman who tried to retrieve the situation by shouting that the worker was desperate to go to the toilet and, amid the roaring laughter of the other workers, that no-one else could leave the boat. The feeling among the workers was now that the management were trying to go too far, a feeling apparently confirmed by the video that the management commissioned and then showed to the workforce. The substance of the video was the amount of working time lost by late starting and early finishing. The film began by noting the different levels of productivity between British and Japanese shipbuilding workers. It continued by showing scenes of the Wear yards with men standing talking or drinking coffee, repeatedly returning to a shot of a clock with a voice asking 'Why are these men still here? Work should have begun twenty minutes ago', etc. The response of the workers was one of outrage. If the film was intended to increase their commitment to work it could not have had a more opposite effect. Questions were asked as to what management spent their time doing?   And why they started at nine o'clock when everyone else started at 07.30? A feeling was rising that management had decided to act daft and the only response that individual workers could initiate was to act twice as daft.   The position of the shop stewards became impossible, with workers raising more and more grievances and management becoming less and less responsive.   Many stewards gave up their posts or volunteered for redundancy, the work having become 'just too much hassle'. This exacerbated the problem, for replacement stewards, when they could be found, were inexperienced in a situation which demanded the maximum of negotiating skills.

It is hard to exaggerate the levels to which feelings rose in the yards of Wearside during the first half of the 1980s. Union response was almost totally disabled by the deteriorating employment prospects within the industry. Thus by the beginning of 1983, 26,000 jobs had been lost within the industry since nationalisation in 1977. A further 3,000 redundancies were announced in the first month of 1983, followed in quick succession by 9,000 more in April of that year.

The managerial offensive began by tightening up on the movement of labour and the 'productive input' of the working day. The durable aspects of worker control began to break down under extreme pressure from above. The intense pressure exerted by senior management generated fear in the lower supervisory grades in the face of the possibility of forced redundancy. Also the threat of the closure of all the yards on the river ensured that for the first time managerial control initiatives were not diluted in their transference to the shop floor.

Importantly these control initiatives were increasingly linked to changes in working practices fostered under the auspices of the phases of the 'Wages and Salaries Restructuring, Harmonisation and Productivity' (W&SRHP) plan already agreed by the Unions. The union agreement to the general idea of such changes in working practices, coupled with the enthusiasm with which they were pursued by higher management in their creation of an atmosphere of fear precluded any collective response. However individual responses were forthcoming. More active expressions of 'botching up' began to emerge, which bordered on sabotage.

As one universally acknowledged responsible worker explained,

> They get you that way, as sick as a parrot. There's sabotage now, I've started rubbing the chalk marks off pipes in the pallet that are ready to go out. (Plumber)

The pipes pre-fabricated in the group shop are numbered with yard and detail position location numbers - to obliterate these would involve a considerable delay in their delivery to the right place. But this was mild by comparison with some of the acts going on. The removal of pieces of machinery, the deliberate fusing of lighting systems in inaccessible places, electric welding machines left arcing to earth until they burned out were just some of the ways that frustrations were vented. There was little comfort in such acts however, as the managerial offensive continued. Foremen were obliged to keep written records of the progress of jobs to be submitted weekly, under relentless pressure. Sometimes they booked jobs in which were not completed and they appealed to or cajoled men to finish quickly. The 'catch phrase' of one foreman at Deptford, when making such appeals, caught on and men greeted each other with A.L.'s words,

> You've got to do it Bob, they'll chew my balls off if you don't. (Foreman)

The workers knew that the pressure was coming from senior management and more specifically its personification in the form of Eric

Welsh (Managing Director), but the effects were felt on the shop floor in the deteriorating quality of relationships between workers and their immediate supervisors.

Access to higher management was restricted and even the personnel department appeared to be aloof. As a worker from the Pallion yard asked,

> why does it take three weeks to see personnel?
> (S.S./Employment Relations Survey, 1986)

When senior management were spotted in the yards their reception was hostile. Thus one worker recalled the reaction of his friend at seeing a group of managers,

> We were working up on one of the masts when he spotted them. He was hanging on with one hand shouting "Bastards, bastards." They took no notice! (Plumber)

The 'big brother' approach was seen as particularly sinister by some,

> They're got videos down there, they can sit in an office and see who isn't where they should be. Their computer monitors the use of power, if there's a shortfall in any area of the yard they want to know why. (Shipwright)

Amid all of this, intense individual struggles went on in circumstances where the union was seen as impotent,

> Health and Safety, all the time I stopped them with that. On one occasion I was working in the double bottoms when a plate slid over the tank top and dropped down a manhole. "I'm not working here", I said to the head foreman, so he got a manager. He asked what could be done to help, could I suggest anything? I told them a lip should be erected around the manholes to stop things sliding down. On another occasion they were lining sections up using lasers. Now I noticed when they first started using lasers they used to rope areas off and put up signs - "Danger Lasers", all that had gone. So I got onto them about it, work stopped while they roped off the main area and put signs up. I don't know what it was we had to beware of, but I got the signs back. The problem was it didn't hit the management, it only annoyed the blokes working on the job - they now had to rope off areas and put up signs as well as their other work. (Plumber)

Again, the problem was how to hit back at management rather than to increase the general level of 'hassle' on the shop floor. It seemed an intractable problem which added to the frustrations all the more. Where direct attacks could be made upon management they were eagerly grasped. One such event gained great notoriety. It occurred on the night shift at Deptford, but by the end of the following day shift was being celebrated in the rest of the yards on the river. The Deptford night shift had been 'getting out of hand' for sometime. On one particular ship no matter how hard the supervisors and management tried the men kept managing to paint "S.S. Rubber Duck" on the hull in large letters. More management were drafted onto the night shift. One night the lads spotted Eric Welsh on the quayside. The spotlights were turned on him and an assortment of bolts, flanges and other objects were thrown at him. He got away but not before a few direct hits were registered. In calmer moments some of the perpetrators confessed that it was a stupid and dangerous thing to do, but that they could not help themselves.

The problem of such individual resistance, as we have seen, is that its target cannot always be hit and thus in some circumstances only serves to make an intolerable situation worse. Moreover with the tightening of control and increasing issue of written warnings individuals were risking 'the sack'. For many of those most active in resisting, this likelihood persuaded them that taking redundancy would pre-empt their increasingly inevitable dismissal and loss of entitlement to any redundancy payment. The importance of redundancy entitlement built up over a number of years in the absence of occupational pensions etc. is often underestimated. It was the threat of losing redundancy entitlement which inclined many of the workers at the yards in the 1980s to leave. Not only was it a way of escaping the 'torture' that the work situation had become,

> Every Monday morning you go in you might as well bend over - you're waiting to be buggered! (Shipwright)

but also it forestalled the loss of entitlement by dismissal. Moreover the plans of the Conservative Government to privatise the Warship yards were well advanced by this time. The fear was that if a buyer could also be found for individual merchant yards these would be sold with no guarantee that long standing redundancy entitlement would be honoured. Again it was the threat of its potential loss which encouraged some workers to take the payment and leave.

Such decisions were not taken easily. For weeks and sometimes months workers and their families agonised over making the right decision. And all the time the pressure at work increased until some could take it no more,'It's become a matter of dignity - I got to get out.' (Plumber) Individual decisions were taken in the light of financial circumstances at home. This inevitably meant that the workforce were divided by their individual home circumstances and many of those who did not leave wished that they could have done. However such was the pressure that some 'had' to leave even in the face of unfavourable circumstances at home. Despite the claims of Maurice Phelps, British Shipbuilders' Industrial Director, that,

> nobody wants to force people out of the industry (Sunderland Echo, 5 May 1983)

the net effect of the managerial offensive on the river was to do just that. As a twenty seven year old shipwright, married for two years with a new mortgage and a pregnant wife, who had just applied to 'take his lot' put it,

> I don't care what anyone says, there has not been one voluntary redundancy on this river. Blokes have been hounded, abused and pushed into it. (Shipwright)

Another responded to the accusation that he was selling his son's future job,

> I wouldn't wish that set-up on my worst enemy let alone my son. He's better off without it. I've got my dignity and my redundancy. (Plumber)

The redundancy issue on the Wear was clearly tied to changes in working practices.

Initially felt as a tightening of managerial control, the offensive developed into formal changes disguised as wage and productivity agreements under the auspices of W&SRHP and with union agreement. The fourth phase of the W&SRHP scheme was outlined to the Shipbuilding Negotiating Committee on 12 October 1983, and the local details of the productivity deal and changes in working practices and technology were formulated over the winter months. The details of this fourth phase of the plan struck at the the very heart of the craft division of labour, involving full interchangeability between craft sections and requiring skilled workers to do their own labouring. There was by this time a feeling that resistance should be offered to any management proposals. But the prospects for a collective stand were not good. Any industrial action was seen by the unions and shop stewards as equivalent to walking out of the yards never to return. As well as the shorter term work based tactical considerations, more long term processes had weakened the potential resources upon which workers could call to fight against changes in the labour process. Several of these issues are apparent under the general tendency towards the growing gulf between the work and non-work community situation of Wearside shipbuilding workers.

Despite claims in the Save Our Shipyards campaign or of banner headlines in the Sunderland Echo of the town rallying to save jobs, division was more characteristic than solidarity. The differences in the home circumstances and financial commitments of individual workers could, as we have seen, exert a determining effect upon their willingness to take their redundancy, and the same was true of attitudes towards industrial action. More generally the increasingly heterogeneous non-work environment of workers had over the years begun to destroy what little 'patterning of paradox' had existed in the past. One feature of the divorce between the work and community situation was used by the management to put pressure upon workers to accept the productivity offer. The consequences of mailing the details direct to each individual home were outlined by one worker,

> When my wife opens the letter and sees the figures that's all she thinks about. She sees it in terms of how much more that amount will buy in the shops. She doesn't see what I would have to do to get it. (Plumber)

Finally in a more general sense the division between work and community and changing patterns of family life have isolated generations from each other. The generations of shipyard workers beginning their working life in the inter-war period have now retired. The relative decline in the industry over which they presided was masked by the absolute growth in the post-war period. For them the crisis of British Shipbuilding is in no way tied to them. Ironically the unchallenged degree of authority that they experienced over the production process is projected onto their sons and grandsons, and it is here that the responsibility is seen to lie,

> .... as time went on you got people who weren't interested and nowadays - there's no buzzer blows in the shipyards, them days eight o'clock in the morning the buzzer blew .... I was walking home one day (I'd been on night shift) and I met a lot of big lads coming along and I said "when the buzzer blows you're supposed to be starting work not getting out of bed", and that is it at the present day - this morning

the shipyards - none of them will be started before nine o'clock because they'll be discussing the Manchester United Cup Final from last night - because they're not on piece, they're on bonus because the whole system has gone rotten .... I could do better than some of the 18 years now and I'm 72 years old .... I'm talking about work, not putting hours in and that's the trouble with them at the present day .... nowadays they couldn't care less - couldn't care less about it. (Retired Plater)

The heterogeneity emerging from the breakdown of the occupational community serves to shatter the potential for solidaristic support. In such an atmosphere and with the shop stewards advocating acceptance, the phase 4 deal was voted for by a majority of the workforce.

The main points in the national agreement included the following sections,

Interchangeability/Flexibility

The nature of the work in the industry is such that it is essential for employees at all levels to work effectively, and to recognise that change will be a normal part of the working life. Therefore, all employees must be prepared to acquire new skills, and to remove customary practices where they are no longer appropriate. To meet the demands of competition it is accepted that new working practices will be adopted which match those of our international competitors and enable companies to respond to changing work priorities, product and work load fluctuations. The key elements of these new practices which need to be implemented urgently and to the fullest effect are:

Interchangeability

1. All levels of staff will be interchangeable as required according to their individual skills and experience.
2. Hourly paid employees will be interchangeable within their main group, i.e. within steelworking, outfitting and ancillary groups.
3. Skilled employees will also be required to be interchangeable across groups and trades, providing they are capable of undertaking the work required, and will also undertake ancillary work as appropriate.
4. Ancillary employees will also be required to undertake tasks within their ability, including work which skilled employees have in

some cases traditionally retained, but which can be completely undertaken by other employees after retraining.
5. All employees will be fully mobile within their company and between areas and departments including maintenance and production.

Flexibility

6. Skilled employees, in order to progress the completion of their own work will undertake their own servicing.
7. As part of the above arrangements, it is agreed that in order that employees will use the full range of their skills and abilities to maximum advantage, companies will have the option of establishing area supervision and integrated groups of workers as required." (British Shipbuilders, 1983: p.3-4)

The local agreement restated in a bolder fashion the points in the national agreement. Thus area supervision and integrated work groups were labelled 'Composite Groups' - they were used to signify the end of the single trade work group, thereby rendering demarcation concerns which arose, in particular between plumbers and fitters at the North Sands yard, an issue which could be handled by an 'independent' foreman. Demarcation increasingly became a matter of individual group dynamics rather than an issue uniting a whole trade. The principle of craft exclusiveness had been surrendered, although the consciousness of individual workers as belonging to a particular trade remained. This again increased the frustrations on the shop floor, and some workers talked of a 'sell out' by their representatives.

The local agreement also went further on the introduction of new techniques, and the point of introduction, before discussion, was conceded,

> We should try new techniques first and get them working while talks are going on about these other matters (Trade Unions, pay, demarcation). That means no delay in using the techniques that have helped foreign shipbuilders grab a bigger share of our markets. (Sunderland Shipbuilders, 1984: p.3)

The agreement at a national level headed off a threatened national strike. The new Chairman of British Shipbuilders was well satisfied,

> After 13 hours of talks a national shipyard strike - accompanied by yard occupations - had been averted. "A hell of a good day's work", said a smiling Mr. Graham Day (Salary £80,000 plus performance bonus) ....
>
> .... The unions had been pressing for an increase on basic rates as a precondition of further productivity talks. Mr. Day has persuaded Mr. Murray, and 29 shipyard delegates who endorsed the outline deal, to accept a productivity agreement as a precondition for getting more money. (The Guardian, 4 November 1983)

Once again the tying of wages to working conditions had helped British Shipbuilders to further the aim defined by Graham Day in the Financial Times,

> .... the craft basis on which British Shipbuilders has operated - rigid demarcation lines, fierce protection of skills and the like - has to be altered., We've got to get from a craft to a system basis. (Stirling & Bridgeford, 1984: p.11)

The workers received £7 a week for accepting the deal, on union advice. The changes were felt very quickly on the Wear, as a painter explained in February 1984,

> It's ridiculous. I've been working in the joiners shop today, sweeping up - me, a skilled painter! (Painter)

As for the composite work groups it was explained in the local agreement that training would be given,

> The groups will be responsible for unit or area completion, usually with one Supervisor, and the people in it will have the skills required. Each person will be expected to carry out whatever work is necessary to complete the job, including work that has been thought of as 'belonging' to only one group. Retraining will be organised .... (Sunderland Shipbuilders, 1984: p.2)

According to Mr. R.D. Clark, the personnel director on the Wear, such training amounted to "multi-skilling", and the management welcomed the rising skill level in shipbuilding. He went on to say that whilst the changes in working practices had been driven through in the face of an adverse economic climate, workers were now happier and more involved in their work because they could follow through the processes on the yard floor.

The reality on the shop floor was rather different. The retraining was seen as a mockery, but workers took the £75 given to those who volunteered. As a shipwright explained,

> I served a five year apprenticeship to become a shipwright but now after three days hanging about with the welders I'm a welder, three days I'm a rigger, two days I'm a burner and two days and I'm a plater! (Shipwright)

Mr. Clark made the claim that the workforce were happy with the changes occurring only one month after Sunderland Shipbuilders had commissioned a piece of survey research looking at worker attitudes in the firm. In the light of the results of that research (which he had at the time of the interview) his analysis seems odd to say the least. Dissatisfaction with the situation in the yards clearly ran through most of the replies to a large majority of individual questions. Thus for example,

Question 5

> "Sunderland Shipbuilders is a pretty good place to work - I would recommend a friend or member of my family to work here."

	% Agree 1 and 2	3	% Disagree 4 and 5
Pallion	16	9	74
Deptford	17	11	71
N. Sands	11	7	81
Main Office	36	20	44
Aggregate	18	10	70

As the survey research firm commented,

> [There is a] clear indication that the considerable majority of employees feel that this is not a good place to work. In other questionnaires we have carried out, it is possible to observe that whilst there are many complaints and grumbles about one's workplace it is still possible to feel that overall it is a fairly good place to work, and consequently that one would recommend it to family and friends. It is in answer to this question that we see that the concerns that the workforce have gone

particularly deep. (Sunderland Shipbuilders/Employment Relations, 1986: p.2)

In answer to the statement that, "Senior management can be trusted to make sensible decisions for the Company's future", 79% of Deptfords manual workers disagreed, and the figures for Pallion and North Sands yards were higher still at 80% and 81% respectively. As far as industrial relations were concerned, the results were even more clear cut. Thus,

Question 12

How would you describe relations between management and trade unions at Sunderland Shipbuilders at present?

	% Agree 1 and 2	3	% Disagree 4 and 5
Pallion	1	3	95
Deptford	3	5	89
N. Sands	2	3	89
Main Office	9	10	82
Aggregate	2.5	4	90

(S.S.E.R., 1986: p.9)

The results are stark and suggest that the workforce were far from happy with changes in the yards. Moreover given the context of the survey, coming as it did in 1986 after several rounds of large scale redundancies when some of the more critical workers had already left in desperation, and, with shop stewards advocating that men should not co-operate with the survey, it is likely that some of the more critical workers left in the yards did not complete the questionnaire.

The depth to which the morale of the workforce had been driven is even more apparent in the replies and comments to the 'free answers' and 'open questions' sections of the survey. In all three yards the largest single response to the question of what was liked about working for Sunderland Shipbuilders was 'Nothing'. This was written by 66 men from Deptford, 60 from North Sands and 209 from Pallion. The next most popular 'like' in all yards was that 'It is a job/better than dole'.

The individual quotations again make the situation crystal clear. Some of these expressed a deep sense of injury to the self,

What do I have to do to get management to realise I am a human being, not a mindless unfeeling robot! HELP!

> Attitude of management to workforce is one of hatred and hysterics.
> Being treated unfairly (you're got to work here to understand that).
> Men - totally demoralised - need to be encouraged and nurtured - sick of being stamped into the ground.
> This is the worst job I've had in 45 years in shipbuilding. (Sunderland Shipbuilders/Employment Relations, 1986, p.12)

Other comments were more concise,

> Management stinks - are corrupt.
>
> Management back-stabbing. (Sunderland Shipbuilders/Employment Relations, 1986, p.12)

Management behaviour towards the workforce was seen variously as ignorant and flippant, high-handed, dogmatic, bullying, arrogant, petty, persecuting. Even attempts at being witty carried the same message,

> Treated like idiots, led by idiots, paid like idiots. Thank Mr. Welsh for his effort on our behalf. (Sunderland Shipbuilders/Employment Relations, 1986: p.12)

Specific issues featured in replies too, the ending of canteen facilities producing hot meals for manual workers yet their continuance free to staff members was a large concern. Similarly, the non-payment of £500 bonus which had been 'promised' by Eric Welsh was mentioned several times with comments such as, Where's our £500 - thieves?

A whole section of replies referred to the work itself, where comments included,

> Not being able to develop new skills. Quality control system not working. Seeming lack of standards in inspections which causes lack of confidence when working with owners reps and having to reply "I don't know" to 90% of any questions relating to specific standards of tolerance. Misuse of skills. Lack of training. Responsibility of job taken away from tradesman. Taken away job satisfaction. No faith in new workpacks. Too much new work. Departments working against each other. Rundown of craft trades. Too many supervisors know nothing of the particular trade they're responsible for.

The list goes on, throwing serious doubt on the claim that the workforce was 'happier' with the new working practices which seemed indeed to have been 'driven through'. The management had by 1986 been able to drive through almost every change that they had desired. Composite group working had become the norm and a computerised stock control system 'Artemis' had been installed. Movement was being made towards a continental split shift system worked on a four set, three shift basis. The craft administration had apparently given way to the constant-flow principle based on the composite work group, and CAD/CAM systems dominated the stages of both pre-outfitting and the more established prefabrication of structural steel units. As an article written by a manager of North East Shipbuilders Limited in the Durham University Industrial Society Magazine put it,

This whole operation is an exercise in precision." (D.U.I.S., 1987, p.12-13)

"An exercise in precision" - is this how it actually worked at the point of production? As has been outlined the changes were forced through with little regard for the views of the workforce, and the new system of working was imposed without detailed consultation. The result was a hybrid of the new system of organisation of work and some of the older detail working practices. These were executed in an atmosphere in which no one wanted to be identified with mistakes, the consequences of which, if they occurred in the early phases of the transformation of plans into reality, could be far more wide ranging than in the earlier systems. The consequences of this in relation to the requisite degree of precision were profound. A plumber explained how the new system worked in practice,

1. The plans arrive and are to be converted into detail sketches. The sketchers draw the individual pipes to be fabricated. But as they would be no good if they end up too small, they add 100mm extra.
2. The sketch is numbered and entered on the computer and the sketch goes to the group shop for "fabbing".
3. When the pipe is fabbed it is then fitted with a tag detailing its location and palatised among many more.
4. The palate is delivered to its location which is not necessarily the right one or even the right yard.
5. When the palate is delivered the paper tags are often torn or get soggy in the rain or just fall off. So a labourer has to rummage through the palate for the right pipe.
6. When the pipe is found it's too long (remember the sketcher left 100mm extra). Therefore if another one looks a better fit you

take that. Or you get a hacksaw and cut it or take it back to the shop to be cut. As you would have done in the old days. (Plumber)

In this example then, the supposed divorce between conception and execution and the fragmentation of work locations and tasks is frustrated by the decisions of the sketchers and the consequent decision of the craftsman to use the pipe that 'looks the better fit'. The formal system is not translated unproblematically into a systemised response at the point of production; the discretion of the individual worker is to some extent left intact. A point borne out in the company's survey where 78% of the workers at Pallion and 77% and 72% at Deptford and North Sands respectively replied that they always felt personally responsible for the job they did. (Sunderland Shipbuilders/Employment Relations, 1986, p.21)

The persistence of the craft ethos among the manual workforce and their immediate superiors represented itself in an even more dramatic way at times. Thus when under pressure from superiors to speed up the work in order to finish a ship nearing the end of its completion time there was a tendency for the new system to break down and the old patterns of working to re-emerge. In such a situation foremen would order workers to bypass the computerised stock control and allocation system and physically go and obtain their materials and tools, on their authority, as they did under the old system.

Moreover, the specific craft identities deemed irrelevant to the composite work groups also reassert themselves as the basis of the physical procurement of tools and materials. Thus plumbers for example complained that stock-keepers in the stores belonging to the A.E.U. would not hand over materials to them, but if a 'friendly' fitter could be found they just walked in the back of the store as was the practice in the past. The point to be made about both these examples of the re-emergence of older working patterns is not that the workers are fighting at the point of production to retain their 'archaic' craft specific skills, but rather, they are fighting to get the job out on time. In the yards it was not the intensity of the conflict between capital and labour that led workers to revert to more traditional working patterns. Rather it was the case that in spite of everything else that management had done, the workers still saw themselves as having a responsibility towards their work and getting the job done.

The feeling of personal responsibility for one's work, a hallmark of the craft worker, was not easily extinguished, even in the face of technical changes in the labour process. This is the key to understanding the high levels of both conflict and co-operation which were, during this period, displayed by the same individuals. The co-operation sprang from a personal responsibility to see the job through. The conflict arose not primarily because of objective technical changes, but rather, due to the management offensive in relation to its direct control strategy and more generally in relation to its whole human relations approach. This offensive represented the substantive manifestation of the external pressures working upon the industry. These were the modernisation of capital and working practices as elements in achieving large growths in productivity in the context of overall reduction of capacity and cost.

A belated appreciation of the realities of the managerial offensive was given in the House of Commons in July 1987 by the town's two Labour M.P.s. Chris Mullin, for Sunderland South, described the management as "bone headed" and went on to say,

> In Sunderland the yards had a management that is more interested in pursuing the class war than in shipbuilding. They have exploited the crisis in shipbuilding to inflict further humiliation on a workforce that has already made great sacrifices. (Sunderland Echo, 10 July 1987)

Bob Clay, M.P. for Sunderland North, spoke of the management's,

> arrogance, secrecy and hostility to the workforce .... The number of managers that have been turned over in Sunderland in British Shipbuilders even exceeds the number of Government Ministers we have had dealing with these debates, or the number of chairman of British Shipbuilders we have had at a national level.
>
> How can you expect workers in a shipyard to feel any confidence in the future when they see managers come and go in sometimes extremely mysterious circumstances. There needs to be a whole inquiry even now into the way British Shipbuilders has been managed. (Sunderland Echo, 10 July 1987)

There was no inquiry however, and the M.P.s were berated in the media for damaging the image of Sunderland Shipbuilders. The hidden abode of the workplace was to remain obscured from public view on the pretext that to discuss such issues would damage the company's image. By this time however, the ferociousness of the managerial offensive had abated somewhat. The desired agreements over working practices had been achieved and the requisite number of voluntary redundancies had been forthcoming. Union resistance to managerial initiatives had been weak and short lived. However the workers still found themselves in a state of desubordination (Miliband, 1978), the changes in the labour process had not totally destroyed either the craft ethos or a willingness to exercise non-formal controls over the mobility of labour. One such example where the management did not appear to realise that control needs to be created and recreated and is rarely finally won, was in relation to the four set, three shift basis of working.

The system was introduced without union agreement and on a purely voluntary basis late in 1986. Most workers were opposed to its introduction, however as the direct controls over physical attendance were relaxed they found that the system could be used. Because of the four set pattern, within an individual shift there was nearly always one section of the workforce which had a legitimate right to be in the amenity block or moving to or from it. Thus the overlapping nature of coffee and dinner breaks was used to good effect by workers who could escape a booking by choosing, in explanation, the 'right set' to belong to. So well was this tactic used by the workforce that the pattern of shift working was withdrawn by the management early in 1988 as unworkable. The nature of the respite from constant managerial pressure was well understood by workers,

> Aye, they're leaving us alone at the moment, they've got what they want .... it'll start again soon though, there's talk of more redundancies again. (Plumber)

The changes in the organisation and control of the division of labour in the Wearside shipbuilding industry, which took place between the time of publication of the first British Shipbuilders Corporate Plan in 1978 and 1988, were massive. Formal agreements between management and union, which in the past had only been realised partially at the point of production, were implemented in full. The Management drove through changes in the organisation and control of labour which formally aimed to increase productivity in the context of a projected decline in state support. In this respect the enthusiasm with which they pursued their work was directly translated into a level of ferocity on the shop floor. This was a move which was seen by Robert Atkinson (former chairman of British Shipbuilders.) as largely pointless and one that he was unwilling to undertake. As he put it on the "World in Action" programme in June 1984,

> .... In early April 1983 I made it clear that the problem was the world recession and the absurd dumping of ships by Korea and Japan, and the solution lay totally outside of the control of British Shipbuilding. It was Government, it was EEC and it was O.E.C.D.. (Commentary) The Department (of Industry) took a different view and looked around for a

chairman who would share that view. They came up with Canadian lawyer Graham Day .... During the two months that they spent at British Shipbuilders before Sir Robert left the two men rarely spoke to each other....I wouldn't be a party to decimating that great British Industry. I really believe that certain Ministers would like to see it rundown and have nothing to do with Government. (World in Action, 11 June 1984)

This view was to prove correct.

Conclusion

Thus it was this generation of workers in the yards who were to bear the final conclusion of the decline of the British industry which began at the turn of the nineteenth century. In this context the apparent acquiescence displayed by these workers is to be seen as 'submission agreement' rather than 'sympathetic agreement'. Individually their resistance to the changes has been both non-conflictual by intent in terms of their continuing tendency to assume responsibility for their work. But also the more overt challenges of management have been tenaciously resisted as an exercise in the dialectic of control and de-subordination. If the work became deskilled the workers did not and this survival of the craft ethos continued to threaten managerial control. Ideologically the workers had nowhere to go. Nationalisation was, in their experience, the vehicle of their oppression. A feeling that you cannot fight the state, borne out by the result of the miners strike, again diffused the possibility of collective action. Yet the attacks by the representatives of labour on those selling their 'birthright' by taking their redundancy is misplaced. It was the failure of the labour and trades union movement to take initiatives on behalf of the workforce during the years of strength which resulted in such an apparently easy victory for those running down the industry.

Given this rundown the changes in the organisation of the division of labour confronted workers merely as an attempt to humiliate the captives before their final execution. In a situation where any resistance to the will of management was deemed illogical or deviant the aspirations of the workers were, in contrast, modest. As Derek Duffy of the Deptford yard put it,

We are not political men. All we want is the right to work .... All I want is to come to work, build ships, and take a pay packet home on a Friday night. (Sunderland Echo, 12 October 1984)

By Christmas 1988 it became clear that for these workers that was too much to ask for.

Direct quotation of workers comes from: Roberts, I.P. (1988), A Question of Construction: Capital and Labour in the Wearside Shipbuilding Industry - 1930's to the Present, PhD, University of Durham.

Bibliography

Allen, E., Odber, A.J. and Bowden, P.J. (1957), *Development Area Policy in the North East of England.* Newcastle: N.E. Ind. and Devt. Assoc.

Allen, J. (1990), 'Introduction to Section 6: Localities and Social Change', in Anderson, J. and Ricci, M.

Allen, J. and Massey, D. (1988), *The Economy in Question*, Sage.

Amin, A. and Malmberg, A. (1992), 'Competing structural and institutional influences on the geography of production in Europe.' in *Environment and Planning A*, vol. 24, pp 401-416.

Amin, A. and Tomaney, J. (1993), 'Illusions of prosperity: the political economy of Urban and Regional regeneration in North East England', in D Fasenfest (ed), *Community Economic Development: policy formation in the US and UK*, Macmillan, London, pp 65-89

Amin, A. and Smith, I. (1990), 'The British Car Components Industry: leaner and fitter?', P.Stewart et al (eds). op cit.

Amin A and Tomaney J (1991), 'Creating an enterprise culture in the North East? The impact of urban and regional policies of the 1980s', *Regional Studies*, 25:5, pp 479-88

Anderson, J. and Ricci, M. (eds.) (1990), *Society and Social Science: A Reader*, Open University Press, Milton Keynes.

Armstrong, K. and Beynon, H. (1977), *Hello, are you Working? Memories of the Thirties in the North East of England.* Whitley Bay: Strong Words Publications.

Ashton, D. et al (1988), 'Local Labour Markets and their Impact on the Life Chances of Youth' in Coles, B. (ed) *Young Careers*, Open University Press, Milton Keynes.

Attwood, M. and Hatton, F. (1983), 'Getting On - Gender Differences in Career Development: A Case Study of the Hairdressing Industry', in Gamarnikow, E. et al (eds), *Gender, Class and Work*, Heinemann, London.
Barnett, C. (1986), *The Audit of War: The Illusion and Reality of Britain as a Great Power*, Macmillan, London.
Bates, I., et al (eds) (1984), *Schooling for the Dole*, Macmillan, London.
Becker, G. (1965), 'A theory of the allocation of time', reprinted in A.M. Amsden (ed.) *The Economics of Women and Work*, Harmondsworth, Penguin.
Bell, D. (1962), *The End of Ideology*, Collier Macmillan, New York.
Bell, D. (1974), *The Coming of Post Industrial Society*, Heinemann, London.
Bell, D. (1980), 'The Social Framework of Information Society' in Forester, T. (ed) *The Micro-Electronics Revolution*.
Benwell CDP (1978), *The Making of a Ruling Class*. Newcastle. Benwell Community Development Project.
Berg, M.(ed) (1991), *Markets and Manufacture in Early Industrial Europe*, Routledge, London.
Beynon, H. et al. (1990), 'Coming to terms with the Future in Teesside', in Anderson, J. and Ricci, M.
Blackwell, T. and Seabrook, J. (1985), *A World Still to Win: The Reconstruction of the Post-War Working Class*, Faber London.
Blyton, P. and Turnbull, P.(eds) (1992), *Reassessing Human Resource Management*. London, Sage.
Borough of Sunderland (1978), *Town Centre District Plan : Report on Initial Participation*, Sunderland.
Borough of Sunderland (1981), *Town Centre District Plan* (Two Vols.), Sunderland.
Boyle, R (1990), 'Regeneration in Glasgow' in D Judd and M Parkinson (eds.) *Leadership and Urban Regeneration*, London, Sage.
Boyle, D. (1989), *Building Futures: A Layman's Guide to the Inner City Debate*, W.H. Allen, London.
Braverman, H. (1974), *Labour and Monopoly Capital*, Monthly Review Press, New York.
British Shipbuilders. (1983), *National Framework Agreement for Survival*, unpublished.
Brown, R.K. and Brannen, P. (1970), *Social Relations and Social Perspectives amongst Shipbuilding Workers, Sociology*, Vol. 4, No. 2.
Bryne, D. (1989), *Beyond the Inner City*, Milton Keynes. Open University Press.

Bryne, D. (1991), 'TWDC: Property Development and petty markets versus maritime industrialism' in R Imrie and H Thomas (eds.) *British Urban Policy And The Urban Development Corporations*. London, Paul Chapman, pp 89-103.

Burrows, R. (ed.) (1991), *Deciphering the Enterprise Culture*, London, Routledge.

Byrne, D. (1992), 'What Sort of Future?' in Colls, R. and Lancaster, B (eds) *Geordies: Roots of Regionalism*, pp 35-52. op.cit.

Cambridge Econometrics (1993), *Regional Economic Prospects*, latest report summarised in *Regions*, RSA, no. 184, pp 16-22

Campbell, M. (ed.) (1990), *Local Economic Policy*, Cassell Educational, London.

Caslin, T. (1987), 'De-industrialisation in the UK' in H Vane and T Caslin, *Current Controversies in Economics*, Basil Blackwell, Oxford

Castells, M. (1985), '*Economic Restructuring, High Technology and the New Urban Process*'. Paper delivered at the International Social Science Council Symposium on Giant Cities, Barcelona, 1985.

Cawson, A. (1985) 'Corporatism and Local Politics' in W Grant (ed.) *The Political Economy of Corporatism*. London, Macmillan, pp 148-147.

Central Statistical Office (1993), *Regional Trends* London: HMSO.

Centre for Urban and Regional Development Studies (1992), *North East of England: Economic Assessment*, a study prepared for the Northern Regions Councils Association, University of Newcastle Upon Tyne

Champion, A. G. and Townsend, A. R. (1990), *Contemporary Britain: a geographical perspective*, Edward Arnold, London

Chaney, D. (1990), 'Subtopia in Gateshead: The MetroCentre as a Cultural Form', *Theory, Culture and Society*, vol. 7, no.4, pp.49-68.

Clough, R. (1982), 'Tyne and Wear Enterprise Trust ' in *Northern Economic Review*, Winter.

Cochrane, A. (1991),'The Changing State of Local Government: Restructuring for the 1990s' in *Public Administration*, Vol 69. Autumn.

Cockburn, C. (1987), *Two-Track Training*, London, Macmillan.

Coffield, F. et al, (1986), *Growing Up at the Margins*, Open University Press, Milton Keynes.

Cohen, A.P. (1982), 'School for the Dole', *New Socialist*, 3.

Cohen, P. (1982), 'School for the Dole', *New Socialist*, 3.

Cohen, P. (1983), 'Losing the Generation Game', *New Socialist*, 14.

Cohen, P. (1984), 'Against the New Vocationalism', in Bates, I. et al, *Schooling for the Dole*, Macmillan, London.

Colenutt, B. and Ellis G. (1993), 'The Next Quangos in London' in *New Statesman and Society*, 26/3/93.

Colls, R. (1987), *The Pitmen of the Northern Coalfield: Work, Culture and Protest, 1790-1850*, Manchester University Press, Manchester.

Colls, R. and Lancaster, B (1992), *Geordies: Roots of Regionalism*. Edinburgh University Press.

Cooke, P. (1988) 'Municipal enterprise, growth coalitions and social justice' in *Local Economy* Vol 3 No 3, pp 191-199.

Cooke, P. (1983), *Theories of Planning and Spatial Development*. Hutchison.

Cooke, P. (1985), 'Radical Regions? Space, Time and Gender Relations in Emilia, Provence and South Wales', in Rees et al., op cit.

Cooke, P. (ed.) (1989), *Localities : The Changing Face of Urban Britain*, Unwin Hyman, London.

Copsey, M. and Hollands, R. (1988), 'Skill Shortages and Training: The Northern Picture', Trade Union Studies Information Unit, Newcastle, January.

Cousins, J, Davis, R, Paddon, M and Waton A (1974) 'Aspects of contradiction in Regional Policy : The case of North-East England' in *Regional Studies*, Vol 8, pp 133-144.

Crosbie, T. and Morgan, K. (1993), 'Vocational and Educational Training in the UK' in P. Auer and G Schmid (eds) *'Challenges and Responses: further education and training for the employed in Europe'*, Wissenschaftszentrum, Berlin.

Crowther, S. and Garrahan, P. (1988), *'Corporate Power and the Local Economy'*, Industrial Relations Journal, volume 19, number 1, pp.51-59.

Dale, R. et al (1990), *The TVEI Story*, Open University Press, Milton Keynes.

Daly, M. (1990) 'The 1980s - a decade of growth in enterprise: data on VAT registrations and deregistrations', *Employment Gazette*, November p553-565.

Daly, M. (1991), 'The 1980s - a decade of growth in enterprise: self-employment data from the Labour Force Survey' *Employment Gazette*, March p109-134.

Darendorf, R. (1959), Class and Class Conflict in *Industrial Society*, Stanford University Press, Stanford.

Davies, J G (1972), *The Evangelistic Bureaucrat*. London, Tavistock.

Department of Employment Gazette, (1988) Vol. 96, November.

Department of Employment Gazette, (1993), March, s21-s22.

Department of Social Security. (1993), *Households Below Average Income: A Statistical Analysis 1979 - 1990/91*. London: HMSO.

Dicken, P. (1988), *Global Shift*. London, Harper and Row.

Dickens, P. (1990), *Urban Sociology: Society, Locality and Human Nature*, Harvester/ Wheatsheaf, Hemel Hampstead.

Dintenfass M (1992), *The Decline of Industrial Britain*, Routledge, London
Disraeli, B. (1962), *Coningsby, or The New Generation*, Signet/New American Library, New York.
Downing, H. (1981), 'Developments in Secretarial Labour: Resistance, Office Automation and the Transformation of Patriarchal Relations of Control', unpublished PhD Thesis, Centre for Contemporary Cultural Studies, University of Birmingham.
Dunleavy, P and King, D. (1990), 'Middle-level Elites and Control of Urban Policy-Making in Britain in the 1990s'. Paper presented to the PSA Urban Politics Group Meeting. LSE. June.
Durham University. (1987), 'Shipbuilding', *Durham University Industrial Society Magazine*.
Education Group, Centre for Contemporary Cultural Studies (1991), *Education Limited: Schooling and Training and the New Right Since 1979*, Unwin-Hyman, London.
Ekins, P. and Max-Neef, M. (eds.) (1992), *Real-life Economics: Understanding Wealth Creation*, London, Routledge.
Elson, D. and Pearson, R. (1989), *Women's Employment and Multinationals in Europe*, Macmillan Press.
Faulder, A. (1992), 'Public Inquiry into proposals for Port Wakefield' *Proof of Evidence*, City of Wakefield District Council.
Fawcett Society. (1985), *The Class of '84: A Study of Girls on the First Year of the Youth Training Scheme*, London, Walworth Rd.
Featherstone, M. (1990), *Consumer Culture and Postmodernism*, Sage, London.
Finch, J. (1983), *Married to the Job: Wives' Incorporation in Men's Work*, London, George, Allen and Unwin.
Fine, B and Harris, L. (1985), *The Peculiarities of the British Economy*, Lawrence and Wishart, London.
Finegold, D. and Soskice, D. (1988), 'The Failure of Training in Britain: analysis and prescription', *Oxford Review of Economic Policy*, volume 4, number 3.
Finn, D. (1984), 'Leaving School and Growing Up: Work Experience in the Juvenile Labour Market', in Bates, I. et al, *Schooling for the Dole*, Macmillan, London.
Finn, D. (1987), *Training Without Jobs*, Macmillan, London.
Foley, P. (1990), 'UK open for business', *Lloyds Bank Economic Bulletin*, no. 138
Foster, J and Wolfson, C. (1989), 'Corporate Reconstruction and Business Unionism: the lessons of Caterpillar and Ford', *New Left Review*, Number 174, pp.51-66.

Fothergill S and Gudgin G (1982), *Unequal Growth: urban and regional employment change in the UK*, Heinemann, London

Fraser, C.M. and Emsley, K. (1973), *Tyneside*, City and County Histories series, David and Charles, Newton Abbot.

Gamble, A. (1981), *Britain in Decline*, Macmillan, London.

Gamble, A. (1986), 'The political economy of freedom', in ed. R. Levitas, *The Ideology of the New Right*, Cambridge, Polity Press.

Garrahan, P. and Stewart, P. (1992), *The Nissan Enigma*, Mansell, London.

Garrahan, P. and Stewart, P. (1991), 'Problems along the Japanese Road', *The Guardian*, 14 October.

Garrahan, P. and Stewart, P. (1992), 'Management Control and a New Regime of Subordination' in N. Gilbert and R. Burrows (eds) *Fordism and Flexibility*, Macmillan.

Garrahan, P. and Stewart, P. (1992c) 'Work Organisations in Transition: the human resource management implications of the Nissan Way', *Human Resource Management Journal*, volume 2, number 2, pp. 46-62.

Giddens, A. (1986), *Sociology: A Brief But Critical Introduction*, Macmillan: London.

Giddens, A. (1990), *The Consequences of Modernity*, Polity Press, Cambridge.

Gorz, A. (1982), *Farewell to the Working Class*, Pluto, London.

Green, A. (1983), 'Education and Training: Under New Masters', in Wolpe, A-M, and Donald, J. (eds), *Is There Anyone Here From Education?*, Pluto, London.

Green, A. (1990), *Education and State Formation*, Macmillan, London.

Gregson, N. (1987), *Locality Research: A Case of Conceptual Duplication*, Paper 28, CERDS, University of Newcastle, Newcastle.

Gudeman, S. and Rivera, A. (1990), *Conversations in Colombia: the Domestic Economy in Life and Text*, Cambridge University Press.

Guest, M. (1989), *HRM: Its implication for industrial relations and trade unions*, in Storey, J(ed), op cit.

Hahn, F. (1988), 'On market economies' in ed. R. Skidelsky, *Thatcherism*, London, Chatto and Windus.

Hakim, C. (1979), 'Occupational Segregation', *Department of Employment Research Paper*, No. 9. London: HMSO.

Hall, S. and M. Jacques. (eds) (1983), *The Politics of Thatcherism*, Lawrence and Wishart, London.

Hamnett, C. et al. (eds.) (1989), *Restructuring Britain: The Changing Social Structure*, Sage/Open University, London.

Harding, A. (1991), 'The rise of urban growth coalitions, UK-style ?' in *Environment and Planning C:Government and Policy*. Vol 9 pp 295-317.

Harrison, B., n.d., *Teesside* (City and County Histories), David and Charles, Newton Abbot.

Hart, M. (1989), 'Belfast's economic millstone? The role of manufacturing since 1973', conference paper, Geographical Society of Ireland, University of Jordanstown, 15th April.

Harvey, D. (1989a), 'Transformation in urban governance in late capitalism' in *Geografiska Annaler* 71 (B) pp 3-17.

Harvey, D. (1989b), *The condition of postmodernity: An inquiry into the origins of cultural change*. Oxford, Blackwell.

Hetherington, P and Robinson, F. (1988), 'Tyneside Life' in F Robinson (ed.) *Post-Industrial Tyneside*. Newcastle, City Libraries.

Hewison, R. (1987), *The Heritage Industry*, Methuen, London.

Hinde, K. (1993), *Labour Market Experiences following Plant Closure: the case of Sunderland's shipyard workers*, Research Paper 3, Newcastle Economic Research Unit, University of Northumbria, Newcastle upon Tyne

Hirst, P. and Thompson, G. (1992), 'The Problem of "globalisation": international economic relations, national economic management and the formation of trading blocs.' in *Economy and Society*, Vol.21, No.4.

Hobsbawm, E. and Ranger, T. (eds.) (1983), *The Invention of Tradition*, Cambridge University Press, Cambridge.

Hollands, R. (1990), *The Long Transition: Class, Culture and Youth Training*, London, Macmillan.

Hollands, R. (1991a), 'Losing the Generation Game Revisited: Youth, Politics and Vocationalism', *Youth and Policy*, 33, June.

Hollands, R. (1991b), 'Working Class Youth Identities: Schooling and the Training Paradigm' in Education Group, Centre for Contemporary Cultural Studies, *Education Limited: Schooling and Training and the New Right in England Since 1979*, Unwin Hyman, London.

Holley, S. (1983), *Washington: Quicker by Quango. The History of Washington New Town, 1964-83*, Washington Development Corporation.

Horne, D. (1984), *The Great Museum: The Re-Presentation of History*, Pluto Press, London.

Howard, J. et al. (1986), *Employment and Unemployment on Wearside*, A report prepared for the EEC and the Borough of Sunderland by Sunderland Polytechnic.

Hudson, R. (1991), 'The North in the 1980s: New Times in the "Great North" or just more of the same' in *Area*. March, pp 47-56.

Hudson, R. (1991), 'The North in the 1980s: New times or just more of the same?', *Area*, March, pp 17-26

Hudson, R. (1989), *Wrecking a Region: State Policies, Party Politics and Regional Change in North East England.* London: Pion.

Humphries, S. (1981), *Hooligans or Rebels?*, Basil Blackwell, Oxford.

Hutton, J., Hutton, S., Pinch, T. and Shiell, A. (1991) (eds.) *Dependency to Enterprise*, London, Routledge.

Huws, U. (1983), *Your Job in the Eighties*, Pluto Press, London.

Jahoda, M. (1982), *Employment and Unemployment: a Social-Psychological Analysis*, Cambridge, Cambridge University Press.

Jessop, B. et al. (1988), *Thatcherism*, Polity Press, Cambridge.

Kaye, H. J. (1987), 'The Use and Abuse of the Past: The New Right and the Crisis of History', in Miliband, R., et al. (eds.), *The Socialist Register 1987*, Pluto Press, London.

Keat, R. and Abercrombie, N. (eds) (1991), *Enterprise Culture*, London, Routledge.

Knell, J. (1992), 'Skill, Employer Strategies, and Labour Market Policy; Evidence from West Yorkshire', *Leeds University Discussion Paper*, Industrial Relations/HRM Series, No. 3.

Knell, J. (1993), TNCs and Human Capital Formation', *Human Resource Management Journal*, Vol.3, No. 4, Summer.

Laclau, E. (1987), 'Class War and After', *Marxism Today*, 31.

Lever W (1991), 'De-industrialisation and the reality of the post-industrial city', *Urban Studies*, 28:6, pp 983-99

Lewis, J. and Townsend, A. (eds) (1989), *The North-South Divide: Regional Change in Britain in the 1980s.* London: Chapman.

Linge, G. and Van der Knapp, G.(eds) (1989), *Labour, Environment and Industrial Change*, Routledge, London.

Lloyd, M and Newlands, D. (1988), 'The growth coalition and urban economic development' in *Local Economy* No 3, pp 31-39.

Loebl, H. (1988), *Government Factories and the Origins of British Regional Policy 1934-1948* Aldershot: Avebury.

Logan, J and Molotch, H. (1987), *Urban Fortunes; The Political Economy of Place.* Berkley, University of California Press.

Lowe, A. (1988), 'Small hotel survival - an inductive approach', *International Journal of Hospitality Management*, Vol. 7, no 3, p197-223.

MacDonald, R. (1991), 'Youth, Class and Locality in Rural England', *Youth and Policy* No 33.

MacDonald, R. and Coffield, F. (1991), *Risky Business: Youth and the Enterprise Culture*, Falmer Press, London.

Martin, R. and Rowthrone, B. (eds) (1986), *The Geography of Deindustrialization*, Macmillan, London.
Massey D (1984), *Spatial Divisions of Labour: social structures and the geography of production*, Macmillan, London
Massey, D. and Allen, J. (eds) (1988), *Uneven Re-development: cities and regions in transition*, Hodder and Stoughton.
Massey, D. and Meegan, R. (1984), *The Anatomy of Job Loss*, Methuen, London.
McCord, N. (1979), *North East England: An Economic and Social History*. London: Batsford.
McCutcheon, J.E. (1960), *A Wearside Mining Story*, Seaham.
Meegan, R. (1993), 'Urban Development Corporations, Urban Entrepreneuralism and Locality' in R Imrie and H Thomas (eds.) *British Urban Policy And The Urban Development Corporations*. London, Paul Chapman. pp 58-73.
Meiksins-Wood, E. (1986), *The Retreat From Class*, Verso Press, London.
Mess, H.A. (1928), *Industrial Tyneside: A Social Survey*. London: Ernest Benn.
Metcalfe, H. (1988), 'Employers Response to the Decline in School Leavers into the 1990s', *IMS Report No. 152*.
Michie, J. (1992), *The Economic Legacy, 1979 - 1992*, London, Academic Press.
Milburn, G. and Miller, S. (1988), *Sunderland: River, Town and People*, Sunderland, Sunderland Borough Council.
Milburn, G. and Miller, S.T. (1988), *Sunderland: River, Town and People*, Borough of Sunderland, Sunderland.
Miliband, R. (1969), *The State and Capitalist Society*, Quartet Books, London.
Miliband, R. (1978), A State of Desubordination, *British Journal of Sociology*, Vol. 29, No. 4.
Moore, C. and Pierre, J. (1988) 'Partnerships or Privatisation: The political economy of local economic restructuring' in *Policy and Politics*, Vol 16 No 3.
Morgan, K and Sayer, A. (1988), *Microcircuits of Capital*.
Morris, L. (1990), *The Workings of the Household*, Oxford, Polity Press.
Morris, J. et al (1992), Japanese Investment in Wales: Economic and Social Consequences, Report by the Cardiff Business School, University of Wales.
MSC. (1976), *Instructional Guide to Social and Life Skills* (MSC).
MSC. (1977), *Young People and Work*, Holland Report, MSC.
MSC. (1981), *A New Training Initiative*, MSC, December.

MSC. (1982), *Youth Task Group Report*, MSC, April.
MSC. (1983), *Guide to Managing Agents*, MSC, July.
National Consumer Council (1990), 'Cars: the cost of trade restrictions to customers', International Trade and the Consumer, *Working Paper Number 4*.
NEDC/MSC. (1984), *Competence and Competition*, Institute for Manpower Studies.
Newcastle City Council. (1990), *Activities and Initiatives Report*. Newcastle City Council Economic Development Committee.
Newcastle City Council. (1991), *Newcastle's Submission to the Secretary of State for Environment in response to the City Challenge Initiative*. Newcastle City Council, July.
Newell, H. (1991), *Field of Dreams*, D.Phil thesis (unpublished), University of Oxford.
Nissan (1991), Information Pack and Press Release
Nissan (no date), Corporate Philosphy.
Nolan, P. (1989), 'Walking on Water? Performance and industrial relations under Thatcher,' *Industrial Relations Journal*, Vol. 20, No. 2.
Nolan, P. and O'Donnell, K. (1991), ' Flexible Specialisation and UK Manufacturing Weakness: a comment on Hirst and Zeitlin', *Political Quarterly*, volume 62, number 1.
Northern Economic Planning Council. (1966), *Challenge of the Changing North*. Newcastle, NEPC.
Northern Economic Planning Council. (1969), *Outline Strategy for the North*. Newcastle, NEPC.
Northern Ireland Economic Research Centre. (1992), *LEDU Monitoring and Evaluation Report*, Belfast
Northern Region Strategy Team (1977) *Strategic Plan (5 volumes)* London, HMSO.
Northern Region Strategy Team. (1977), *Strategic Plan for the Northern Region, vol 2, Economic Development Policies*, HMSO
Oliver , N and Wilkinson, B. (1988 and 1992), *The Japanisation of British Industry*, Blackwell.
OPCS. (1990), *Standard Occupational Classification*, HMSO.
Pahl, R.E. and Wallace, C. (1985), 'Household work strategies in economic recession', in N. Redclift and E. Mingione (eds.) *Beyond Employment: Gender, Household and Subsistence*, Oxford, Blackwell,
Parsons, W. (1988), *The Political Economy of British Regional Policy*, Routledge, London.
Pawley, M. (1990), 'Big Sheds', The Late Show, 30 December 1990, BBC2.

Pearson, R. (1989), *Women's Employment and Multinationals in the UK; Restructuring and Flexibility* in Elson, D. and Pearson, R. (eds), op cit.

Pearson, G. (1985), 'Lawlessness, Modernity and Social Change: A Historical Appraisal', *Theory, Culture and Society*, vol. 2, no. 3, pp.15-36.

Peck, J. (1992) ,'TECs and the local politics of training' in *Political Geography*. Vol 11 No 4.

Peck, F and Stone, I. (1993), 'Japanese inward investment in the northeast of England: reassessing 'Japanisation' ' in *Environment and Planning C: Government and Policy*, Vol 11, pp. 55-67.

Peck, J. (1993), "Labour and Agglomeration: labour control and Flexibility in Local Labour Markets' Forthcoming in *Economic Geography*.

Peck, J and Lloyd, P. (1989), "*Conceptualising Processes of Skill Change: A Local Labour Market Approach*" in Linge, G. and Van der Knapp, G. (eds), op cit.

Peck F (1990), 'Nissan in the North East: the multiplier effects', *Geography*, 75:4, 354-57

Peck F and Stone I (1992), *New Inward Investment and the Northern Region Labour Market*, Research Series No. 6, Employment Department, Sheffield

Peck F and Stone I (1993), 'Japanese inward investment in the North East of England: Re-assessing Japanisation', *Environment and Planning C: Government and Policy*, 11:1, pp 55-67

Pickvance, C.G. (1985), 'Spatial Policy as Territorial Politics', in Rees, et al., op cit.

Polanyi, K. (1946) *Origins of our Time: the Great Transformation*, London, Victor Gollancz.

Policy Reserach Unit, Leeds Polytechnic. (1989), '*Wakefield Employment Skills Survey*', Report commissioned by Wakefield Metropolitan District Council.

Pollard, S. (1991), '*Regional Markets and National Development*' in Berg, M.(ed), op cit.

Pollert, A. (ed.) (1991) *Farewell to Flexibility*, Oxford, Blackwell.

Raby G (1977), 'Contraction poles: an exploratory study of traditional industry decline within a regional industrial complex', CURDS discussion paper, Newcastle University

Rainbird, H. (1991) 'The self employed: small entrepreneurs or disguised wage labourers?' in ed. A. Pollert, op cit.

Rees, G., et al. (eds.) (1985), *Political Action and Social Identity: Class, Locality and Ideology*, Macmillan, London.

Ritchie, J. (1991) 'Enterprise cultures: a frame analysis' in ed. R. Burrows.

Roberts, I.P. (1988), *A Question of Construction: Capital and Labour in the Wearside Shipbuilding Industry, 1930s to the Present.* PhD, Univesity of Durham.

Robins, K. and Webster, F. (1989), *The Technical Fix: Education, Computers and Industry*, Macmillan, London.

Robins, K. (1990), 'Global Local Times', in Anderson, J. and Ricci, M., pp.196-205, op cit.

Robinson, F. (ed), (1988), *Post-Industrial Tyneside*, Newcastle Libraries, Newcastle.

Robinson, F. (1990), *The Great North.* Report commissioned by BBC North East. Centre For Urban Development Studies, University of Newcastle.

Robinson, F. and Goddard, J. (1982), *Economic Prospects for the North.* Newcastle: BBC North East.

Robinson, F., Wren, C. and Goddard, J. (1987), *Economic Development Policies: An Evaluative Study of the Newcastle Metropolitan Region.* Oxford: Clarendon.

Robinson, F. and Shaw, K. (1991), 'In search of the Great North', *Town and Country Planning*, October, pp 279-83

Rowe, D.J. (1990), 'The North East', in F.M.L.Thompson (ed.), *The Cambridge Social History of Britain, 1750-1950, Vol. 1 : Regions and Communities*, Cambridge University Press, pp.415-70.

Rowthorn, B. (1986), 'De-industrialization in Britain' in R Martin and B Rowthorn (eds), *The Geography of De-Industrialisation*, Macmillan, London

Rushton, P. (1989), 'The Poor Law, the Parish and the Community in North-East England, 1600-1800', *Northern History*, vol. 25, pp.136-52.

Sadler, D. (1992), *The Global Region: production, state policies and uneven development*, Pergamon, Oxford

Samuel, R. (1988), 'Little Englandism Today', *New Statesman and Society*, 21st October.

Savage, M. (1989, 'Spatial Differences in Modern Britain', in Hamnett et al.

Sayer, R A. (1985), 'Industry and space; a sympathetic critique of radical research.' in *Environment and Planning* D, Vol 3. pp3-29.

Secretary of State for Industry, Trade and Regional Development (1963), *The North East: A Programme for Regional Development and Growth* ('Hailsham Plan'). Cmnd. 2206. London: HMSO.

Shaw, K (1990) 'The Politics of Public-Private Partnership in Tyne and Wear' in *Northern Economic Review* No 19 pp 2-16.

Smith, T Dan (1970) *Dan Smith:An Autobiography.* Newcastle, Oriel Press.

Smith, A. D. (1991), *National Identity*, Penguin, London.

Smith, I. (1986), 'Takeovers, Rationalisation and the Northern Region Economy', *Northern Economic Review*, number 12, pp 30-38.

Smith I and Stone I (1989), 'Foreign investment in the North: distinguishing fact from hype', *Northern Economic Review*, 18, pp 50-61

Spence, J. (1987) Industrial Relations in Wearside Shipbuilding: 1945-1981, in Potts, A., *Shipbuilders and Engineers North East Labour History Society*.

Stewart, P. et al (eds.) (1990), *Restructuring for Economic Flexibility*, Avebury/Gower.

Stirling, J. and Bridgeford J., (1984) British and French Shipbuilding: The Industrial Relations of Decline, *Industrial Relations Journal*, Vol. 16, No. 4.

Stone, I. and Stevens, J. (1985/6), 'Employment on Wearside', *Northern Economic Review*, Winter, 12.

Stone, I. and Stevens, J. (1986) 'Employment on Wearside: trends and prospects', *Northern Economic Review*, no. 12, p. 39-56.

Stone, I. (1993) 'Remaking it on Wearside - de-industrialisation and re-industrialisation', *Northern Economic Review*, Spring, no. 20, p.6 - 22.

Stone I (1989), *Shipbuilding on Wearside: reviewing the prospects*, Report for Sunderland Borough Council, Sunderland

Stone I (1994, forthcoming), 'The UK Economy', in F Somers (ed), *European ComunityEconomies: a comparative study*, Pitman, London

Stone I and Stevens J (1986), 'Employment on Wearside: trends and prospects', *Northern Economic Review*, 12, pp 39-56

Storey, D (1983) 'Local Employment Initiatives in North-East England' in K Young and C Mason (eds.) *Urban Economic Development*. London, Macmillan.

Storey, J. (1987), 'Developments in the management of human resources: an interim report,' *Warwick Papers in Industrial Relations* No. 17, IRRU, School of Industrial and Business Studies, University of Warwick, November.

Storey, J.(ed) (1989), *New Perspectives on Human Resource Management*, Routledge, London.

Storey D (1982), *Entrepreneurship and the New Firm*, Croom Helm, London

Storey D et al. (1982), *Manufacturing Employment Change in Tyne and Wear since 1965*, CURDS, Newcastle University

Stubbs, C. and Wheelock, J. (1990), *A Women's Work in the Changing Local Economy*, Aldershot, Avebury.

Sunderland Borough Council (1969/70), *Youth Employment Committee Annual Report*.

Sunderland Shipbuilders (1984), *Productivity Agreement*, unpublished.

Sunderland Shipbuilders/employment Relations (1986), *Industrial Relations Survey*, unpublished.
Swingewood, A. (1977), *The Myth of Mass Culture*, Humanities Press, New Jersey.
SYEP (1984), *Views on YTS*, Sunderland Youth Employment Project.
Taylor, R. (1982) *Workers and the New Depression*, Macmillan, London.
The Guardian, 4.11.83.
The Guardian 24.1.89
The Guardian 24.1.91
The Guardian 24.10.91
The Guardian 24.6.91
The Guardian 26.4.91
The Guardian 3.2.92
The Guardian 5.11.91
The Newcastle Initiative (1988) *The Newcastle Initiative*. Newcastle, TNI.
The Sunday Telegraph, 21.6.92.
The Sunderland Echo, May 5 1983, July 10 1987.
The Wearside Opportunity (1990) *A Vision for the Future*, Sunderland, TWO
Tomaney, J. (1990), 'The Reality of Workplace Flexibility', *Capital and Class*, number 40, pp.29-60.
Tonkin, E., et al. (1989), *History and Ethnicity*, Routledge/ASA Monograph 27, London.
Touraine, A. (1974), *The Post-Industrial Society*, Wildwood, London.
Trade Union Studies Information Unit (1985), *Tyne and Wear in Crisis*. Newcastle: TUSIU.
Training Agency (1990), *Training and Enterprise: Labour Market Assessment 1990/91*, Training Agency.
TUSIU (1988), *An Analysis of Private Training Agencies on YTS in Newcastle*, TUSIU, Newcastle.
Tyne and Wear Development Corporation (1989) *A Vision for the Future*. Newcastle, TWDC.
Unemployment Unit, *Unemployment Bulletin*, No 28, August.
Urry, J. (1981), 'Localities, Regions and Social Class', *International Journal of Urban and Regional Research*, vol. 5, pp.456-74.
Waring, M. (1989) *If Women Counted*, London, Macmillan.
Watts D (1981), *The Branch Plant Economy: a study of external control*, Longman, Harlow
Wheelock, J. (1990), *Husbands at Home: The Domestic Economy in a Post-Industrial Society*, Routledge, London.

Wheelock, J. (1992a) 'The household in the total economy' in eds. P. Ekins and M. Max-Neef, p. 124-135, op cit.
Wheelock, J. (1992b) The flexibility of small business family work strategies in eds. K. Caley, F. Chittenden, E. Chell, C. Mason, *Small Enterprise Development: Policy and Practice in Action*, Paul Chapman Publishing Ltd, p. 151-165.
Wheelock, J. (forthcoming) 'Household responses to urban change: the clash between incentives and values' in eds. P. Healey et al., *Urban Management*, Belhaven.
Wheelock, J. (1990), 'Capital Restructuring and the Domestic Economy: Family, Self-Respect and the Irrelevance of "rational economic man"', *Capital and Class*, vol 41.
Wickens, P. (1987), *The Road to Nissan*, Macmillan.
Wiener, M.J. (1982), *English Culture and the Industrial Spirit, 1850-1980*, Cambridge University Press, Cambridge.
Wilkes, L. and Dodds, G. (1964), *Tyneside Classical: The Newcastle of Grainger, Dobson and Clayton*, John Murray, London.
Wilkinson, S (1992) 'Towards a new city ? A case study of image-improvement intiatives in Newcastle upon Tyne' in P Healey et al (eds.) *Rebuilding The City*. London, E and FN Spon pp 174-211.
Wilkinson, E. (1939), *The Town that was Murdered: The Life Story of Jarrow*. London: Gollanz.
Williams, R, (1983), *Towards 2000*, Penguin, Harmondsworth.
Williams, A. (1991), 'What is wealth and who creates it? in eds. J. Hutton et al. p. 1-20, op cit.
Williams, K. et al (1992), 'Against Lean Production', *Economy and Society*, volume 21, numer 3, pp 321-354.
Williams, K. et al (1992b), 'Factories or Warehouses: Japanese Manufacturing FDI in Britain and the United States', *Occasional Paper on Business, Economy and Society*, Polytechnic of East London.
Willis, P. (1977), *Learning to Labour*, Saxon House, Westmead.
Willis, P. (1979), 'Shop-floor Culture, Masculinity and the Wage Form', in Clarke, J. et al (eds), *Working Class Culture*, Hutchinson, London.
Willis, P. (1985), *The Social Condition of Young People In Wolverhampton in 1984*, Wolverhampton, Wolverhampton Borough Council.
Wolman, H and Goldsmith, M. (1992), *Urban Politics and Policy: A Comparative Approach*. Oxford, Blackwell.
Wood, S. (ed). (1989), *The Transformation of Work?*, Unwin-Hyman, London.
Wright, P. (1985), *On Living in an Old Country: The National Past in Contemporary Britain*, Verso, London.

Wyn, H. (1991), 'Women, the state and the concept of financial independence' in ed. J. Hutton et al. p. 105-113, op cit.

Yeandle, S. (1984), *Women's Working Lives*, London, Tavistock.

Young, D.I. (1991), *Enterprise Years: a Business Man in the Cabinet*, London, Headlines.

YTS Monitoring Unit (1985), *The Great Training Robbery Continues*, TURC Publishing, Birmingham.

YTURC (1985), *Easy Come, Easy Go...The Sorry Tale of a Private YTS Training Agency*, TURC Publishing, Birmingham.